GREAT NORSE, CELTIC AND TEUTONIC LEGENDS

WILHELM WÄGNER

Introduction by
W. S. W. Anson

DOVER PUBLICATIONS, INC.
Mineola, New York

Bibliographical Note

This Dover edition, first published in 2004, is an unabridged republication of the text of the work originally published in 1907 by the Norrœna Society, London, as *Romances and Epics of our Northern Ancestors / Norse, Celt and Teuton / Translated from the works of Dr. W. Wägner / With introduction by W. S. W. Anson,* which formed Volume 12 of the *Norrœna Anglo-Saxon Classics (Royal Edition) / Hon. Rasmus B. Anderson, LL.D., Editor in Chief / J. W. Buel, Ph.D., Managing Editor.* An earlier publication credits the translation to M. W. Macdowall.

Library of Congress Cataloging-in-Publication Data

Wägner, Wilhelm, 1800–1886.
    Great Norse, Celtic, and Teutonic legends / Wilhelm Wägner ; introduction by W.S.W. Anson.
        p. cm.
    Originally published: Romances and epics of our northern ancestors, Norse, Celt and Teuton. London, New York [etc.] Norrœna Society, 1906, in series: Norrœna, the history and romance of northern Europe.
    ISBN 0-486-43489-3 (pbk.)
    1. Romances. 2. Literature, Medieval. I. Title.

PN683.W3 2004
839.5—dc22

2003068770

Manufactured in the United States of America
Dover Publications, Inc., 31 East 2nd Street, Mineola, N.Y. 11501

GREAT NORSE, CELTIC AND TEUTONIC LEGENDS

CHRIEMHILD DENOUNCES HAGEN AT THE BIER OF SIEGFRIED.

(After the painting by Emil Lauffer.)

Many painters have used Chriemhild's (Kriemhild) denunciation of Hagen as the subject of their greatest efforts, since the incident, aside from its tragic and pity-compelling character, involves accessories colorful as they are dramatic. The legendary killing of Siegfried, and the leading up to that foul deed, has an allegoric significance, for the events may be taken to represent the transition from Paganism to Christianity. The artist conceiving this higher meaning, has therefore chosen to bring these opposing powers into his picture, grim Hagen typifying the former, while the murdered Siegfried, at the feet of a crucified Saviour, clasps the symbol of the faith that triumphs in death.

See page 140

Contents

The Amelungs.

Legend of Dietrich and Hildebrand.

The Nibelung Story.

The Hegeling Legend.

List of Photogravures

Introduction.

LEGEND IS not history; but in legend we find embodied historical truths, manners and customs of past ages, beliefs and superstitions otherwise long forgotten, of which history itself takes no account. Legend has preserved for us, maybe in romantic dress, maybe under altered names and circumstances, stirring pictures of heroes and heroines, who once have lived and suffered, fought and conquered, or have faced death with trustful courage; pictures, too, of men of equal prowess, as strong in evil as in might, who, victorious for a time, have yet ever met a stronger power than theirs, stronger in virtue, stronger in might.

As we write, the shadowy forms of terrific Alboin raising aloft his goblet fashioned from royal skull; the noble Siegfried with his loved Chriemhild and the jealous Brunhild; brave King Dietrich; the gentle, patient Gudrun and her beauteous mother Hilde, all flit before the mind, framing themselves into a vivid picture, such as must have lived in the imagination of our early forefathers, stirring them on to noble actions, restraining them from evil working. Thus has good in all ages fought against ill, and all races of men have sung its victory in strains but slightly varying. And so will it ever fight, no matter how our more elaborate ideas of what is good or evil may vary; the nation always glorifies the great and noble according to its own unreasoning reason.

This volume contains the principal hero-lays of the six great epic cycles of the Teutonic Middle Ages. Beside these French poems, stand the Breton ones of King Arthur and his Knights of the Round Table, which later on took up the legend of the Holy

1

Grail into their very heart, and at this period found their way to Germany, where they met with a more romantic and poetic treatment at the hands of the court minnesingers. But these foreign importations never found a true home amongst the German people; they never became *popular*. The native hero-lays on the other hand, even though less beautiful in conception and in form, lived on through centuries, and even to this day exist, though disguised and degraded. For in the market-places of Germany, and at the few old English fairs that yet remain, the pedlar bookseller gives in exchange for the farthing piece printed versions of many of these old legendary tales: Siegfried's battle with the Dragon, the Rose-garden, Alberich and Elbegast's adventures, and other wondrous histories of Teutonic epical origin. But this literature is fast dying out, if, indeed, it may not by this time be said to be already dead. In Iceland, however, and in the Faroe Isles, tradition still holds her throne unconquered. She yet sings to the listening grey-beards, to the men and women, and to the growing youth, of Odin and his mighty rule, of Honer and the wicked Loke, of Thor and Frey, and Freyja Queen of Heaven, of the Fenriswolf and the Midgard-serpent. In the long winter nights she still tells of bold Sigurd's (Siegfried) deeds and battle, of Gudrun's faithful love and dumb grief beside the body of her lord, of Gunnar's marvellous harping in the garden of snakes, and the listeners hold it all in their memory, that they may sing and tell it to their children and their children's children. And so do they cherish the time-old legends of their fathers, that the ardent youth may still he heard to adjure his bride to love him "with the love of Gudrun," the master revile his dishonest workmen as "false as Regin" (the evil dwarf), and the old men to shake their heads and say of the daring lad, that he is "a true descendant of the Wolsungs." At the dance, Sigurd-songs are yet sung, at Christmastide a grotesque Fafner takes his part in the mummery. Thus old German tradition in her wane has found an asylum, perhaps a last resting-place, in the far North, driven from their first home by strangers, the myths of Greece and Rome. Every schoolboy can tell of Zeus and Hera, of Achilles and Odysseus, every schoolgirl of the golden apples of the

Hesperides, of Helen, of Penelope; yet to how many of our older folks, even, are the grand forms of Siegfried, Chriemhild, and Brunhild more than mere names?

It is true that a tendency is now springing up in England and in Germany once more to enquire into these old tales, nay beliefs, of our common ancestry. It is true that we have a Morris and they a Wagner; but we should wish to see the people of both nations take a more general interest in a subject of such intrinsic worth to them, their long-forgotten heritage. It is not the history of class-books that they will find in it—it is that of their fathers' manners and customs, of their joys and sufferings, their games and occupations, festivals and religious observances, battles, victories and defeats, their virtues and their crimes. Such is the golden field that lies beneath our feet, which, unheeded, we have let lie fallow, till it has almost faded from memory.

To what extent these legends formed a part of their religion proper it is impossible for us now to say. Of later origin and more poetic treatment, they stood in a similar position towards the old Teutons as the later Greek heroic legend stood to the Greeks of history. Some say, and the learned Grimm amongst them, that the heroes were historical men raised to the dignity of gods, others that they were humanized gods themselves; but may be neither theory is exactly true, though both contain a portion of the truth. In the hero-legends we certainly find heroes possessed of the distinctive attributes of certain gods, and we are tempted to add others to their characters, but we consider that these divine qualities were looked upon rather as divine *gifts* of the gods, and did not thereby exactly deify the recipients. It was similar with the Greeks, and perhaps with all nations at a stage when their heroes really formed an essential element in their belief. The gods were never human heroes, the heroes never became gods, though each approached the other so nearly that we are often misled into assuming that they were identical.

W. S. W. ANSON.

THE AMELUNGS.

CHAPTER I.

HUGDIETERICH AND FAIR HILDBURG.

WHILE ORTNIT'S ancestors ruled over Lombardy, the great Emperor Anzius lived at Constantinople, and governed Greece, Bulgaria, and many other lands. When he died, he confided his son, Hugdieterich, to the care of his faithful friend, Berchtung, duke of Meran, whom he had himself brought up, and afterwards covered with honours.

Berchtung felt that his first duty was to choose a wife for his ward, and that only a princess of equal rank and great beauty and wisdom would be a suitable helpmeet for so mighty a prince. He had travelled far and wide, and amongst all the princesses he knew there was one and only one that he could propose as a wife for his liege lord. But there were many difficulties in the way. Berchtung confided his troubles to the prince, and told him how much he wished to bring about a marriage between him and Hildburg, daughter of King Walgund of Thessalonica; but he feared it would be impossible, for Walgund loved the maiden so dearly that he had shut her up in a high tower, and permitted no one to speak to her except the old watchman, himself, her mother, and her maid. This he did, fearing lest she should marry and leave him.

Hugdieterich listened to the strange story with great interest, and determined to get a sight of the maiden if he could. So he set to work to learn all that he might of women's works and women's ways, even going so far as to dress himself in women's

4

garments. After which he announced his intention of going to Thessalonica to make fair Hildburg's acquaintance.

He arrived in due course at Thessalonica, disguised as a great lady, with a numerous train of female servants. Hearing of the new arrival, the king and queen invited the stranger to visit them. She did so, and gave their majesties to understand that she was Hilgunde, sister of the emperor Hugdieterich, and that she had been outlawed by her brother. She begged the king to protect her, and to provide her with a lodging in his palace, and at the same time presented the queen with a costly piece of embroidery, as a sign of her good will. Her request was granted. The queen then begged her to teach her ladies to embroider as she did herself. After this all went so well that Berchtung and his men-at-arms were sent back to Constantinople, their protection being no longer needed.

Fair Hildburg heard what was going on, and begged her father to allow her to see the embroideries, and the artist who worked them. No sooner had she done so than she wished to learn the art. Walgund gave his consent, thinking the stranger a very suitable companion for his daughter, and Hildburg found great pleasure in her company. It was not until weeks afterwards that she discovered who her teacher was, and when she did their friendship became stronger than before, until it grew into acknowledged love.

The fear lest their secret marriage should be discovered, one day reached a climax.

"What will become of us?" cried Hildburg. "My father will never forgive us. He will order us both to be slain."

"Then, at least, we shall die together," replied Hugdieterich, "but I hope for better things. The guards and your personal attendants are on our side, and I expect Berchtung very soon to come and take me home to Constantinople, on the plea that my brother has forgiven me. I shall then send an ambassador to ask for your hand in marriage; and when your father knows our secret, he will not refuse his consent."

Berchtung came as Hugdieterich had expected, and fetched him away; but the wooing had to be put off till a more convenient season, as war had broken out on the frontier, and the emperor was obliged to take the field. Meantime Hildburg was in greater danger at home than her husband in the midst of battle. She had a son. He was born quietly in the tower, without any one except the three faithful friends who guarded the princess there knowing aught about it. It was not until months after this event that the queen, her mother, sent to say that she was coming to visit her daughter. She followed almost on the heels of the messenger. The porter pretended to have great difficulty in unlocking the door, and by the time he succeeded, the watchman had smuggled the child down to a safe hiding-place beside the moat. It was already evening, so the queen spent the night with her daughter. When she was gone next morning, the faithful servant hastened to where he had hidden the child, and it was not to be found. After long and anxious search, he returned to his mistress, and told her that he had taken the boy to a nurse, who had promised to bring him up carefully and well.

Soon after this, Berchtung arrived at Thessalonica to thank the king in his master's name for the reception he and his family had given the princess, his sister, and to ask for the hand of the Lady Hildburg, with whom the emperor had fallen in love from his sister's description. The king put off giving any immediate answer to this request, and asked Berchtung to a great hunt he intended to give in his honour on the following day.

It was a lovely morning when the hunters set out for the forest. They rode on cheerily, and had a good day's sport. At length chance led the king and Berchtung past the tower where sad Hildburg spent her weary days in waiting for the husband who came not. As they rode along, they discovered the fresh track of a wolf leading towards a spring. They followed the spoor, which led them to a den in a thicket close by, and in the den was a strange sight.

In the center of the nest, and surrounded by a litter of wolf-cubs so young as to be still blind, lay a beautiful child. He was playing with the little wolves, pulling their ears, and chatting in baby language such as only mothers and nurses can translate. But evidently his companions did not like his attentions, and the mother-wolf's ire was so roused against him, that it wanted very little more to make her spring upon the child, and put a sudden end to his play. The old wolf came up at the same moment, so that the danger was much increased. Seeing this, the two hunters flung their spears with so much skill as to kill both the old wolves on the spot. Then the king lifted the baby in his arms as gently as if it had been his own child.

"It's very strange," he said, "how much I feel drawn to this boy. But he must be hungry, poor little man. My daughter's tower is close to here; we shall find some fresh milk there, and she will be glad to see the little fellow; she is so fond of children, and seldom gets a chance of seeing them."

They walked on slowly, Berchtung carrying the child, while the king examined the wolf's track with great interest and attention.

"Look here," he said, "is it not strange? The tracks lead straight from the den to the moat; I wonder if the wolf stole the child from anywhere near this."

Fair Hildburg was not a little astonished when she heard her father's tale. She took the child in her arms, and at once recognised him by a birth-mark on his arm in the shape of a red cross. She struggled to conceal her feelings, and offered as calmly as she could to take care of the child, and only begged her father to send a nurse as quickly as possible.

When he got home, the king told the queen of his adventure, and she was very curious to see the child. She sent for a nurse, and accompanied her to the tower. Arrived there, the queen sought her daughter, and found her busied with the child.

"How I wish," said the queen, taking it in her arms, "that I knew who the boy's mother is! She must be in such distress."

"Yes," answered Hildburg; "but look at his clothes, how fine they are! They show that he is of princely descent."

"Oh dear," sighed the queen, "what a lucky woman I should think myself if I had a grandson like that!"

Hildburg could keep her secret no longer. She threw herself into her mother's arms, and told her, with many tears, that she was secretly married to Hugdieterich, and that the child was theirs. The queen was startled, angry,—but—it was done, and could not be undone. It was at least a comfort to think that the child's father was a mighty emperor. She told her daughter she would say nothing; but would think what was best to be done.

Walgund felt strangely attracted by the child. He came to the tower almost every day to visit it and his daughter. On such occasions the queen would tell him how much she wished for a son-in-law and such a grandchild as this. She reminded him that they might in their old age fall a prey to the barbarous tribes in the neighbourhood, if they had not some young, strong man to take their part, and added that in her opinion Hugdieterich would not be amiss. In short, the queen prepared the way so well that when Berchtung made his formal offer for the princess' hand, the king after slight hesitation gave his consent, on the sole condition that Hildburg was not averse to taking Hugdieterich as a husband. The queen then told her lord the whole story.

"Wonderful!" he exclaimed, too much astonished to be angry.

Hugdieterich arrived soon afterwards, and was publicly married to the Lady Hildburg. After the wedding festivities were over, he set out for Constantinople, accompanied by his beautiful wife, and the little boy, who was named Wolfdieterich, in remembrance of his first adventure.

With the empress went Sabene, one of the notables of Thessalonica, as her father had much confidence in his wisdom, and wished him to be his daughter's counsellor in any matters of difficulty. He made himself so useful, that he soon became necessary to her, and at the same time won the confidence of honest Duke Berchtung so completely that he persuaded the emperor to make Sabene regent during their absence on a foreign campaign.

The high position he had gained through the duke's kindness, made the false-hearted man bolder and more self-confident than ever. One day he went so far as to speak unbecomingly to the empress. The noble lady reproved him severely, and he fell at her feet, begging her pardon, and entreating her not to tell the emperor of his impertinence. She promised, but commanded him never more to appear in her presence.

When Hugdieterich returned victorious, Sabene was the first to meet him. He gave him an account of his stewardship, and at last remarked, as though by chance, that there was a great deal of dissatisfaction amongst the people regarding Wolfdieterich, the heir-apparent, who rumour said was not the king's child, but the son of an elf, or, worse still, of an alraun, who had been palmed off upon the royal family by a witch. Hugdieterich laughed at the story as at a nursery tale. The only effect it had on him was to make him take his son from under the charge of Sabene, and give him into the care of faithful Berchtung, that he might learn all knightly exercises with the duke's sixteen sons.

Time passed on, and the empress presented her husband with two other sons, named Bogen and Waxmuth, who were also sent to Berchtung to be educated. The old duke loved all his pupils dearly, but Wolfdieterich was his special favourite, for he showed himself full of every quality that makes a true knight and noble warrior. The busy emperor seldom found time to go to Lilienporte, the castle of Meran, and Hildburg was a still less frequent visitor, so that Wolfdieterich had grown accustomed to look upon Berchtung as his father, and the duchess as his mother. His brothers, Bogen and Waxmuth, had long since returned to Constantinople, where crafty Sabene did all that he could to gain their friendship and confidence. Their mother was sorry to see it; and fearing lest evil should come of it, she told her husband all that had happened between them many years before. Hugdieterich's wrath blazed forth, and Sabene scarcely escaped alive. He fled from the country, and sought refuge amongst his kindred in the land of the Huns.

Hugdieterich, worn out by many anxieties and battles, grew old before his time. When he felt his end approach he arranged all his affairs with the utmost care. He bequeathed to his eldest son Constantinople and the larger part of the empire, while the two younger sons were given kingdoms farther to the south, and the empress and Berchtung were to see the will carried out. But scarcely was the emperor laid in the grave, when the notables of the land met in council, and demanded the recall of Sabene, because otherwise they feared he might carry out his threat of bringing the wild Huns upon them. The empress did not feel herself strong enough to withstand the clamour of the nobles, so she sent for the traitor.

WOLFDIETERICH AND HIS ELEVEN.

NO SOONER had Sabene returned than he began to scheme again. He spread amongst the people his silly tales about the origin of Wolfdieterich. He said that the empress had been secretly wedded to an elf while she lived in that solitary tower; and that it was elfish spells that had prevented the wolves from tearing the child in pieces. The populace believed the story more easily from its utter incredibility, and demanded that Wolfdieterich should remain at Meran. Sabene even succeeded in making the royal brothers, Waxmuth and Bogen, believe his tale, and give him the power for which he hungered. Sure of his own position, he acted with the utmost harshness. He bade the empress leave the palace and go to her son at Meran. He only allowed her to take with her a maidservant, a horse, and her clothes. Everything else that she possessed, whether through her father or her husband, had to be left behind. The two young kings did not interfere on her behalf, for Sabene had shown them that her treasures would be very useful to them in equipping an army, supposing Wolfdieterich and the Duke of Meran attacked them.

When Hildburg arrived at Hugelwarte, an outwork of Lilienporte, she was travel-stained and sorely spent. At first duke Berchtung refused to admit her, because she had recalled Sabene contrary to his advice. But at last, filled with pity for the unhappy woman, he led her into the castle, and treated her there with royal honours. The duchess received her surrounded by seventeen young men, who all called her mother. The empress did not at once recognise her son, who was the tallest and stateliest amongst them; but as soon as each knew the other, Wolfdieterich, throwing himself into her arms, tried to comfort her by promising to restore her to her former rank and splendour.

Duke Berchtung at first counselled peace, because the position of the two kings seemed to him so strong and unassailable; but at length, carried away by his foster-son's enthusiasm, he not only gave his consent, but placed his sixteen sons and their sixteen thousand followers at the disposal of the prince. It was settled, while the men were being called together, that the duke and Wolfdieterich should set out for Constantinople, and see whether they might not attain their end by peaceful means.

The day after their arrival, they met Sabene and the kings in council. Berchtung was received with all honour, while nobody seemed even to see his companion. When Wolfdieterich rose, and demanded his rightful share of the royal heritage, Bogen answered that a changeling had no right to any share; and Sabene added that he ought to apply to the alraun, his father, for a kingdom in the realms of hell. Wolfdieterich laid his hand on his sword; but his foster-father's words and looks of entreaty sufficed to calm him down and prevent any open expression of anger. The kings and Sabene did their utmost to persuade the duke to join their party, but in vain; and when the council broke up, the old man went away, hiding his displeasure as best he could. He and Wolfdieterich mounted their horses and returned to Lilienporte without loss of time.

After a few days' rest they set out again for Constantinople, but this time in battle array. On reaching the borders of Meran, they found the royal forces drawn up to meet them. As evening was closing in, they encamped in a wide valley surrounded on all sides by a forest. Next morning the troops rose refreshed, and each side made sure of victory.

The battle-song was now raised, and echoed amongst the mountains like rolling thunder. Next instant the armies met. Wolfdieterich was always to be seen in front. All at once he turned to Berchtung, and said:

"Do you see Sabene and my brothers on yonder hill? I will go and see whether they or the alraun's son are the better men."

With these words, he set spurs to his horse and dashed through the enemy's ranks. Old Berchtung, who had vainly tried to restrain him, now followed with his sons and a small body of his men-at-arms.

As they neared the hill, they found themselves surrounded by the Greeks on every side. The carnage was terrible. Six of Berchtung's sixteen sons fell at his side, while a stone struck Wolfdieterich on the helmet, and stretched him senseless on the ground. But the old duke and his other sons picked him up, and brought him safely off the field. All night long they fled, and after resting only a few hours during the day, resumed their journey. On their arrival at Lilienporte, they found that many of their men had got there before them.

"We will await the traitors here," said Berchtung. "They may break their teeth on our stone walls, and then go away worse than they came. We have supplies enough to last four years, and can bid them defiance."

Soon after this, the enemy appeared before the fortress. Sabene demanded that the prince should be delivered up to them, and threatened that if this were refused he would burn the castle and all within it. The only answer made by the besieged was a sortie, led by Wolfdieterich in person. He still was hopeful of victory, but numbers prevailed. He had to retreat, and with difficulty regain the fortress. From that day he lost the confidence and gaiety of youth, and became grave and silent; his trust in the sure success of a righteous cause was gone. He lost his faith in Divine justice, and said he had fallen a victim to the resistless power that men call Fate.

SIGEMINNE.

THE SIEGE had already lasted three years, and yet there was no hope of an end. The food had grown scanty; and if the enemy chose to make famine their ally, the castle must finally capitulate. The duke vainly sought for some plan of deliverance. One day Wolfdieterich came to him, and said that he intended to slip out of the fortress by night, make his way though the enemy's camp, and go to Lombardy there to ask the help of Ortnit, the powerful emperor of the West. The old man did his best to dissuade the lad, reminding him that their provisions would last yet a year, and that the enemy, already weakened by sickness, might raise the siege before long. The young hero was not to be held back; at midnight he took leave of his foster-father and his other faithful friends.

"May God protect you, my dear lord," said Berchtung, clasping him in his arms. "You will have to cross the deserts of Roumelia, which are uninhabited, save by wild beasts and evil spirits. There you will find Rauch-Else, who lies in wait for young warriors.

Beware of her, for she is a witch, cunning in enchantments. If you are fortunate enough to reach the emperor Ortnit, do not forget your trusty henchmen, me and my ten remaining sons."

So they parted. They arranged that the besieged should make a sally through the principal gate of the fortress, to draw off the enemy's attention to that quarter, while Wolfdieterich got away by a postern door at the back. He was nearly out of the enemy's camp when he was recognised. Immediately mounting his horse, he drew his sword and cut his way through their midst, and once in the dark forest beyond, he was safe from pursuit. All night long Wolfdieterich rode through the wood. He heard the were-wolves howling in the distance but none came near to seek his life. As morning broke, he found himself by the side of a broad moorland lake. All sorts of strange creatures rose out of it, and sought to bar the road. Two of them he killed, but he let the others escape. He wandered three days in the wilderness, finding nothing for his horse or himself to eat. He shared the bread he had in his wallet with his steed. It was but a little at best; and the faithful creature was at last too exhausted to carry him farther, so he dismounted and led it by the bridle.

On the fourth evening, fatigue overpowered him so much that he was forced to rest. He lighted a fire with the brushwood scattered about. The warmth did him good, for a cold mist hung over the face of the earth. He and his horse quenched their thirst at a neighbouring rill, after which he lay down, and making a pillow of his saddle, thought over his sad fate. Sleep was beginning to steal upon his senses, when he was suddenly roused by a noise in the dry grass. Something black, and horrible to look upon, crept nearer and nearer. It raised itself in the air; its height was appalling. It spoke to him, not with a human voice; the sound was more like the growling of an angry bear.

"How dare you rest here!" said the monster. "I am Rauch-Else (rough Alice), and this ground belongs to me; besides which, I have another and a wider realm. Get up, and go at once or I will throw you into the quaking bog."

Wolfdieterich would willingly have obeyed, but he was too tired. He could not move. He therefore begged the bear-like queen to give him something to eat, telling her that his cruel brothers had deprived him of his inheritance, and that he was now starving in the desert.

"So you are Wolfdieterich," growled the bear-woman. "Well, Fate has marked you out to be my husband, so you may count upon my aid."

Upon which she gave him a juicy root, and scarcely had he eaten one mouthful when his courage returned, and his strength seemed tenfold what it had ever been before. It even came into his mind that he could conquer the Greek forces single-handed, and set his eleven faithful servants free. In obedience to Rauch-Else's command, he gave the rest of the root to his horse, which first smelt it carefully, and then ate eagerly. No sooner had it done so, than it began to paw the ground, and neighed with eagerness to resume its journey.

"Speak, will you be my true love?" asked the bear-woman, coming up to the youth, and preparing to clutch him to her heart with her terrible claws.

"Keep back," he cried, drawing his sword. "Demon that you are, seek a husband in hell, where alone you will find a helpmeet worthy of you."

"Have I not fed and succoured you?" asked Rauch-Else; "was that done like a demon? I have long waited for you to come and free me from an evil spell. Love me, and save me."

It seemed to the warrior as if her voice had all at once grown soft and human in its tones.

"Yes, yes," he said, "if only you were not so rough and hairy."

He had hardly spoken, when the black fleece slowly slipped to her feet, and a beautiful woman stood before him, her brow encircled by a diadem, and her green silken garment confined at the waist by a jewelled belt. Her voice was sweet and thrilling as she repeated her former words.

"Speak, young hero, will you love me?"

His only answer was to clasp her in his arms and kiss her.

"You must know," she said, "that although Rauch-Else was my name here in the wilderness, I am really Sigeminne, queen of Old-Troja. Your 'yes' has set me free from the spell of the enchanter, so we can now set out for my country, of which you shall be king."

Full of joy and thankfulness, they started on their way, followed by Wolfdieterich's horse. At last they heard the sound of waves breaking upon the shore, to which they soon afterwards descended. There they found a curious vessel awaiting them. The prow was formed of a fish's head, large and pointed. At the helm stood a merman, whose outstretched arm was the handle by which the rudder, or fish's tail, was worked. Instead of sails, the vessel was rigged out with griffin's wings, the advantage of which was, that they enabled it to go against both wind and tide, when such a course was thought desirable. The merman was so marvellously fashioned out of cedar-wood from Mount Lebanon, that it could steer wherever the travellers wished without their help. There were other wonders on board the ship, such as a cap of darkness, a ring with a stone ensuring victory to the wearer, a shirt of palm-silk, and many other things. The shirt seemed as though it would only fit a little child; but when Sigeminne put it on her lover, it grew bigger and bigger, until it fitted him exactly.

"Take great care of it," she said, "and wear it whenever you are in any danger, for it will protect you alike from steel and stone, from fire and dragon's tooth."

Wafted by the griffin's wings, the vessel clove the western sea, swift as the wind, and soon brought the travellers to Old-Troja. There the people received their beloved queen with shouts of joy, and cheered loud and long when she introduced the stately warrior Wolfdieterich as her future husband. The marriage was solemnized with great festivities, and a life of joy began for the new king. By the side of his fair wife he forgot all his misfortunes and sorrows, and, alas! even the Eleven Friends he had left in peril of their lives. Now and then, when he was alone, the memory of all that had come and gone would cross his mind like something he had dreamt, and then he would reproach himself with neglecting his duty; but Sigeminne had only to take his hand, and he once more forgot that honour and duty alike bade him he be up and doing.

Once when he, his wife, and the whole court were out hunting, a wondrous stag with golden horns broke out of a neighbouring thicket. He did not seem to be afraid, but, after looking at the hunters, turned back to the wood. "Up, good folk," cried Sigeminne. "Whoever kills that stag, and brings me the golden antlers, shall stand high in my favour and receive a ring from my own hand."

A number of huntsmen started in pursuit, first among them Wolfdieterich. The stag led him by many devious paths, only to disappear at last. Wolfdieterich returned to the tents much disappointed. When he got there, he found all in confusion; for that terrible magician, Giant Drusian, followed by many armed dwarfs, had fallen on the camp during the absence of the king and his warriors, and had carried off the queen. No one knew where he had taken her to. Wolfdieterich was now as much alone in the world, and as wretched, as he had been that terrible day in the desert. One thought filled his mind—the thought of Sigeminne. He would seek her through the world; and if he could not find her, he would die!

He exchanged his royal robes for a pilgrim's dress, and hid his sword in a hollow staff, which served to support him on his journey. Thus accoutred, he wandered through many lands, asking everywhere for the castle of Giant Drusian. At length he leant from a tiny dwarf, that the man he sought lived in the lofty mountains far over the sea, and that many dwarfs owned him for their lord. He set out again, and journeyed on and on, till at length the castle came in sight. He sat down to rest by a spring, and gazed longingly at the place where, as he believed and hoped, he should find his wife. His fatigue was so great that he fell asleep, dreamt of her, and was happy in his dreams.

All at once he was awakened by a rough voice, and a blow on the ribs.

"Who, ho! pilgrim," said the voice. "Have you snored long enough? Come home with me, and have some food. My wife wants to look at you."

Wolfdieterich sprang to his feet, and followed the giant who had wakened him so roughly, and who now strode before him to the castle. He knew that he had reached the end of his pilgrimage, and entered the wide hall with thanksgiving and joy.

There sat Sigeminne, her eyes red with weeping; and as she looked to him, he saw that she knew who he was. He pulled himself together with a violent effort not to betray his identity.

"There, wife," growled Drusian, "there's the priest you wanted to see, that he might speak to you about his religion. What a mite he is, to be sure, and as dumb as a lizard into the bargain! There, bag-of-bones," he added, turning to the pilgrim, "sit down by the fire, and see if some of our good food will not warm your thin blood."

The pilgrim did as he was desired, for, anxious and excited as he felt, he was starving. Dwarfs brought in food and drink, and he ate till his hunger was satisfied. The giant questioned him up and down, and received short answers, some of them, it must be confessed, far enough from the truth!

As twilight deepened, Drusian seized the lady by the hand, and pulled her from her seat, saying, "There, you see the son of the alraun, who freed you from the bear-skin, he will not succeed in freeing you from me a second time. He fears a broken skull too much. The term you asked for is over now, so come with me."

He would have dragged Sigeminne from the room, but the pilgrim had already thrown aside his disguise, and drawn his sword from the hollow staff.

"Back, monster," he shouted, "that is my wife." With these words he sprang upon the giant. The suddenness of the attack made the latter jump back, exclaiming, "Why, alraun, are *you* Wolfdieterich? If that is the case, we must have everything fair and in order. You must arm and fight with me—if you are brave enough, that is to say. Sigeminne shall be the wife of the conqueror."

The hero consented to fight the duel, and the dwarfs brought him three suits of armour to choose from. One was of gold, the second of silver, and the third of iron, very heavy, but old and rusty. He chose the last, but kept his own sword. Drusian also put on his coat of mail, and caught up his battle-axe.

After some time, Wolfdieterich's shield was broken by a violent blow from his opponent's axe. The hero seemed lost; but avoiding the next blow, and grasping his sword with both hands, he struck so hard a stroke that the sharp blade cut deep down through neck and shoulder. Scarcely had the monster fallen, when the dwarfs swarmed round the victor with their small daggers and spears to avenge their master. The fine needle-points pierced the rings of his armour, but the palm-silk shirt protected the solitary warrior from every wound. At last he forced them back, and husband and wife were able to clasp each other's hands, and to assure one another of a love that would last till death.

"Let us away from this cursed house," cried the hero, "who can tell but the dwarfish rabble are spinning new toils for us."

They hastened out into the deserted court, and then sought a stable, in which they found two saddled horses. These they mounted, and rode away.

After a long and tiring journey, they reached Old-Troja, where the return of the queen and her brave husband was greet with joy.

Sigeminne ruled her people with a gentle hand, but justly and firmly; no wonder, then, that they loved her. After her return, she was even sweeter and more thoughtful for others than she had ever been before; but she was pale and thin, and what was worse, grew paler and thinner day by day. One evening, when she and her husband were sitting alone together, she raised her sweet face to his and said, "When I am gone, you must go back to your own country and people, for then you will be looked upon as a stranger and usurper here, and the land might be wasted by civil war."

The thought of her death cut him to the heart, but he strove to look cheerful for fear of distressing his wife. He redoubled his anxious care of her, but all in vain; her doom was sealed. He had been strong enough to conquer the giant and save his wife, but he was powerless to save her now. She died in his arms, and he laid her in her early grave.

THE KNIFE MAN.

ONCE, WHEN he was standing sadly by her last resting-place, he suddenly remembered that she had bidden him go back to his own country when she was dead; and then the thought of his mother and his Faithful Eleven rushed back into his mind. He also recollected that he had never carried out his plan of calling the Emperor Ortnit to their assistance.

"I shall never forget you, dear wife," he murmured, "but I should be unworthy of your great love for me if I did not at once set out to bring freedom to those who have been true to the death in their fidelity to me."

He turned away, and hastened to make ready for his journey.

He passed through many lands, rich and poor. One evening he saw a castle before him, and asked a passing traveller to whom it belonged.

"Sir," replied the man, crossing himself, "ride on quickly, if you be a Christian, for that stronghold is where the heathen king Beligan lives, with his daughter Marpilia, a maiden learned in magic arts. He slays every Christian he can catch, and sticks his head on a spike placed on the battlements for the purpose. Look, there is one place empty still; beware lest your head be sent to fill it."

The hero explained that he felt no fear of that, as his armour was good, and he must have sharp weapons who sought to pierce it. But the traveller assured him that the king so thoroughly understood the art of dagger-throwing that none could escape from him alive.

Wolfdieterich and the man parted company. The former would have ridden past the castle, had not the owner come out to meet him, and invited him to spend the night with him; an invitation the hero was far too brave a man to decline. The daughter of his host, a young and beautiful girl, received him at the gate, and led him into the hall. While they supped together, Wolfdieterich, on being questioned, told them whence he came, and whither he was going; and Beligan saw from his answers that he was a Christian. The heathen king then informed his guest, with a diabolical smile, that he had come just in time to provide a head to make up the required number on the battlements. Wolfdieterich understood what was meant, but showing no signs of fear, he raised his goblet to his lips, and emptied it to the health of his host and his daughter.

Bedtime came, and Beligan, taking him aside, told him that he had found grace in the eyes of his daughter Marpilia, and that he might marry her if he liked, receiving both castle and kingdom as her dowry, on one condition—that he would worship Mahmet. Wolfdieterich asked for time to think over the proposal; but the heathen smiled, and said—

"You may have to-night to consider the plan; that is long enough."

He then offered him a goblet of wine, into which he had secretly thrown a powder.

"Drink, friend," he said, "and you will sleep long and soundly to-night."

The hero was on the point of obeying, when Marpilia, who had re-entered, snatched the goblet out of her father's hand, and emptying it on the floor, exclaimed,—

"Not so, father. I intend to teach the stranger better things to-night."

She led her guest to his room, and said—

"I have saved you from a great danger. My father was about to give you a sleeping potion, that he might slip into your room in the night and cut off your head, as he has already done to many a Christian. I now offer you my hand and kingdom, if you will only pretend to follow our faith."

Wolfdieterich thought of Sigeminne, and turning to Marpilia did his best to convert her to his faith. They spent the whole night talking on these subjects.

The next morning Beligan came, and invited his guest to join him at breakfast, and after that, in a little game of throwing the dagger, explaining that such was their custom. As soon as breakfast was over, they went into the court, where the king's servants stood around them in a wide circle. The hero laid aside his armour and sword as he was desired and received a buckler and three sharp and pointed daggers. The heathen took his stand opposite, armed in like manner. The latter flung the first dagger at his opponent's foot, and he avoided it by springing to one side.

"By the beard of the Prophet," cried the heathen, "who taught you that? Are you Wolfdieterich, from whom it is foretold that evil shall befall me?"

Wolfdieterich would not confess to his name, but stood ready again for the fight. The second dagger scratched his head, carrying off a bit of the scalp; the third he caught on his buckler.

It was now the hero's turn to throw. His first dagger pinned the heathen's foot to the ground; the second scratched his side; but the third, which he flung with the cry, "I am Wolfdieterich!" struck him to the heart. He was now attacked on all sides, but succeeded in putting his opponents to flight. He then reentered the castle, put on his armour, took his horse out of the stable, and was about to mount, when he suddenly saw that a wide lake surrounded the castle on every side, and a gale of wind was blowing the great waves so high that there seemed no chance of escape. At the edge of the water stood Marpilia, describing circles in the air and on the ground with a magic wand, and murmuring to herself the while. Riding up to her, he caught her in his arms, and swung her before him on his horse.

"If I am to drown, witch, you shall not escape," he said.

With these words he spurred his horse into the wild waves, and saw that the waters stretched out farther and farther, until they seemed a sea. He looked around, and saw that only one chance was left him. He flung the witch-woman off his horse; instantly the storm ceased, the waters retired, and he was once more on dry land.

But Marpilia was not drowned. She appeared before him again in all her beauty, stretching out her arms as if to embrace him, but he threatened her with his drawn sword. Then she changed into a magpie, flew to the top of a high rock, and sought from thence to entangle him with new enchantments, each more terrible than the other. At last, thoroughly spent with fatigue, he exclaimed, "Help me, Thou Three in One, or I die."

Scarcely had he uttered the words when the witch vanished, the sun shone once more upon mount and vale, and before him lay the broad road that led to Lombardy.

After meeting with many adventures by land and water, he travelled through a wild mountain region, and there he fell in with a giantess, an old friend of his father, who received him very kindly, and told him, amongst other things, of the said fate of Ortnit and Liebgart. Although her tale diminished his hopes of help, he was yet determined to continue his journey. The giantess said it would take an eternity travelling as he did, horses were so slow! With that she picked up both horse and rider, and carried them pick-a-back on her broad shoulders three hundred and fifty miles in one day, over mountains, valleys and rivers, and set him down in the fair land of Lombardy.

THE LIND-WORM.

IT WAS a beautiful moonlight night when Wolfdieterich reached Garden. He dismounted, and standing under the shadow of an olive-tree, he looked about him. He saw two women walking on the sea-shore. One of them was tall and stately. When she threw back her veil, he nearly uttered a cry of astonishment, she was so like Sigeminne. Had the grave given up its dead, or had some deceitful elf taken the beloved form to lead him into danger?

He stood breathless to listen, and heard Queen Liebgart, for it was she, complain to her serving-maid of the manifold sorrows and indignities she had been forced to endure.

"The cowardly vassals!" she said. "They have courage enough to frighten a weak woman, but no one dares to do the only thing that I desire on earth—to avenge the death of their king on the monster that killed him. And yet I have promised, although unwillingly, to give my hand to the true knight and hero that will do this thing!"

"There is only one man," said the maid, "who could do the deed, and that is the Greek Wolfdieterich, whose fame is spread abroad in every land."

"The avenger is come, great queen," said the hero, stepping out of the shade where he had stood. "I will venture my life to conquer the dragon."

The two women started back in alarm.

"It is Wolfdieterich!" cried the maid. "He once saved me from a band of robbers."

"Thanks, noble hero," said Liebgart, "and may Heaven protect you on your quest! But—the monster will take your life as it did my husband's. Nay, go your way in peace, and leave me to my fate."

But when the Greek showed her that his mind was firm, Liebgart gave him a ring which the dwarf had told her would bring good luck to the wearer, wished him all success, and then returned to Castle Garden.

Without more delay the hero turned his horse to the mountains, and made the best of his way to the lind-worm's hole, which at length he reached. He peeped into the dark cavern, and saw five dragons' heads staring and hissing at him. These were the young "worms"—the old one had gone out to seek for food. The hero was about to slay them there and then, but it suddenly occurred to him that it would be better if the old worm knew nothing of his coming, and it would be an easy task to kill the little ones when the mother was dead. So remounting his horse, he set out in search of the monster. As he rode on slowly, he saw a beautiful child standing on a rock. It called to him,—

"You are come to revenge my son Ortnit; beware that you sleep not, for if you sleep my son will remain unrevenged, and you will fall a prey to the dragon."

"My good friend," laughed the hero, "you are too young to be a father. I advise you to look out for yourself. You would be a sweeter morsel for the monster than I!"

And setting spurs to his horse, he rode away laughing. Like Ortnit, he came first to the high cliffs, and then to the meadow, where clover grass and flowers grew in wonderful profusion. A linden-tree shaded part of it from the heat of the mid-day sun. The hero was tired after his long journey and wakeful night. He stretched himself in the shade to rest, while his horse grazed in the meadow. Fatigue, the fresh sweet air, and the song of the birds in the branches overhead, all combined to make him drowsy, so he gradually fell asleep.

Perfect peace reigned in the quiet spot. It seemed as though it might last for ever, but suddenly it was broken by a horrible hissing, a crashing of rocks and breaking of trees. The dreadful monster, the terror of the land, was drawing near. At the same moment Alberich exclaimed: "Wake, noble hero; sleep no more; the lind-worm is upon you."

The dwarf repeated his warning several times in vain. The faithful horse galloped up to his master, and kicked him, but he did not awake. It was not until the dragon gave utterance to a loud and hideous roar, that made the rocks crack and the mountains tremble, that the hero was at last aroused from his trance. He sprang to his feet and attacked the monster; but his weapons were all too weak for the work they had to do—they broke like reeds on the creature's hide, without doing it any injury. So he flung the handle of his broken sword in the monster's face, and commended his soul to God, for he was defenseless. The worm caught him up in the coils of its long tail, and at the same moment seized the horse in its great jaws. Then it bore its victims away to its den, and threw them down as food for its young. After which it went away again in search of more food. The little dragons tried to devour Wolfdieterich, but could not, he was so well protected by his shirt of palm-silk, so they thrust him aside unconscious, and turned their attention to the horse, which they soon disposed of.

In the middle of the night Wolfdieterich came to himself, and began to look about him carefully. The moonlight penetrated the cavern, and showed him at a little distance something that shone bright red. He moved towards it cautiously for fear of waking the dragons, and found that the object which had attracted his eye was a huge carbuncle in a sword-hilt. He at once knew that this must be the sword Rosen, and took possession of it, as well as of the rest of Ortnit's armour, that he found lying uninjured amongst other coats of mail, which however were all more or less broken. With the armour he found a ring. this he put upon his finger. His preparations were no sooner completed than daybreak came, and with it the old lind-worm. He at once attacked her, and, thanks to the magic sword, slew her and all her brood after a hard struggle. Thoroughly exhausted,

he threw himself under a tree, where he lay panting and breathless. There Alberich found him, and revived him with food and
wine.

Before the victorious hero set out on his return to Garden, he
went back into the dragon's den to get the heads of the monsters; but when he had cut them off, he found that they were
much too heavy to carry, so he contented himself with taking
their tongues. These he put in a leather bag that one of
Alberich's dwarfs brought him for the purpose, and then began
his journey, which was made longer and more wearisome by
having to be done on foot. He often lost his way amongst the
wild mountains, and did not reach his destination for many days.

When he got to Garden, he found the castle full of feasting
and mirth. Wondering much, he went to a pious hermit who
lived near, and asked him the meaning of what was going on.
From him he learnt that the Burgrave Gerhart had slain the
lind-worm, and was to be married to beautiful Liebgart that very
evening. Wolfdieterich then begged the holy man to lend him
priestly garments, and having received those that had formerly
belonged to brother Martin, the hermit's predecessor, he put
them on over the armour he had found in the dragon's cave, and
repaired to the castle.

He entered the great hall and saw Burgrave Gerhart, nicknamed "Hawk's Nose," seated next to the pale queen, who, with
her maidens, filled the glasses of the guests. Above the
Burgrave's chair were the dragon's heads, symbols of his victory.
When the queen saw the pretended hermit, she took him a cup
of wine, which he emptied at a draught, and then gave back,
after having slipped into it the ring she had given him on the
evening he started on his quest. Liebgart did not notice the ring
till she had returned to her seat by Gerhart's side. Then she
trembled violently, but forcing down her emotion, she desired
the hermit to approach, and tell her from whom he got the ring.

"Lady, you gave it me yourself," he said, throwing aside his
disguise.

Every eye was fixed on him as he stood in the middle of the hall,
clad in Ortnit's wondrous armour, and looking more like a god than

a mortal man. When, advancing to the queen, he laid her husband's ring in her hand, and told her how and where he had found it, many voices cried, "Hail to the avenger of our king, the slayer of the dragon and its brood! Hail to the new king of Lombardy!"

Burgrave Gerhart was not to be put aside so easily. He pointed to the dragon's heads as proofs of his right; but when Wolfdieterich produced the tongues from his wallet, there was no more to be said but for Burgrave Gerhart to beg the hero's pardon. This he received on condition of swearing fealty.

Wolfdieterich was now proclaimed king of Lombardy, and was told that he was expected to marry the queen.

"My lords," he said, "as ruler of this kingdom, I am also the servant of my people, and am bound to labour for their welfare. But as regards personal matters, such as the choice of a wife, I must be free, and the queen must also be free to choose as she lists. She is yet mourning the loss of her first husband. But if she holds me worthy to succeed him, and thinks that my love and reverence will comfort her for his loss, I offer her my hand for life."

Liebgart, remembering what Ortnit had said to her, placed her hand in the hero's, and was married to him before long.

Wolfdieterich was no longer the impetuous boy who had left Lilienporte, but a man who could act with wisdom, prudence and forethought. He felt that his first duty was to restore peace and quiet to Lombardy, and that only after that was done would he be at liberty to consult his own wishes, and start to the assistance of his faithful servants. A year was spent in this labour, and then he told his wife that he must go to Lilienporte. She wept and said that she feared lest, like Ortnit, he should never return, but in the same breath confessed that he was right, and helped him to make ready for his journey and that of his army, which was to number sixty thousand men.

THE ELEVEN.

Winds and waves were in their favour, and the army landed at a short distance from Constantinople. Whilst the men encamped in a wood, the king set out in peasant's clothes to pick up all the news he could learn. After spending hours wandering about the city, and hearing nothing that was of any use to him, he chanced to meet Ortwin, a gaoler, and a former acquaintance of his. The man carried a basket filled with black bread. The hero went to him and asked him to give him a loaf for Wolfdieterich's sake. The man looked at him keenly, and recognised him.

"Ah, sire," he said, "things have gone badly here with us. The good old empress died during the siege of Lilienporte. When the fortress capitulated, the noble duke Berchtung and his sons were put in irons and flung into a dark and dismal dungeon. Death soon put an end to the old man's pain, but the ten young lords are still kept in strict confinement, and I may bring them no better food than a daily supply of this black bread and water."

Wolfdieterich was miserable when he thought that he was not without guilt with respect to his mother and his old friend. He could do nothing for them now, but he might still do something for the ten faithful servants who yet remained. He arranged with Ortwin that they should have better food, and should be cheered by the hope of a speedy deliverance. The old gaoler went on his way, and the king returned to his people.

He found his men already under arms, for they told him that Sabene had discovered not only that they were there, but what had brought them.

The armies met, and the battle raged long and furiously, without either side getting the better of the other. But at last the fortune of the day turned. The citizens of Constantinople rose in revolt against the tyranny that had ground them down so long, hastened to the prison, and set Berchtung's ten brave sons at liberty. Having done this, they put themselves under their command, and marched to the assistance of Wolfdieterich. It was a glorious victory. The hero was proclaimed emperor on the battle-field.

Soon after their return to the capital, Sabene and the royal brothers were brought before their judges. The first was sentenced to death, and was at once led away to instant execution; the death of the two latter was likewise demanded by both people and army, and Wolfdieterich knew that they were guilty of causing the death of their mother and that of old Berchtung, and had brought upon him all the troubles and difficulties of his early youth. Yet he could not decide what was best to be done, and reserved judgment until the following day.

That night, as the victor slept the sleep of the just, his mother appeared to him in a dream, saintlike and beautiful in aspect. She said: "Spare my children, and my blessing shall rest on thee."

And immediately Bechtung appeared at her side: "God has mercy upon His erring children; do not shed thy brother's blood."

As the hero gazed at the apparitions in intense amazement, Liebgart joined them, and said gently: "Hast thou not gained kingdom, glory and me, through the ill deeds of thy brothers. Return them, therefore, good for evil."

Morning broke—the figures vanished, leaving Wolfdieterich resolved what he should do. He called the nobles together, and before them all pardoned Bogen and Waxmuth, restored them their dignities and lands, to be held thenceforth as great fiefs under him. At first no one approved of his clemency, but on hearing his explanation all were silenced.

As soon as his arrangements were completed, Wolfdieterich returned with his army to Lombardy, and was welcomed by Liebgart with the greatest joy. After resting there for a while, he, his princes, and their followers went to Rome, where he was crowned emperor. At the feast which followed the coronation he appointed the ten sons of good Duke Berchtung to be rulers of great fiefs. Herbrand, the eldest, received Garden and its territory. Through his son Hildebrand, of whose valiant deeds we shall hear later on, he was the ancestor of the Wülfings. Hache was given Rhineland, with Breisach his capital. His son Eckehart was the protector of the Harlungs, Imbreke, and Fritele. He is celebrated in song and story as the trusty Eckehart. Berchther, the third son, succeeded his father at Meran. The other sons were as well endowed, but not as famous as their brothers, so their names and possessions need not be told.

Wolfdieterich and Liebgart had a son, whom they named Hugdieterich after his grandfather. He grew up to be a mighty hero, and was the father of a valiant race.

CHAPTER II.

KING SAMSON (SAMSING).

IN THE good old times a mighty jarl (earl) ruled over the rich town and district of Salern, which was one of the largest fiefs of a great kingdom. The jarl governed so strictly and justly that peace and plenty cheered the hearts of all that dwelt in the district. He kept up a large army to defend his coasts from the onslaught of the Vikings, who often descended on them in great numbers in hopes of plunder.

Amongst the followers of the jarl was the warrior Samson, nicknamed "The Black," because of his coal-black hair and beard. He was always the first in battle, and had even been known to disperse whole battalions with his single arm. He was terrible to look upon. His dark eyes flashed under heavy beetling brows. His bullneck and powerful limbs bore witness to his remarkable strength. No one could withstand him in battle. He hewed men down, whether armed or unarmed, with as great ease as if they were made of touchwood. In private life, on the other hand, he was gentle and kindly, unless contradicted; then, indeed, he would keep silence, but would none the less carry out his own will, regardless of the cost to others. As can be readily imagined, few people ventured to oppose him without reason.

One day the jarl, who had just been made king, was sitting at a feast in celebration of a great victory. His warriors were round him sharing in his joy, Samson in their midst. Suddenly he rose, and, taking a cup of wine in his hand, offered it to the king, and said, with all courtesy:

"Sire, many a victory have I helped to gain for you, and now I come to offer you this cup and to ask you to grant me a boon."

"Speak on, brave hero," answered the king, "and tell me what you desire. Hitherto you have asked no reward for your great deeds of valour. What you already have was given of my good will, unasked by you. So demand what you like, I can deny you nothing."

"Good, my lord," said Samson. "I do not want any more castles or lands, I am rich enough; but I am very solitary at home,

now that my mother has grown old and cross. Your daughter
Hildeswid is a sweet little thing, and I should much like to make
her my wife. Now you know how you can pleasure me by grant-
ing this request."

Rodgeier was so astonished at this address that he nearly let
the cup fall.

"You are a famous warrior," he said; "but the maiden is of
royal birth, and only a king can lead her home. You are in her
service as well as mine. So take this plate of sweetmeats and
bear it to her in the women's house. Then come back here, and
drown all memory of your strange request in a bowl of good
wine."

Samson took up the sweetmeats silently, and bore them to the
princess, who was busy embroidering with her maids. He placed
the dish before her, saying,—

"Eat, sweet one, for I bring you good news. You are to follow
me to my home, and live there as my good wife. Dress now, and
bid one of your maidens come with you."

On seeing the girl's hesitation, he added,—

"If you do not go willingly, you will force me to kill the jarl,
and burn the palace, with all that are in it."

He looked so fierce and grim as he spoke, that Hildeswid
trembled with fear, and obeyed him without a word.

He took her by the hand and led her down to the court, where
a groom was holding his horse in readiness. In the clear light of
day, and in the presence of many watchmen, none of whom
dared remonstrate, Samson placed the princess before him on
the saddle, and rode away with her into the wood and towards
his home. When he reached his dwelling the door was locked,
and he knocked so thunderously that the sound was heard to a
great distance. No answer. He knocked again and again. A
hoarse voice at last was heard from within, proclaiming that the
door should not be opened whilst the owner of the house was
from home.

"Mother," cried Samson, "pull back the bolts, for it is I—your
son—I have brought you a princess to be your daughter, and to
tend you in your old age."

The door opened, creaking and groaning, as though unaccustomed to move on its hinges, and a thin old woman came out on the threshold, dressed in rags.

"What?" she cried. "Do you bring guests with you? That woman in her grand clothes, her maid, and an idle groom. How could you do it, son? You know how poor we are;" and she looked up at her tall son with a cunning leer.

"But, mother," said the warrior, "where is the gold I sent you? Where are the servants I gave you? And what have you done with the gorgeous raiment I sent to clothe you?"

"I hid the gold away in my chest," answered the old woman; "for one never knows whether one may not become a pauper in one's old age. I dismissed the servants you gave me very soon, for I thought they would have eaten me out of house and home; and as for the clothes, I have laid them aside to wait for better times."

"Ah well, mother," said Samson, "if that sort of thing makes you happy, you can do as you like with your own; but now open the door and let us in. We are tired after our long ride, and would fain have a good dinner."

They went into the house and sat down. The old woman placed before them a hunch of rye bread and a jar of water. Samson would have made but a poor meal, had his groom not brought out a cut of venison and some wine, with which he had taken care to provide himself before leaving the palace. After he had stilled his hunger, Samson begged his lady's permission to go out and see if he could not find a stag to store the larder. The groom went down to the cellar, where he was fortunate enough to find a cask of ale; and the old mother withdrew to her own apartments, leaving the princess alone with her maid.

The wide hall was dark and eerie, and full of strange flickering shadows, that grew more mysterious and ghostlike as the evening closed in, and the owls might be heard hooting in the pine-trees near. Hildeswid could bear it no longer. She sent her maid to ask the old woman to come back to the hall; but she did not, nor did the maid return. The poor child's terror was so great that she determined to go in search of her mother-in-law.

She wandered through one empty, dreary, dusty room after another, till at last she entered a large vaulted chamber, and there she saw the old woman crouching over a great chest full of gold and precious stones, muttering to herself. Approaching her, Hildeswid heard her gloating over her treasures, and saying how much they would be increased when she added the princess's ornaments to the number, which could so easily be done by strangling the girl. Hildeswid uttered a low cry of terror, and the old woman looked round. Then, with a shriek of "thief, robber, wretch!" she threw herself upon the unhappy child, and tried to throttle her; but at that moment Samson came in and stopped her.

"Mother," he said, "you cannot remain here. I will take you and your treasure to my other house on the edge of the wood. There you can live in peace."

Meanwhile King Rodgeier had discovered that his daughter had been carried off. He sent out one body of his men-at-arms after another to fetch her home; but they all failed, and he prepared to go himself.

Riding along towards Samson's grange, he and his men saw a little house by the side of a great wood. They entered, and asked the old woman they met in the house to tell them where Samson lived. She denied that she had ever heard of such a man; but when the king offered her a handful of gold, she at once pointed out the path that led to his grange, and even went a bit of the way to see that they made no mistake.

The king and his fifteen companions had not gone very far when they met the hero. His helmet and armour were coal black, like his beard and hair; his steed was also black, but on his shield was emblazoned a lion on a golden field. There was a sharp, short fight in which Samson came off conqueror.

When the battle was over, he set out for his mother's house. On entering the hall he found her there busily counting the gold the king had given her.

"Mother," he said, "for the sake of that gold you betrayed your own son, and you richly deserve to die; but as you are my mother, I cannot punish your treachery."

The old woman went on counting her hoard as calmly as before.

"Mother," he began again, "you betrayed your son for gold,

and you should die by my dagger; but you are my mother, and I cannot slay you. Now listen to me: take your gold and leave this place, lest harm befall you."

The old woman poured her treasures into a huge sack, and answered,—

"This should all have been yours, if you had not brought that little fool into the house. I will go, and take my wealth to the king."

"I have slain him and his men," said Samson quietly; but he looked so stern that his mother changed colour, and muttered,—

"Very well then, I will go and seek an heir who will give both me and my treasures house-room."

Three times Samson's hand sought sword and dagger, but he mastered his anger, and rode away through the dark pine forest to his home.

When he got there, he found Hildeswid hard at work with her maidens.

"Wife," he said, going up to her, "my mother betrayed me for love of gold—my sword and dagger both thirsted for her blood—but I would not, could not slay her. If *you* are false to me—then—they *must* do their work."

He looked terrible in his wrath, but she took off his helmet and coat of mail, kissed him and led him to his seat. And he at once grew gentle, and told her that he wanted to win glory and honour for her sake, and that he hoped soon to see her acknowledged queen of her father's realm.

When the death of Rodgeier was made known in Salern by the only one of his men who had escaped to tell the tale, a Thing was summoned in order that a new ruler might be chosen. The votes were all in favour of Brunstein, brother of the late king, a man of great wisdom in counsel, and a lover of justice. There would now have been peace in the realm, had it not been for Samson, who made raids into the land and carried off cattle and supplies. So Brunstein called together all the bravest warriors of his own and other lands, and made them lay their hands in his and swear to take Samson alive or dead, or themselves die in the attempt. Then, led by the king, they set out and rode over mountains and plains and through the dark forest, and all without finding the object of their search. One evening they reached a strong fortress, and being very tired, rested there for the night. After supper they went to bed and slept. Every one slept, even the guards, when they had carefully locked and bolted the great gates.

That night Samson came. Finding he could not break the gates, he set fire to them, and while they were still burning, pulled them down, and leaped into the place. The watchmen awoke and blew their horns; but as there were many thatched roofs within the walls, all of which caught fire, the king and his men naturally thought a large army had broken in upon them, and were filled with terror. The gigantic figure of Black Samson appearing now here, now there, amongst the flames, added to their fear, and all that were left of them took refuge in flight.

The king, followed by six faithful attendants, made his way into the forest, and after riding a long time came in sight of a goodly grange. He entered, and found that the mistress of the house was his niece Hildeswid. He asked after Samson, but she said he was out. He then begged her to leave her husband and go with him; but she refused, advising him to go away as quickly as he could, lest he should fall into his enemy's hands.

Brunstein confessed that she was right, and took his departure, but it was even then too late. Samson had returned, and, seeing them, at once set out in pursuit. No courage or strength, however great, could avail against his terrible arm. Brunstein and five of his warriors fell never to rise again, while the sixth got away with great difficulty and not without severe wounds. Samson started in pursuit. When he got out of the wood, he saw thirty horsemen galloping towards him. On their banner, a lion was displayed on a golden field.

"So, ho," cried the hero, "you are Amelungs. Welcome, Uncle Dietmar. I rejoice to see you and your men."

When they had rested and refreshed themselves in Samson's grange, Dietmar explained, that having heard that his nephew was outlawed and in need of help, he had come to visit him and see whether he could be of any use. Samson was much pleased, and announced his intention of taking the open field now that he was no longer alone in the world. So he and his companions

set out next morning. No one ventured to oppose him, and he
soon had so large a district under his command that he was able
to take up the powers and dignity of duke. After that he made
his way towards Salern, and sent on messengers to desire the
citizens to elect him king, under pain of having their town and
possessions burnt about their ears.

After much conferring together, the burghers came to the
conclusion that they could not do better than obey; for while
Samson had been their friend, their town had been more flour-
ishing than at any other time. So they sent to beg him to come
and rule over them.

When the hero found that all was going as he wished, he sent
for his wife, and, side by side, they rode into Salern, where they
were received with acclamation.

The new ruler governed with a strong hand, and administered
justice equally to all, both high and low. He showed a grateful
remembrance of every kindness he had met with in his adver-
sity, and kept peace on his borders. He grew old in the punctual
fulfilment of these duties; and when he felt that he was no
longer strong enough to do the work alone, he appointed his
eldest son to be his assistant and successor. But he did not like
it to be supposed that he was too old and weak to be of use; and
so when his second son asked him what share he was to have in
the royal heritage, he answered him nothing, but called together
the whole army and made them an address.

He told them that when he was young every one had sought
to do great deeds, but now people had grown lazy. The long
peace, that had brought material blessing on the realm, had also
brought the curse of a love of ease and pleasure; and for fear this
evil should increase, and the country become an easy prey to
some greedy neighbour, he summoned every warrior to appear
before him in three months' time, each accompanied by his
men, and bearing a courageous heart within his breast, for he
was going to lead them against a powerful foe.

The same day that Samson made this announcement to his
army, he wrote a letter to the proud yarl Elsung of Bern
(Verona), a man of about his own age, and with an equal love of
great and heroic deeds. In this letter he demanded that Elsung

should pay him tribute as his liege lord, and should give his daughter, Odilia, to his second son. All this he demanded as a right, due from a vassal to his king.

When the jarl read the letter, he was very angry, and made immediate preparations for war. He began by ordering five of Samson's ambassadors to be hung on the spot, and the sixth to be sent back to his master with his tongue cut out.

No sooner were the three months over than King Samson started for Bern at the head of his men.

The armies met, and there was a great battle. The slaughter on either side was hideous. At length Samson's wondrous strength enabled him to slay the yarl, and gain the victory. The Bernese, seeing that their ruler was dead, thought it most prudent to choose Samson for their king, and thus put an end to all ill-feeling between the two nations.

When this business was settled, the victor sent for the jarl's daughter, Odilia, and told her that he intended her to be the wife of his second son, to whom he was going to make over her father's realm. The maiden wept, and said that she could not marry so soon after her father's death; but Samson's rage at meeting with contradiction was so terrible, that the girl in mortal fear consented to wed the prince. His berserker wrath appeased by her obedience, the king at once regained his usual genial manner, kissed her, and assured her of his protection.

The marriage arranged, Samson set out on his return to his own land, accompanied by his eldest son. Before he had gone very far, he felt his wounds painful. They would not heal, and caused him so much suffering that he had to halt at a little town on the way, and there he died, naming his youngest son ruler of the Rhineland, with Fritilaburg as his residence.

CHAPTER III.

DIETWART.

THERE WAS once an emperor of Rome (Romaburg) called Dietwart. His name was known far and wide for his great deeds.

At last, wishing to marry, he sent an embassy to King Ladmer of Westenmer to ask for the hand of his daughter. Ladmer professed himself highly honoured that so great an emperor should wish to be allied with his house, and begged that Dietwart would come to Westenmer and see the princess; that done, the two young people might make up their minds whether they were suited to each other. Dietwart consented, and after a stormy passage arrived at his destination, accompanied by a hundred of his bravest warriors.

Ladmer received his guest with all courtesy, and told him how glad he would be to have him for a son-in-law, but that the choice of a husband lay with the princess herself, for he would never constrain his daughter to marry against her will.

At the feast given in his honour, Dietwart dressed himself like his men; but the princess, whose duty it was to offer wine to her father's guests, soon saw which was which, and filled his goblet first. That evening her father asked her what she thought of the stranger, and she replied,—

"He seems to be a great prince, but I do not know his ways; and until I know that they are pleasant in my eyes, I will not marry him, as I might be very unhappy far away from all I love, in a foreign land."

Her father kissed her, and told her she must do as she pleased, but in his heart of hearts he hoped she would say "yes."

A great hunt was arranged for the following day, the object of which was the destruction of a number of stags, for they had grown so numerous that they had done a great deal of mischief in the neighbourhood.

Now it happened that Princess Minne was a mighty huntress, so she begged her father to let her join him on that day also, for she loved the sport, and, as he knew, her arrow could reach its goal as surely as that of any man. Dietwart did not much relish seeing her so employed. He thought it was not maidenly, and confided to his friends that he would rather seek a wife among the daughters of the great princes at home, than wed such a hoyden as the Lady Minnie. But however that might be, it was his duty, and theirs, as men, to see that the giddy girl got into no danger through her foolhardiness.

As they were going down a narrow glen, Minnie wounded a splendid stag, and the dogs set out in pursuit; while the princess, drawing another arrow from her quiver, hastened after them. Suddenly the dogs set up a simultaneous howl, and rushed out of the thicket. The ladies of the court shrieked aloud. "The worm," they cried, "the lind-worm! Come back, Lady Minnie, come back!" and at the same moment, turning quickly, they fled across the valley, and took refuge on the top of a neighbouring hill.

A frightful hissing, cracking and trampling was heard, and the dragon crept out of the thicket, its jaws wide open ready to seize its prey. It was a sight to make the bravest man tremble. Princess Minnie shot three arrows, one after the other, straight at the monster; but they glanced harmless off its horny scales. She turned to fly, but her foot caught in a branch, and she fell to the ground. She seemed lost, for the dragon was making ready to spring upon her. Dietwart and his men were close at hand. The latter threw themselves on the worm; while the former took his stand before the girl to defend her. It was a horrible sight.

Lances, swords, arrows were no defense. They could not pierce the monster's scales, and one brave man after another was caught in its claws, or was torn by its terrible teeth, which in shape resembled the anchors of a ship. Dietwart rushed to the assistance of his friends. He struck at the lind-worm's neck with his lance, but the point slipped from the scales, and the dragon tore his breast with its claws. It opened its great jaws as wide as it could, to seize and devour him; but the hero thrust the shaft of his spear into its gigantic mouth, and worked it round and round with such force that the point came out at the other side. A stream of poison, and flames of fire issued from the creature's nostrils, and the hero fell fainting to the ground, the dying monster on the top of him.

Dietwart was roused from his insensibility by feeling himself violently shaken. When he opened his eyes, he saw the princess struggling to free him from the dragon's body. Some woodmen came up and helped her. When at last he rose to his feet, he was so weak that he could not stand; and the men made a litter of wattled boughs, on which they carried him to the palace. The wound on his chest was carefully bound up, and no one thought much of it, because the flesh alone had been torn; but it festered badly, and the edges turned black, as though they had been burnt. The doctors declared that some of the dragon's poisonous breath had touched it, and they feared for the hero's life. The king, the court, nay the whole country, mourned for the man who had rid them of the monster.

One morning, as Dietwart lay sunk in a feverish doze after the intense pain of the night, he felt a hand busied about his wound. Strange to say, the hand felt both softer and gentler than that of the doctor. He opened his eyes, and recognised the princess. He watched her carefully remove the bandages, and drop some liquid from a bottle into his burning wound. The pain at once left him. He would have thanked her, but she signed to him to be silent. After she had replaced the bandages, and motioned to the nurses to be still, she went away as gently as she had come. The wounded man felt as free from pain as if an angel had brought him some of the water of life. He fell into a quiet slumber. At night the pain returned, but the next morning Minnie came back, and poured balm into his wound. On the third morning she came again. He felt so much stronger, that he could not refrain from seizing her hand and pressing it to his lips. She withdrew it gently, and went away signing to him once more to hold his peace.

The doctor rejoiced to the rapid recovery of his patient. When told what had happened, he said that the royal maid had received the miraculous balm from her mother on her deathbed, and that she was forbidden to use it except in cases of great necessity, and for those she loved.

"For those she loved?" repeated the hero; and he felt strangely happy.

When he was well again, he one day met her alone in the garden, and told her of his love. They talked together for a long time; and when good King Ladmer heard of their engagement, he gave them his blessing. The marriage feast was soon afterwards held, and there, in the middle of the table, as one of its

greatest ornaments, was one of the dragon's teeth set in silver—
a nice little tooth it was, weighing at least half a hundred weight.

The husband and wife set out for Rome. The winds and waves
favoured them, and they soon reached Dietwart's native land.
The legend informs us that they lived very happily together for
four hundred years, and had forty-four children, of whom one
son, Sigeher, alone survived them. But it does not tell us
whether the Lady Minnie took kindly to her household duties,
or always remained fonder of field sports than of needlework.

LEGEND OF
DIETRICH AND HILDEBRAND

CHAPTER I.

DIETMAR, SECOND son of Hugdieterich, ruled with a strong hand at Bern, and refused to acknowledge his elder brother Ermenrich, or any other king as his suzerain. He was a mighty warrior, and so terrible in battle that few of his enemies dared look him in the face. But at home he was gentle to all, especially to his wife Odilia, daughter of Elsung, or, according to another saga, daughter of a Danish king. His eldest son, Dietrich, was the joy of his heart. At twelve years old the lad had the strength of a mighty warrior. His fair hair fell over his shoulders in heavy curls. His figure was tall and slender, yet strong and well-knit. He had regular features, but when he was angry, he was terrible to look upon. From his earliest childhood any one might see that he would become a lion-hearted hero. It was even said that his breath was like glowing fire when he was angry, and this the people thought an undoubted proof that he was descended from a demon ancestor.

When Dietrich was five years old, a famous hero came to his father's court. This was Hildebrand, son of Herbrand, and grandson of the faithful Berchtung. As we said before, Herbrand's fief consisted of the district and castle of Garden. He had brought up his son in the traditional way, so that he grew up to be a perfect warrior, and a wise man. King Dietmar was so pleased with his guest that he appointed him to be his son's

41

teacher and governor. This was the beginning of a friendship between master and pupil that lasted till death parted them.

THE SWORD NAGELRING.

NOW IT came to pass that a giant and giantess invaded Dietmar's land; and slew, burnt, and plundered the people. They were so strong that no one could resist them. The king went against them at the head of an army; but could not find them. He saw everywhere on his borders the desolation they had caused; but none could tell him where they were concealed. At this ill-success young Dietrich and his master were as much distressed as the king himself. They determined to search for the giants till they found them, though the search should cost them years.

They wandered over mountains and valleys seeking the monsters, but seeing nothing of them. One day they set out to hunt with their hawks and hounds, and came to a great forest, in the middle of which was a green meadow, where they thought they should find plenty of game. They uncoupled the hounds, and rode, one to the left and the other to the right of the meadow, holding their weapons in readiness. As Dietrich slowly advanced, keeping a sharp look out, a dwarf crossed his path. Stooping from his horse, he caught up the mannikin and placed him in front of him. The little prisoner made so loud a moan, that Hildebrand heard him, and galloped across the meadow to see what was the matter. Catching sight of the dwarf,—

"Hello!" he cried. "Hold the rascal tight. He knows all roads, both on, and under the earth. He is Elbegast, the prince of thieves, and is certain to be a friend of the robbers."

The dwarf shrieked louder than before, and declared that far from being their friend, he had suffered much wrong at the hands of the giant Grim and his sister Hilde, that he had even been obliged to forge for them the good sword Nagelring, and the strong helmet Hildegrim, and had been forced to lead them to their victims by hidden ways known only to himself. He swore to help the warriors if they wished to fight the unholy pair.

The mannikin was therefore set at liberty. He drew a long breath, and said:

"You could not catch me now, if I wished to escape you; but I will serve you faithfully, that I may be freed from the power of the giants. Come back to this place at day-break to-morrow, and I will give you the sword Nagelring, without which you could not conquer the monster. I shall steal it from him as truly as I am Elbegast, the prince of thieves. Then I will show you his foot-marks in the dewy grass, that you may track him to his hollow mountain, where, if you slay him and his wicked sister, you will find rich booty to reward you."

The dwarf had no sooner uttered these words than he vanished. The next morning, before daylight, the prince and his companion came to the edge of the green meadow talking of this and that. They agreed that the word of a mountain goblin was not to be trusted, and that thievish Elbegast would probably be false like all his kindred. Their conversation was interrupted by a strange clanking sound, and at the same moment they noticed the rosy dawn overspreading the sky. They started to their feet, and looked about. Elbegast came up to them dragging a huge sword. Dietrich seized it with a cry of joy, unsheathed it and swung it in the air.

"Now," cried Elbegast, "you have the strength of twelve men, and can fight the monster on equal terms. Look carefully and you will see the marks of his shoes distinctly printed on the dewy grass. I had to make his shoes of iron, for he is miserly, and said that leather was too dear. Follow the tracks, and they will lead you to the entrance of his cave. I can go with you no farther."

He vanished, and the heroes followed the giant's tracks in obedience to the dwarf's advice.

At length they reached a great cliff, but there was no opening to be seen large enough to serve as a door. A few cracks might be noticed here and there in the stone, so small that only a dwarf or a lizard could have crept in; certainly not a man in armour, and still less a giant. Hildebrand thought that a bit of the rock might perhaps be fitted into the cliff instead of a door. He tried to shake and loosen any projecting piece of the cliff that he could clutch. His efforts were not in vain. An enormous block of stone stirred and rocked beneath his hands, and just as Dietrich came to his assistance, it fell thundering into the valley below. The sunlight penetrated the darkness of a deep cavern, in the background of which a great fire was burning. Grim was lying on a bed of bear and wolf skins close to the flames. Wakened by the falling rock, he raised himself on his elbow, and perceiving the warrior's approach, looked about for his sword; not finding it, he snatched up a burning log, and rushed upon Dietrich. His blows sounded like claps of thunder, and fell as thick as hail; it was only the young warrior's nimbleness that saved his life, which was endangered not only by the force of the blows, but by the smoke and the burning sparks that flew from the log. Hildebrand would have gone to his pupil's assistance had not the latter forbidden him. And indeed he soon had enough to do to defend himself, for the giantess now appeared, and catching Hildebrand up in her arms, held him tight. It was a deadly embrace. The warrior could not breathe. He struggled in vain to free himself from the sinewy arms that held him. At last the giantess threw him on his back, pressing his hands and arms as though in a vice, and making the blood spurt from under his nails. She looked about for a rope with which to bind and hang him. Hildebrand called to his companion to help him in his need. Dietrich seeing his friend's danger leaped over the giant's weapon with a despairing spring, and at the same time seizing his sword in both hands, split the monster's head from the crown to the collar-bone. Then turning upon the giantess, he slew her after a short but sharp engagement.

Hildebrand now staggered to his feet, and said that from henceforth he would regard his former pupil as his master, because that woman has been harder to deal with than any foe he had ever met before. Dietrich and Hildebrand took the treasure they found hidden away in a side cave, as their meed of victory, and brought it home to Bern.

King Dietmar rejoiced in the glory of his heroic son, whose name had become famous in every land; but he did not live long after these events. He died loved and honoured by all. When Dietrich ascended the throne, he gave his young brother

Diether into Hildebrand's charge, begging his friend to teach the boy to be a hero and a worthy scion of his noble race.

And Hildebrand did his best, with the help of his wife, the good high-souled Ute (Uote), whom he married soon after. Together they taught the boy to love what was good and true, to be brave, and to be not only an admirer but a doer of high deeds.

SIGENOT.

SOON AFTER Grim and Hilde had fallen under Dietrich's sword, their nephew, strong Sigenot, a giant who lived in the Western Mountains, came down into the forest to visit his relations. When he discovered their dead bodies in the cave, he howled with rage and swore to avenge their death. A dwarf for whom he called told him of the fight between his uncle and aunt and the heroes, but Sigenot would not believe the story. He thought that Grim and Hilde had been murdered in their sleep by Dietrich and his comrade for the sake of their hoard.

Years passed on. One evening the heroes were seated together in the great hall of the palace, drinking their wine and talking.

"Master," said King Dietrich, "I never saw a living wife embrace her husband so passionately as Hilde did you that day in the cave. I think the Lady Ute would be angry if she heard how the giantess hugged you."

"What a monster she was," answered Hildebrand with a shudder, "and you freed me from her clutches."

"Yes," said the king, laughing, "it showed my generosity. I returned you good for evil that time, for you know I might have remembered how many thrashings and floggings you had given me when a boy. Now, confess, was I not generous?"

"I am quite willing to do so," replied Hildebrand with a smile, and then added gravely: "but do not pride yourself too much on the past, for the giant Sigenot has long been watching for us in the mountains, that he may fall upon us and avenge his uncle Grim's death. From what I hear, he is so strong that no mortal man can withstand him, and even an army would fall before him like corn under the sickle."

"Hey! what new story is this?" cried the king. "So Grim's avenger is lying in wait in the mountains? Why did no one tell me before? I will start to-morrow in search of him, and free my realm from the monster."

"What!" cried one of the guests.

"Are you going to attack the giant?" asked another.

"The murderous Sigenot!" added a third.

"Listen to me, Dietrich, my pupil," said Hildebrand solemnly, "he is not heroic, but foolhardy, who undertakes to do the impossible, and it is impossible to conquer that giant."

"Listen, dear master," answered Dietrich; "do you remember how you taught me that he is a hero who undertakes what is apparently impossible, because he trusts in his strength, and in the justice of his cause? He is a hero, whether he gains the crown of victory or meets with death. My cause is just, because I go forth to free my realm and my people from the power of the monster."

"Sire," cried Hildebrand, "you are no longer my pupil, but my comrade, and as your comrade I will accompany you to the great battle."

The king answered after a short pause, "My master used to say, 'One against one is the way of true warriors; two against one is the way of cowards'—so I must go alone."

"If you do no return in eight days," returned the master, "I will follow you, and be your liberator, or your avenger, or your companion in death."

"Why make so much ado?" cried Wolfhart; "the king will strike old Long-legs dead, or else uncle Hildebrand will do it, and if they both should fail, I will follow them, and I wager my head that I will lead him like a captive bear by a rope to the castle here, and then hang him over the battlements, where he may stay till his gossips in hell come to fetch him home."

Dietrich then set out on his journey. On the evening of the third day he came in sight of the Mountains. He felt so cheery and so strong that he would not have feared to offer battle to all the giants in the world. As he was lying on the grass, sunk in happy reverie, he saw a stately elk, sprang on his horse, and followed it until he came up with it, when drawing his sword he stabbed it in the neck, so that it fell dead. He lighted a fire, roasted a bit of the elk for his supper, and ate it, washing it down with some cups of wine he drew from the skin at his saddle bow.

A cry of agony disturbed him in the midst of his enjoyment. He looked up, and saw a naked giant covered from head to foot with bristly hair, who was holding a dwarf firmly bound to the end of his iron club. The mannikin shrieked to the warrior for help, affirming that the monster was about to eat him alive. Dietrich at once advanced towards the wild man, and offered him a fair exchange. He said he might have the elk instead of the dwarf, and that he would find it a larger and juicier mouthful.

"Get out of the way, you dog," bellowed the giant. "Get out of the way, or I will roast you at your own fire, and eat you up, armour and all."

The hero's anger was stirred at this address, and he drew Nagelring from its sheath, while the giant swept the dwarf from off his club as easily as a snowflake. Then the battle began, and raged until both combatants were so weary that they had to rest awhile. The king again offered to make peace with the monster, because he had come out to fight with the master and not with the servant. A shout of scornful laughter was the answer he received, and then the giant cried in a mighty voice that made the trees tremble to their roots, "Do you think that a little midget like you could conquer Sigenot? He would bind you to a stake as easily as I should that dwarf, and would leave you to die in agony."

And now the fray was renewed. The dwarf, who had freed himself from his bonds, kept well behind Dietrich, and advised him what to do.

"Hit him over the ear with the hilt of your sword, the blade is of no use with him."

Dietrich did as he was advised, and the monster fell with a crash beneath his blow. The sword-hilt had penetrated deep into his skull; a second and a third blow put an end to him.

"Now quick, let us away," cried the dwarf, "before Sigenot, king of the Mountains, comes down upon us. Should he find us here, we are lost."

Proud of his victory, Dietrich explained the object of his quest. "Noble hero," said the mannikin, "you cannot escape your fate. If by a miracle you are victorious, we poor dwarfs will be freed from an intolerable tyranny, in gratitude for which boon we will be your faithful friends as long as you live. Our father, Alberich, left the rule over thousands of our people in equal proportions to me, his eldest son, Waldung, and to Egerich, his younger son. But in spite of our caps of darkness, and all our magic arts, Sigenot has enslaved us, and holds us now in such vile bondage that many die of hardships, and many more are devoured by him."

"Well," said Dietrich, "show your gratitude by pointing out the way to Sigenot."

The dwarf showed the hero the snow-topped mountain where his enemy lived, drew the cap of darkness over his head, and disappeared.

Dietrich set out, and about mid-day arrived at the regions of ice and snow. Long grey moss hung pendant from the branches of the pines, and covered the stems to the root. A thick mist suddenly rose, and hid the mountain. All at once the mist parted like a curtain, and Dietrich saw a beautiful woman in snow-white garments, a diadem of precious stones on her head, and round her throat a necklace that shone like the stars. She raised her finger warningly, and said, "Ride back, hero of Bern, or you are lost. The destroyer is lying in ambush for you."

She glided past with inaudible steps, and vanished among the glaciers, leaving Dietrich lost in astonishment, and wondering whether it were the goddess Freyja, or the elf-queen Virginal that he had seen.

He was startled out of his reverie by a shut, and at the same moment perceived the gigantic warrior hastening to meet him.

"So you have come at last," he cried, "to give me an opportunity of revenging the murder of Grim and Hilde."

They began to fight without more ado. As Dietrich tried to make use of what he thought a favourable chance, the blade of his sword Nagelring was caught in an overhanging bough. All his efforts to withdraw it were in vain. At last the steel broke, and at the same moment a blow of the giant's club stretched the hero senseless on the ground. His helmet was unhurt, but the blow had been so heavy that it left him unconscious. The giant now fell upon him, kneaded his defenseless body both with his hands and his knees, and then dragged him away into his dismal den.

Master Hildebrand waited for eight days with great impatience; then, finding that the king did not return, he took leave of his wife, and set forth in search of him.

In the wood near the snow-capped mountain Hildebrand found the king's horse, and further on the broken sword. He could no longer doubt what his friend's fate had been. Vengeance, not deliverance, was now alone what he hoped for, and he rode on unheeding the warning that the little dwarf Waldung called after him.

On perceiving the new comer the giant rushed upon him. The battle between them was long and fierce, and Sigenot disdained no weapon or defense. He tore up bushes and even trees, and threw them at the hero. When Hildebrand at last tried to defend himself by a ruse, the club came down upon his head, and struck him senseless to the ground. "Come on, long beard," shouted Sigenot, "Hilde and Grim are avenged at last."

So saying, he bound the fallen warrior hand and foot, and seizing him by the head, flung him over his shoulder, and bore him to his cave, singing loudly the while.

The giant's dwelling was large and lofty. The roof was supported by stone pillars, and a carbuncle in the centre shed a pleasant light over the foreground, while the back of the cavern was dark and gloomy in the extreme. On entering, the giant threw down his burden with such force that Hildebrand thought every bone in his body was broken. Sigenot then went to a side cave to fetch an iron chain with which to bind his prisoner, saying that he would not be long away.

When a weak man is in sore traits, he at once gives himself up for lost. Not so the hero. He never abandons hope until he has tried every mode of rescue, however poor. It was thus with Hildebrand. Looking around him, he perceived his good sword, which the giant had seized as rightful booty, lying in a distant corner, and he thought that he might yet fight and gain the victory, if he could only cut the cords that bound his wrists. He sawed the cords on his wrists against the pillar, and cut them through. No sooner were his hands free, than he undid the ropes and cords about his feet, and snatching up his sword, hid behind the pillar, which he intended to use as a protection, his shield having been left in the wood.

Sigenot returned with the chains, and looked about in astonishment. His prisoner was gone. Suddenly he caught sight of him behind a pillar, and the battle raged anew. The ground trembled beneath the giant's tread, and the rocks re-echoed the sound of blows. The combatants were now fighting in the dark background of the cave, led there by the gradual retreat of Hildebrand, when suddenly the hero heard his name called from the depths beyond. He recognised the king's voice, and the knowledge that his friend yet lived gave added strength to his arm. A few minutes more, and the giant was stretched at his feet.

The victory was won. He cut off the monster's head, and while resting for a moment after his exertion, he heard Dietrich's voice exclaiming:

"Hildebrand, dear master, help me out of the serpent's hole. There are still some adders here, alive, though I have slain and eaten many more."

Finding that the king was confined in a deep hole, Hildebrand looked round for a rope or a ladder, with which to help him out. Whilst engaged in this search, he was joined by the dwarf Waldung, who gave him a ladder of ropes, by means of which the king was rescued.

"Hildebrand," said Dietrich, taking a long breath of the fresh pure air, "you are not my comrade, but my master."

After this, the heroes followed the dwarf into his subterranean kingdom, where he provided them with food and drink, and offered them costly treasures. The noblest gift that Dietrich accepted was his sword Nagelring mended, hardened, and newly adorned with gold and precious stones, so that it was more beautiful as well as stronger than before. The heroes now returned to Bern, where they were received with great joy.

CHAPTER II.

QUEEN VIRGINAL.

ONCE WHEN Dietrich and Hildebrand were hunting in the wild mountains of Tyrol, the king confessed that he had never been able to forget Queen Virginal, who had come out to warn him of Sigenot's approach.

"You would find it as easy to gain the love of a star as to wile Queen Virginal away from her glaciers and snow mountains," said Hildebrand.

While the heroes were thus talking together, a tiny little mannikin dressed in full armour suddenly stood before them.

"Noble warriors," he said, "you must know that I am Bibung, the unconquerable protector of Queen Virginal, ruler of all the dwarfs and giants in these mountains. With my help she chased thievish Elbegast away from her dominions; but the wretch has now invaded her realm with the help of the magician Ortgis, his giants and his lind-worms. He has forced her by his black art to pay him a shameful tribute. He obliges her every full moon to give him one of her beautiful maidens, whom he then imprisons, fattens, and eats for his dinner. So Jeraspunt, her palace, is filled with weeping and mourning. My lady, hearing that you conquered the dread Sigenot, entreats you to come to her aid; therefore hasten to Jeraspunt and rescue our great queen."

The heroes consented, and asked to be shown the way. The dwarf guided them till they came within sight of a wondrous building shining on the heights in the light of the evening sun. Hildebrand broke the silence that had fallen on them by exclaiming, "Truly if the Lady Ute were not my wife, I should be inclined to try my luck with Queen Virginal; but as things are, I will do my best to help you to win her. Well, Bibung!—why, where in the world has the rascal got to?"

"The unconquerable protector of the queen has a wholesome terror of Ortgis," laughed Dietrich. "But now let us on to the palace."

"Night is the time for witches to journey, not honest men,"

said Hildebrand, "so let us stretch ourselves on the soft moss, and rest until morning."

The next morning was dull and misty, and a snow storm beat in the faces of the warriors as they climbed the steep mountain on foot, by a road impassable for horses. On and on they went, a weary way. As they stopped to slake their thirst at a spring, they heard a woman's voice shrieking for help. A girl rushed up to them and entreated their aid against terrible Ortgis, to whom she had been delivered according to the treaty, and who was now hunting her down with his dogs. At the same moment the holloa of the huntsman was heard, and in another the battle of the heroes with Ortgis and his followers had begun. Gigantic as were Ortgis and his train, they soon fell under the swords of the heroes. One man alone escaped, but he was the worst of the whole crew, for he was Janibas, son of Ortgis, and a great magician like his father.

Dietrich and Hildebrand determined to take shelter in the castle of Ortgis which was nigh at hand. When they knocked at the door several armed giants rushed out upon them, but at length they too were conquered. A horseman in black armour had kept behind the rest during the battle. He murmured something in a strange language, and obedient to his voice, new giants arose out of the earth, to take the place of the slain; still the heroes were victorious. The black horseman continued to murmur, and horrible lind-worms crept out of the ground, and with them Dietrich and Hildebrand had to fight all night long. The black horseman disappeared at last, when the first rays of the rising sun lighted up the castle in the valley. At the same moment the heroes saw an enormous old lind-worm crawling away with an armed man in its jaws. It wanted to creep away unnoticed, but the warriors immediately attacked it. The dragon let its victim fall, and hurled itself, hissing, upon Dietrich who stood nearest. With one claw it tore away his shield and ripped up his coat of mail; at the same time it caught up Hildebrand with its tail and flung him to a great distance. But Dietrich thrust his sword right through its jaws, and so deep into a neighboring tree, that the creature was pinned down, and died a few minutes after, roaring like thunder.

The maiden they had saved from Ortgis had watched the combat from afar. She now approached and bound up Dietrich's wounds, pouring in a healing balm. Meanwhile, Hildebrand had picked up the man the dragon had let fall, and recognised him as Ruotwin, the son of Helfrich of Tuscany, who was his mother's brother.

Ruotwin joined the other two, and promised to help them to punish the wizard Janibas. Further help appeared in the person of Helfrich. The whole party now moved on towards the magician's castle, the gates of which stood open. The court was full of armed men, amongst whom was Janibas in black armour, riding on a coal black steed. He murmured magic words, and lions rushed out on the heroes. These great beasts were slain, and so were the men-at-arms who followed them. Janibas alone escaped.

Dietrich and his followers entered the castle, where they found three of the queen's maidens cooped up for fattening, and set them free. After which, they burnt the magician's fortress, that it might not serve as a refuge to Janibas if he returned to that part of the country.

The whole party then started for Aron, the castle of Helfrich, where the heroes were to rest before continuing their journey to the palace of Queen Virginal. A short respite from their toil was the more necessary as Dietrich's wounds were very painful; but their hostess' good nursing had soon the happiest effect in subduing the fever, and healing the wounds. At last the day was fixed for their departure, and Helfrich had settled to go with them, and lead them to Jeraspunt. While they were making their final arrangements, a dwarf galloped up to the door, and throwing himself from his horse, entered the hall, his mantle torn and dusty, and his countenance as pale as death.

"Help, noble heroes, help!" he cried. "Janibas has come against Queen Virginal in battle array. He has ordered her to deliver all her maidens up to him, and also the carbuncle in the coronet. If he gets that into his power, no one can withstand him, for it would give him complete command over all the mountains, and over all the giants, dwarfs and lind-worms that inhabit them. Woe to them, if they fall into his hands."

Dietrich at once declared his readiness to go alone to the

queen's help, if the others were not prepared to start on the instant.

"What, alone!" cried the dwarf. "If you go alone you are a dead man. Even I, her majesty's special defender, had to turn my back, and fly before the foe; what then would become of you?"

Nobody could help laughing at the mannikin's conceit; but there was no time to lose, and all the warriors hastened to arm and start for the palace.

The heroes and their friends had a long and hard pull up the mountain side, over snow fields and glaciers, in the midst of which great crevasses yawned in unexpected places, but they were cheered on their way by catching from every height a glimpse of Jeraspunt. At length they came so near that they heard shrieks and howls, and other sounds of battle. A few minutes later the terrible scene was visible. Some of the palace guard were killed and mangled, others were yet defending themselves. Gigantic dogs, monsters of every sort, and hordes of savage warriors formed the enemy's ranks. Many had forced their way through the broken gate, and were raging, storming, and howling round the queen's throne.

The sovereign lady sat there unmoved, surrounded by her trembling maidens; a carbuncle glowed in the diadem that graced her head, and a silver veil was wrapt about her. Her only protection seemed to be a magic circle that her assailants could not pass. Whether the magic lay in her wonderful beauty or in the spiritual love that shone in her face, it were impossible to say. No one had yet dared to approach her. Even the heroes halted for a moment on first seeing her, but then recovering themselves, pressed forward.

They made their way in spite of clouds of snow, and lumps of ice, to say nothing of a frightful hurricane that almost blew them away. The mountains trembled under repeated thunder claps, and a bottomless crevasse divided them from the palace. But the same moment Dietrich perceived the black horseman reading his magic spells from an iron tablet. He sprang upon him broke the tablet, and slew the magician. A great clap of thunder rolled over the mountains, avalanches fell, ice fields broke up, and then came a silence as of death. The spell was broken, the yawning gulf closed, and the way to the palace was free. The magician's followers, eager to avenge their master, attacked the heroes and their men, but their efforts were vain. The monsters, who yet lived, had soon to fly and seek refuge in the solitudes of the snow mountains.

Dietrich now approached the queen at the head of his followers. He would have knelt before her, but she rose from her throne, and offering him her hand, greeted him with a kiss. Unable to utter a word, he let her lead him to the throne, and seated himself at her side.

"Know, great hero," she said, "that I have seen your love and your deeds. I give up my rule in Elf-land, and will go home with you, and live amongst mortal men till death parts us."

The palace was cleansed by invisible hands; the gate, and all the broken posts and pillars were mended during the night, and the marriage of the mortal hero with the elf-queen was solemnized soon after. The husband and wife then started for Bern, where Virginal made his home so delightful that it was long before Dietrich thought of seeking more adventures. Meanwhile there was sorrow in the mountains, and in the heart of every elf that lived there. The queen had left her country and her people for the sake of a mortal. All nature mourned her absence, the sunsets had no longer the prismatic hues of former times, and the fairy palace was invisible to all.

Chapter III.

Dietrich's Comrades—Heime.

In all countries and amongst all nations were spread the name and fame of Dietrich of Bern, for he was the favourite hero of many a wandering minstrel, and so it came to pass that numbers of brave warriors used to go and visit him, and take part in the amusements or serious occupations that engrossed the attention of their host during the time of their visit.

Even in the far north his name was famous, not only in the

castle of the noble, but in many a wayside inn and solitary grange.

At the time of which we speak a renowned horsedealer called Studas lived in the heart of a great forest. He cared little for the singing and fiddling of the wandering minstrels, but his son Heime was different. He often declared that he knew he could wield lance and sword as well as the hero of Bern. His father was weary of his vainglorious talk, and one day, when the young fellow was boasting as usual that he was as good a man as Dietrich, if not better, his father exclaimed in a pet:

"Well, if that be the case, go up to the hollow mountain, and kill the dragon that is doing all this mischief in the neighbourhood."

The lad looked up at him inquiringly. The father nodded, and Heime, casting a haughty look at him, turned and went out.

"He will not do it," muttered the old man, "but I think I have cooled his hot blood for him."

Things were going otherwise than honest Studas dreamed in his philosophy. His bold son armed himself, and mounting one of his father's best horses, rode off to the mountain. The lindworm sprang at him with open jaws, but the lad plunged his spear into his mouth with such force that the point came out behind his head. The monster lashed the ground long and furiously with his tail, but at length fell dead. Whereupon Heime cut off his head, and riding home, took it into the grange, and flung the trophy at his father's feet.

"St. Kilian!" cried Studas. "Boy, have you really killed the dragon? Well—"

"Well," answered the bold youth, "I shall now go and slay the hero of Bern. Give me the horse that carried me so bravely to-day. He will take me to Bern, and bring me home again without hurt."

The old man felt his head go round when he heard his son speak in such a way; but he granted the lad's request, and Heime rode out into the unknown world.

In the royal palace of Bern, Queen Virginal was busy filling the goblets of the warriors, who feasted with her husband, and who agreed that great as were the blessings of peace, it was high time they should be up and doing something, lest their swords should rust in their scabbards. In the midst of this conversation the door opened, and a stranger entered in full armour. He was a tall broad-shouldered man, and apparently young.

Hildebrand welcomed him, and invited him to take off his coat-of-mail, telling him that purple and silken garments were more suited to a royal feast than the panoply of war.

"My trade is war," said the stranger, "I am Heime, son of the horse-dealer Studas, and have come to challenge the famous Dietrich to come out with me into the open field, and try which of us is the better man."

He spoke so loud that every one heard, and Dietrich at once accepted his challenge, calling upon his guests to come out and watch the fray. The king then put on his armour, mounted his good horse, Falcon, and in another moment was ready for the combat.

They fought for some time on horseback, but at length the shafts of their spears being broken in the melée, they sprang to the ground, and continued the combat on foot. Again a little time, and after Heime had performed wonderful feats of valour, his sword broke, and he stood defenseless before the angry king. Dietrich swung his sword above his head preparatory to giving his opponent the death-blow, but he had not the heart to do it. He had compassion on the youth and courage of the bold warrior, who stood so fearless before them. Letting his sword fall to his side, the king offered his hand to Heime in sign of peace. This generosity conquered the lad completely. He took the offered hand, said that he confessed himself overcome, and swore that henceforth he would be a faithful servant and follower of the glorious king. Dietrich was pleased to number a man like Heime among his followers, and presented him with castles and rich lands.

WITTICH.

Wittich was the son of Wieland, the smith of Heligoland, by Böswilde (Badhilda). From his earliest childhood his father had taught him the use of the bow, and the greatest praise he ever gave him was to say,—

"You are a bowman like my brother Eigel!"

Young Wittich wanted very much to learn all that he could about his uncle, and Wieland began:

"When your mother's father—Nidud, Drost of the Niars—made me a prisoner long ago, my brother Eigel came to his castle, and entered his service as bowman of the guard. Every one admired his skill. He could shoot away the head of an eagle that was flying high as the heavens. I have also seen him aim an arrow at the right or left foot of a lynx, and pin it to the bough on which the creature sat. And he did other wonderful things too numerous to relate. But the Drost wanted to see something more wonderful still, so he desired him to shoot an apple off the head of his own child at a hundred paces off, telling him at the same time that if he refused, or if obeying, he missed his mark, he would have the boy hewn in pieces before his eyes. Eigel drew three arrows from his quiver, and fitted one to the bowstring. The boy stood motionless, looking at his father with perfect confidence. Could you have done that, my lad? Eh!"

"No father," answered Wittich boldly, "I would have fetched your trusty sword Mimung, and have hewn off the head of that wicked old man; and then, if his Niars had tried to avenge him, I would have chased them out of the country."

"All very fine, young hero," laughed the father, "but remember this; a true hero only speaks of what he *has* done, not of what he *would* have done under such and such circumstances. It would have been better, however, if Eigel had done something of that kind. After he had shot away the apple, he turned to the Drost, and told him, that had he by any accident killed his son, he would have used the two other arrows in shooting him first, and then himself. The Drost took no notice of the speech at the time, but soon afterwards, he exiled the bowman without thanks or payment, and no one knows what has become of him."

The smith brought up his son on tales like this, which naturally excited the boy's ardour for adventure, and made him more and more unwilling to work at the forge. One day the lad spoke out, and asked his father to give him a suit of armour, and the good sword Mimung, that he might hie away to Bern, fight with king Dietrich, and win a kingdom like his ancestors. After many refusals the smith at last gave his consent, and furnished his son with all that he needed for the enterprise, explaining to him the special virtues of each weapon. Finally he told him to remember that his great-grandfather, King Wilkinus, a mighty warrior in his day, had married a mermaid, who, when the king was dying, had promised him, by the memory of their love, that she would help any of their descendants who asked for her aid. "Go down to the seashore, my son," continued the smith, "if ever you are in need, and demand the protection of our ancestors." And then with much sage advice, together with many old stories of things he had seen and known, Wieland took leave of his son.

Wittich rode on for many days before he met with any adventure. At length he came to a broad river, and dismounting, took off his armour, which he laid upon the bank, and began to wade across the water, leading his horse Skemming by the bridle. When half way across, three horsemen in full armour passed by, and seeing him began to taunt him and ask him where he was going. He told them that if they would wait until he had put his armour on, he was ready to try conclusions with them. They agreed, but no sooner did they see him dressed in his coat of mail, and mounted on his good steed, than they bethought them, that as they were in a strange place, it would be better to have a man of such thews and sinews for a comrade than an enemy. So they offered him peace instead of war. He accepted, and after shaking hands, they journeyed on together.

They rode up stream for a long way, and at last they came to a castle. A host of savage-looking men poured out of the gates, and advanced to meet them.

"There are too many for us to conquer," said the eldest of the strangers, "still I think that our good swords may enable us to hew our way across the bridge."

"Let me go and offer them a silver piece as toll," said Wittich, and setting spurs to his horse he rode on.

Arrived at the bridge, he was informed that the only toll demanded or accepted there were the horse, armour, clothes, right hand and right foot of the traveler. He explained that he could not afford to pay so high a price for so small a benefit, and offered them a piece of money. Whereupon they drew their swords and attacked him.

The three warriors meanwhile kept on a neighbouring height, and watched and commented on all that went on below. Seeing that their new friend seemed hard beset, two of them galloped to his assistance, while the third held back in scorn. But before they reached the place of combat, seven of the robbers were slain, and at sight of them the others took flight.

The heroes now rode on to the castle, where they found plenty of food and much booty. While they enjoyed their evening meal, their tongues were unloosed, and each told his name and deeds. Wittich had more to tell about his father than about himself, and then he learnt that the eldest of his new companions was Master Hildebrand, the second strong Heime, and the third Jarl Hornboge, who was also a comrade of Dietrich.

"This is a stroke of good luck for me," cried the young warrior, "for I am on my way to Bern to try my strength against the glorious king, and I have good hope that I may win the day, for my father has given me his sword Mimung, that can cut through steel and stone. Just look at the hilt, is not the workmanship beautiful?"

On hearing this, the three comrades grew more silent, and proposed to go to rest, as they were very tired. Wittich followed their example.

The young hero was soon snoring in company with Heime and Hornboge, but Hildebrand lay awake, a prey to sad forebodings. He knew that Wittich's sword could cut through his master's helmet, and he considered what was to be done. He crept noiselessly from his bed, and taking Mimung, compared it with his own sword. The two blades were wonderfully alike, but not the hilts. So with a grim smile of satisfaction, he carefully unscrewed the blades from the hilts, and exchanged them; then returned to his couch, and soon after fell asleep.

They started again on their journey next morning. In the course of a few days, they met with several adventures that proved to Hildebrand and his comrades that Wittich was of the stuff that heroes are made of.

On hearing of the arrival of his old master and the rest, King Dietrich hastened out into the court to meet and welcome them. But his astonishment was great when the young stranger pulled off his silver gauntlet and handed it to him. In another moment Dietrich had snatched it, and flung it in the youth's face, exclaiming wrathfully:

"Do you think it is part of a king's duty to make a target of himself for every wandering adventurer to strike at? Here, my men, seize the rascal, and hang him to the highest gallows."

"The power to do so is on your side," answered Wittich, "but bethink you, my lord, whether such a deed would not bring dishonour on your fair fame?"

And Hildebrand said, "Sire, this is Wittich, son of Wieland, the celebrated smith. He is no mean man, or secret traitor, but well worthy of a place in the ranks of your comrades."

"Very well, master," replied the king, "I will fight him as he desires, but should he be conquered, I will deliver him to the hangman. It is my last word. Now come to the race course."

The whole town assembled to witness the duel between the king and stranger. The combat raged long, but at last Wittich's sword broke, and he stood defenseless before the king.

"False father, you deceived me," he cried, "you gave me the wrong sword, and not Mimung."

"Surrender, vagrant," cried Dietrich, "and then to the gallows with you."

The young warrior's last hour had come, if Hildebrand had not sprang between them.

"Sire," he said, "spare an unarmed man, and make him one of your comrades. We could not have a more heroic soul in our company."

"No. He shall go to the gallows. Stand back, master, that he may once more lick the dust before me."

The master was sick at heart. He thought of how he had wronged the young hero by changing his sword; "Here, brave warrior, is your sword Mimung," he said handing Wittich the weapon at his side, "and now, Dietrich, do your best!"

The battle began again, and Mimung showed its mettle now. Bits of the king's shield and armour fell away, and a home-stroke laid his helmet open. "Surrender, king!" cried the victorious youth; but Dietrich fought on, in spite of terrible wounds.

Then the master sprang forward.

"Wittich," he cried, "hold your hand, for it is not your own strength, but Wieland's sword that gives you victory. Be our comrade, and then we shall rule the world, for, next to the king, you are the bravest of all the heroes."

"Master," replied Wittich, "you helped me in my need and I will not now deny you." Then turning to the king:

"Glorious hero of Ben, I am your man henceforward, and will be faithful to you as long as I live."

The king took his offered hand in his firm grasp, and made him ruler over a large fief.

WILDEBER, ILSAN AND OTHER COMRADES.

ECKE WAS the eldest son of the once powerful king Mentiger by the mermaid whom he made his queen. He loved Queen Seeburg, who lived at Cologne in the Rhineland. Seeburg had a great desire to see King Dietrich, and Ecke on hearing of it, promised to bring him to her, or die in the attempt. She, on her side, said that she would be his wife if he came home successful. He went, met Dietrich, and after showing prodigies of valour, died at his hands, much to the sorrow of the king, who had learnt to love him during the few hours of their acquaintance.

When Dietrich returned to Bern after slaying Ecke, Heime came out to meet him, and was so outspoken in his joy at seeing him again, that the king, much troubled, gave him his good sword Nagelring as a sign of his friendship. The warrior received it with delight, and kissed the trusty blade twice or thrice, as he said:

"I will wear this sword for the glory of my king, and will never part with it as long as I live."

"You are unworthy of the sword," cried Wittich, who had come up with the other warriors: "Do you remember how you left your weapon in its sheath when the robbers were attacking me, and that Hildebrand and Hornboge alone helped me?"

"Your self-sufficiency had made me angry, as your spiteful tongue does now. I will cut it out."

Both men put their hands to their swords, but the king stepped between them, and desired them to keep the peace in the castle. When he learnt all that had happened, Dietrich told Heime that he might go his way, because it was not seemly in a warrior to leave his comrade unaided in danger. But he added, that when he had shown by brave deeds that he was really a hero, he might return to them once more.

"Well, sire, I think I shall win myself greater wealth by Nagelring than I lose in the castles you now take from me."

Having thus spoken, the bold warrior sprang on his horse and rode away without taking leave of any one. He rode on, till he reached the Wisara (Weser), where he drew a band of robbers around him, and wrought great mischief. He plundered the defenseless country people, and even bold warriors had to pay him blackmail; and thus, through highway robbery, he became the owner of a great hoard of wealth, which he was never tired of increasing.

Dietrich had to tell his friends of his terrible combat with the hero Ecke, in which he had won the beautiful suit of armour he brought home with him, and the good sword Ecke-sax. One day, when the warriors were discussing this subject, a monk entered the hall, and remained standing humbly near the door. He was tall and broad-shouldered, and his cowl was pulled forward so as to hide his face. The servants began to play him tricks, until at last the monk, growing impatient, seized one of his persecutors by the ear, and held him up shrieking in the air.

When the king asked the reason of the noise, the monk stepped forward, and begged a morsel of bread for a half-starved penitent. Dietrich came forward himself, and commanded food and drink to be placed before the brother; but his astonishment was great when the monk pushed back his cowl, and displayed well rounded cheeks that bore no trace of starvation. He was still more surprised when he saw the quantity of food and wine the reverend brother could dispose of.

"The holy man has the appetite of a wolf," murmured the bystanders.

"Five long years have I done penance by prayer, fasting and water-drinking," he said, "and have now license from the venerable prior to go out into the world, and lay penance on other sinners. Now," he continued, going on with his meal, "ye be all miserable sinners with your continual feasting and drinking, and I call upon you to do penance, and be converted, that your sins be blotted out."

Then he intoned, in a loud ringing voice, "O Sanctissima."

Master Hildebrand had joined the group, and now exclaimed: "Why, it is my own dear brother, Ilsan the Monk."

"Culpa mea," cried the monk; "touch me not, unholy brother. Confess, and do penance, that thou go not straight to hell like the others."

"But," said the master, "we are all collected here together to convert, by kindness or force, all monsters, giants and dwarfs; so, my reverend brother, I now beg of you to lay aside your robes, and once more become one of us."

"Convert, say you? Yea, I have license to convert the heathen, and will therefore join you in your pious work."

With these words, the monk flung off his robes, and stood before them dressed in full armour.

"Here," he cried, touching his broadsword, "is my preacher's staff, and here," pointing to his coat of mail, "my breviary. St. Kilian pray for me and for all of us, Ora pro nobis."

He sat down amongst the warriors, who had all known the stout monk Ilsan for many years. He drank and sang, now psalms, now songs, and told merry tales of his life in the monastery.

Evening came apace. Candles and torches were lighted. Suddenly every one was startled by a strange creature pattering in at the door. It was like a bear to look upon. Its head resembled that of a boar, but its hands and feet were of human form. The monster stood as though rooted to the threshold, and appeared to be considering on whom first to make its spring.

"An evil spirit," cried Ilsan; "a soul escaped from the purgatorial fire. I will address it. Conjuro te . . ." He paused, for the monster had turned its face to him.

"I will drag him back to his purgatory again," cried bold Wolfhart, springing over the table, and seizing the creature by its fur. But pull and tug as he might, he could not move it by so much as an inch. It quietly gave the warrior such a kick, that he fell head over heels into the middle of the hall.

Hornboge, Wittich, and other warriors tried to push the monster out with their united strength, but in vain.

"Give room, brave comrades," cried the angry king. "I will see whether the monster is proof against my sword Ecke-sax."

"Sire," interrupted Master Hildebrand, catching him by the arm, "look; do you not see a golden bracelet, sparkling with precious stones, on the creature's wrist? It is a man—perhaps a brave warrior."

"Well," said the king, turning to his strange guest, "if you are indeed a hero, doff your disguise. Join us, and be our faithful comrade."

On hearing these words, the strange guest threw off boar's head and bear's skin, and stood before the king and his followers clad in armour.

"I know you now," said Hildebrand. "You are the brave hero Wildeber, surnamed The Strong. And the gold bracelet is the gift of a swan-maiden, and makes your strength double. But why did you so disguise yourself? Every brave man is a welcome guest to our king."

Wildeber seated himself by the master's side, emptied a goblet of sparkling wine, and said:

"Once, after fighting a hard fight with robbers, I lay down to sleep on the bank of a lake. Suddenly I was awakened by a splashing in the water. Turning my eyes in the direction of the noise, I saw a beautiful maiden bathing. I spied her swangarment lying on the bank, crept up to it softly, took it, and hid it. The maiden sought it everywhere, and when she could not find it, she began to weep aloud. I went to her, and begged that she would follow me home and be my wife. But she wept the more, and said that she must die if she were deprived of her bird's dress. I was sorry for her, and gave it back, whereupon she gave me this bracelet, which increases my strength immensely; but she told me that to preserve it I must wander about as a bear with a boar's head, until the most famous king on earth chose me to be one of his comrades. If I did not obey her, she warned me that the virtue of the jewel would depart, and I should soon be slain in battle. Having thus spoken, she flew away. That is why I came to you in such disguise, brave hero," he continued, addressing Dietrich; "and as you have received me into the ranks of your comrades of your own free will, I hope that the bracelet will retain its magic power as long as I live."

"Pax vobiscum!" stammered the monk, as he staggered away to bed. The other warriors soon followed his example, and silence reigned in the palace.

DIETLEIB.

KING DIETRICH was one day about to mount his horse, and set out to visit his brother monarch, the Emperor Ermenrich, when a warrior rode into the court. The king at once knew him to be Heime. He was not much pleased to see him back at Bern, but when Heime told him that he had been victorious in many battles against giants and robbers, he consented to receive him once more into the ranks of his comrades, and desired him to accompany him and certain of his followers to Romaburg.

At Fritilaburg, where they rested, Dietrich accepted the offered service of a man who called himself Ilmenrik, son of a Danish yeoman Sote; and enrolled him amongst his servants.

When they came to Romaburg, they were received with all honour by the emperor, who gave them both board and lodging. But the emperor forgot one thing in his plans, and that was, to provide food for the servants. Ilmenrik fed them the first night. On the second, his private resources being exhausted, he pawned Heime's armour and horse for ten gold pieces; on the third, he pawned Wittich's goods for twenty; and on the fourth, he got thirty for the weapon and horse of the king. On the fifth day, when the king gave orders for their return home, Ilmenrik asked for money to free the articles he had pawned. Dietrich was astonished and angry when he heard how extravagant his servant's ideas had been. He took him before Ermenrich, who at once said he would pay the sum required, and asked how much it was. The emperor and all his court made merry at Ilmenrik's expense, especially Walter of Wasgenstein (Vosges), who asked him if he was a were-wolf and well up in strange knowledge of all kinds. Ilmenrik modestly answered that he had learnt to perform many feats of strength and skill from his father, such as putting the stone and throwing the hammer; and that he would wager his head against the lord of Wasgenstein's that he could beat him in this. Walter accepted his challenge, and the trial began.

Such skill as Ilmenrik displayed had never been seen before. The heroes all feared for the life of the brave warrior of Wasgenstein. The emperor then called the young victor to him.

"Hearken to me, young sir," he said; "I will buy the head of my vassal from you at whatever price you list. Gold for blood is the old law."

"Fear not, sire," answered Ilmenrik, "the head of the brave hero is in no danger from me. I do not want it. But if you wish to do me a kindness, lend me so much money as I have expended for the keep of the servants, that I may redeem the weapons, garments and horses that I pawned."

"Treasurer," said the emperor, turning to one of his ministers, "weigh out sixty marks of red gold, that the fellow may redeem his pledges, and another sixty marks to fill his purse."

"Thank you, my lord," returned the young man, "I do not need your gift, for I am a servant of the rich king of Bern, who will see that I lack nothing; but if you will keep us another day here, I will, with this sixty marks, treat the servants to a better feast than before, and also my master, all his warriors, and you yourself, should you desire to join the party, even if I have to pawn horses and coats of mail again."

The warriors all laughed at the merry youth, but Heime frowned, and said that if ever he pawned his horse again it should cost him his life.

The feast which the servant prepared them was of royal magnificence. All were pleased except Heime, who secretly feared that his property was again in pawn. The young fellow seated himself at his side, and asked him in a low voice if he knew who had given him that scar on his forehead. Heime answered that it was Dietleib, son of Jarl Biterolf, adding that he would know him again in a moment, and that the scar should be avenged in blood.

Ilmenrik replied:

"Methinks, bold warrior, your memory has gone a-wool-gathering. If you look me in the face, you will see that I am that Dietleib whom you and your robbers attacked as he was riding through a forest with his father. We slew the robber Ingram and his companions, but you escaped with that wound, thanks to the speed of your good horse. If you don't believe me, I have a witness here that will prove my words in the open field. But if you will trust me, the matter may remain a secret between us."

Towards the end of the feast, Dietrich told the youth that he should no longer be a servant, but should be received into the ranks of his comrades; and he, thanking him, answered that he was really Dietleib, a son of Jarl Biterolf, whose glorious deeds were known far and wide.

All the king's followers, except Heime, received the young hero into their ranks with pleasure. He returned to Bern with the king, and proved himself his trusty comrade in many an adventure. But he was of a restless mind, and wished to see more of the world; so after a time he took service under Etzel, king of the Huns, at whose court he found his father settled. Father and son together were the doers of many a daring deed. King Etzel, wishing to keep them in his service, offered them the land of Steirermark (Styria) as a fief. Biterolf gave up his share to his son, who was therefore surnamed the Styrian, but who often appears in story by his right name of Dietleib the Dane.

CHAPTER IV.

KING LAURIN AND THE LITTLE ROSE-GARDEN.

DIETLEIB ONCE came unexpectedly on a visit to Master Hildebrand at his castle of Garden. He looked sadder than of old, and returned the master's greeting without an answering smile. Hildebrand inquired the cause of his sadness, and he replied that he had a sweet and wise sister named Künhild, who had kept house for him in Styria. One day, when she was dancing with other maidens in a green meadow, and he looking on she suddenly vanished from the circle, and no one knew what had become of her.

"Since then," he continued, "I have learnt from a magician that it was the dwarf King Laurin that hid her under a cap of darkness, and carried her off to his hollow mountain. This mountain is in Tyrol, where the dwarf has also a wonderful Rose-garden. Now, good master, I have come to you for advice. How can I free my sister from the power of the goblin?"

"It is a ticklish matter," said Hildebrand, "and may cost many a good life. I will go with you to Bern, to see Dietrich and our other comrades, and then we can agree in council what is the best plan to pursue. For the dwarf is powerful, not only because of the extent of his empire, but from his knowledge of magic."

When the heroes heard what had brought Hildebrand and Dietleib to Bern, Wolfhart spoke first, and said that he would adventure himself alone upon the quest, fetch home the maiden safe and sound, and bring the royal mannikin to Bern bound to his saddle-bow. Dietleib then asked Hildebrand if he knew the way to the Rose-garden. He replied that he did, but that Laurin watched over the garden himself, and exacted the left foot and right hand of any one who was bold enough to venture within its bounds, and spoil the roses.

"He cannot exact this tribute," said Wittich, "unless he gets the better of the warrior in fair fight."

"Well, then," added the king, "we will not touch the lovely flowers. All we want is to save our friend's sister from the hands of the dwarf, and that is a labour beseeming a warrior."

The heroes all swore to do no hurt to the garden, and then Hildebrand consented to be their guide. The adventurers were Hildebrand, Dietrich, Dietleib, Wittich, and Wolfhart.

Their road led them northward among the wild mountains, and over crevasses, ice, and snow. It was a perilous way they trod, but they recked nothing of fatigue or danger, for their hearts beat high with hope. At length they reached the garden; a lovely place, where spring reigned eternally, making it a flowery oasis in a wintry desert. The heroes feasted their eyes on the beautiful sight, and felt as though they had reached the gates of paradise.

Wolfhart was the first to break the spell; setting spurs to his horse, he called to his comrades to follow, and galloped towards the garden. His mad career was soon checked by an iron door with golden letters inscribed on it. He tried to break open the door, but in vain; his comrades came to his aid, and the door was at last beaten in by the four strong men. The garden was still defended by a golden thread, such as used to surround the palaces of the Asas in the olden time. The warriors trod down the thread, and then, in spite of Hildebrand's warnings, began to pluck the roses and trample the garden. Dietrich did not join in the work of destruction, but stood apart under a linden tree.

Suddenly Hildebrand called out, "Draw your swords! Here comes the master of the garden."

They all looked up, and saw something bright advancing rapidly towards them. Soon they were able to distinguish the form of a horseman riding a steed that was swift as the wind. He was small of stature, and habited in a complete suit of armour. His helmet was of specially beautiful workmanship, and was further adorned with a diadem of jewels, in the midst of which a carbuncle blazed like a sun. On beholding the damage that had just been done, he drew rein, and exclaimed angrily:

"What harm have I ever done you, robbers as you are, that you should thus destroy my roses? If you had aught against me, why did you not send me a challenge like honourable men? You must now expiate your crime by each giving me his right hand and left foot."

"If you are King Laurin," answered Dietrich, "we do indeed owe you reparation, and will pay you a fine in gold; but we cannot afford to lose our right hands, for we require them to wield our swords; and as to our left feet, we could not well ride were we deprived of them."

"He would be a coward who talked of paying any fine except in blows," cried Wolfhart; "and I am determined to dash that hop-o'-my-thumb, together with the cat he is riding, against the cliffs over yonder, and then his bones will break into such tiny pieces that even his grasshopper subjects can never collect them."

Upon this Laurin answered in words of defiance, and the combat with Wolfhart began, only to end in the latter's overthrow the moment he felt the touch of the dwarf's spear. Wittich was not more fortunate than his friend, for he also was thrown from his saddle at the first encounter.

Laurin sprang from his horse, drew out a large knife, and approached the hero, who lay senseless on the ground. Dietrich sprang forward to rescue his comrade.

"Do not venture the spear thrust, but close with him," said Hildebrand in a low voice. "Laurin has three magic charms of which you must deprive him; and these are, a ring with the stone of victory on his finger, a belt that gives him the strength of twelve men round his waist, and in his pocket a cap of darkness, which makes him invisible when he puts it on."

After a long and fierce wrestle, Dietrich managed to get possession of the ring, which he at once gave into the master's charge. Again the combat raged, neither side gaining any advantage. At last Dietrich begged for a short truce, which Laurin granted.

The truce over, the two kings renewed the fight. Dietrich caught Laurin by the belt, and at the same moment the latter clasped him round the knees so tight that he fell backwards. The violence of his fall broke the belt he was holding, and it slipped from his hand. Hildebrand then rushed forward and caught it before the dwarf could pick it up. No sooner was this done than Laurin went out of sight. Dietrich still felt the blows he gave, but could not see him. Filled with a berserker rage at his own powerlessness, he forgot the pain of his wounds; he flung away both sword and spear, sprang like a tiger in the direction in which he heard the whistling of the invisible sword, and seized his adversary for the third time. He tore away the cap of darkness, and Laurin stood before him praying for peace.

"I shall first cut off your right hand and left foot, and then your head, and after that you may have peace," cried the angered hero, setting off in pursuit of the dwarf, who now took to his heels.

"Save me, Dietleib, my dear brother-in-law," cried Laurin, running up to that warrior; "your sister is my queen."

Dietleib swung the little creature on horseback before him, and galloped away into the wood. There he set him down, and told him to hide himself until the king's anger was abated.

Coming back to the place of combat, the warrior found Dietrich on horseback, and as furious as before.

"I must have either the dwarf's head or yours," cried Dietrich.

In another moment their swords were flashing; a second fight would have begun had not Hildebrand held back the king by main force, while Wittich did the same to Dietleib. After a little they succeeded in making peace between the angry men, and also in gaining grace for the dwarfs. Later still the warriors might have been seen in friendly converse with each other and with Laurin, who was then and there admitted as one of Dietrich's comrades.

This point settled, the dwarf proposed to show them the wonders of his hollow mountain, saying that Dietleib should then give his sister to him as wife, with the usual ceremonies.

"It is the old law," answered the hero of Steierland, "that when a maiden has been carried away from her home and is recovered by her friends, she should have free choice given her either to remain with her husband, or return to her people. Are you willing that it should be so in this case?"

"By all means," said the dwarf. "Now let us go. Do you see that snow-capped mountain? My palace is there—so to horse, that my eyes may no longer be pained by seeing the wreck you have wrought in my garden. The roses will bloom again in May."

The journey to the snow-capped mountain was much longer than the warriors had imagined. It lasted till noon of the following day. Below the snow, they came to a meadow that was as beautiful as the rose-garden. The air was filled with the perfume of flowers. Birds were singing in the branches, and little dwarfs were to be seen hurrying to and fro. They followed Laurin into the dark entrance of his underground kingdom. The only one of their number who felt the least distrust was Wittich, who had not forgotten the thrust of the dwarf king's spear.

IN KING LAURIN'S REALM.

A SOFT twilight reigned in the vast hall of the palace to which they now came. The walls were of polished marble, inlaid with gold and silver. The floor was formed of a single agate, the ceiling of a sapphire, and from it there hung shining carbuncles like stars in the blue sky of night. All at once it became light as day. The queen came in, surrounded by her maidens. Her girdle and necklace were jeweled, and in her coronet was a diamond that shone like the sun, bringing the brightness of day wherever it came. But the lady herself was more beautiful than aught else. None could take their eyes off her face. She seated herself beside Laurin, and signed to her brother Dietleib to sit down at the other side of her. She embraced him and asked him many questions about her old home and friends. By this time supper was ready. Laurin was a perfect host, and his guests were soon quite at their ease. Even Wittich forgot to be suspicious. When the meal was over, the dwarf king left the hall, and Dietleib seized the opportunity to ask his sister whether she was willing to remain in that underground paradise as its queen. She answered with tears that she could not forget her home and friends; that she would rather be a peasant girl in the upper world than a queen among the dwarfs, and that though she must admit that Laurin was very good and kind, yet he was not as other men. Dietleib then promised to save her, or lose his life in the attempt.

Laurin now returned, and asked the hero if he would like to retire to his bedchamber. He took him there, and remained talking with him for some time. At last he told him that his comrades were all condemned to death, and that he had only spared him because he was his brother-in-law.

"Traitor, false dwarf!" cried Dietleib. "I live and die with my comrades, but you are in my power!"

He started forward, but the dwarf was gone, and the door was shut and locked on the outside.

Laurin then returned to the hall, filled the goblets of the warriors from a particular jar, and entreated them to drink the wine, which would insure them a good night's rest. They did so, and immediately their heads sank upon their breasts, and a heavy drugged sleep fell upon them. Then turning to the queen, Laurin desired her to go to her room, for these men must die in punishment for the wreck they had made of his rose-garden; adding that her brother was safely locked up in a distant room, that he might escape the fate of his comrades. Künhild wept aloud, and said that she would die if he carried out his cruel purpose. He gave her no distinct answer, but reiterated his command.

As soon as the queen had retired, he sounded his horn, and immediately five giants and a number of dwarfs hurried into the room. He commanded them to bind the warriors so tight with cords that they could not move when they awoke. After that he had them dragged to a dungeon where they might remain until he should decide their fate next morning. Having seen his orders carried out, he went to bed, and began to think whether it would be better to let the men off to please the queen, or to punish them for their evil deed. The last seemed to him the wiser plan, and he fell asleep, gloating over the intended slaughter of his helpless victims.

Dietrich awoke soon after midnight; he felt that he was bound hand and foot, and called to his comrades for aid; but they were as powerless as he. Then Dietrich's wrath was roused to such a pitch, that his fiery breath burnt the cords that bound one hand, and left it free. After that, it was a matter of little difficulty to untie the knots at his wrist and feet, and then to set his comrades at liberty. What was to be done now? They could not break open their dungeon door. They had neither weapon nor coat of mail. They were helpless victims. At this very moment, while they were looking at each other in despair, they were startled by hearing a woman's voice, asking in a low whisper if they were yet alive.

"We thank you, noble queen," answered Hildebrand, "we are alive and well, but totally unarmed."

So Künhild opened the door, and appeared on the threshold with her brother. She placed her finger on her lips to enforce silence, and led the way to where the heroes' armour was piled. As soon as they were ready, the queen gave each of them a ring, by means of which he could see the dwarfs, even when they wore their caps of darkness.

"Hurrah!" cried Wolfhart. "We can make as much noise as we like, now that we have our armour on and our weapons in our hands."

Laurin, wakened by Wolfhart's loud tones, knew that the prisoners were free, and at once summoned his dwarfish army to his assistance. The battle began, and raged for a long time without any advantage being gained by either side. Laurin was pleased in his heart of hearts that matters had turned out as they had, for he was a bold little fellow, and liked open war better than trickery. At length the underground forces were routed with great loss, and Laurin himself was taken prisoner.

Dietrich spared the life of the dwarf king at fair Künhild's request, but deposed him from royal power, and gave the mountain to Sintram, another dwarf of high rank, for a yearly tribute. When everything was ordered to their liking, the heroes returned to Bern, taking Laurin with them as a prisoner.

There was great joy in Bern at the return of the heroes, who were much praised for their valiant deeds, while the unfortunate Laurin was laughed at by all. There was only one person who showed him any sympathy, and that was Künhild. One day she met him when he was wandering about alone and melancholy. She spoke to him kindly, tried to comfort him, and told him he would soon gain the king's friendship if he proved himself to be faithful and true.

"Ah," he laughed bitterly; "they think they have kicked a dog who will lick their hands; but a trodden snake bites! You may know what I intend to do. I have sent to inform Walberan, my uncle, who rules over the dwarfs and giants from the Caucasus to Sinai, of what has happened, and he is coming at the head of his forces to be my avenger. He cannot fail to win the day, slay strong Dietrich and his comrades, and lay the whole land waste. When that is done, I will take you back to my kingdom, and replant my Rose Garden, that it may be lovelier in May than it ever was before."

"Laurin," she answered, "you carried me away from home by trickery and magic spells; but I have not been blind to your love, and feel myself honoured by its greatness. I cannot live in your underground kingdom, but I will love you and be your queen in the Rose Garden, if you will think of love and faithfulness, and not of revenge."

She left him, and he sat pondering the matter for a long time.

A few days afterwards, Dietrich came to the dwarf king, and, taking him by the hand, said, that he had been his prisoner long enough, that he must now sit with his comrades, or return to his own home, whichever he liked better.

"And then," continued the king, "I will go with you to your Rose Garden next spring, and see it in its beauty."

The dwarf silently followed the king into the hall. He sat at Dietrich's side at the feast, and thought over the vengeance he would take when his uncle came.

But lovely Künhild appeared and filled his goblet, saying a few kind words the while, and immediately love conquered hatred, and he cried, emptying the goblet to the last drop,—

"Henceforward I am your faithful comrade in life and death."

Whilst the warriors were still at the feast, a messenger from King Walberan came in, and declared war on Dietrich in the name of his master, unless Laurin were at once restored to his kingdom, and unless the hero of Bern sent Walberan all the money and all the weapons in the country, as well as the right hand and left foot of every warrior who had taken part in the destruction of the Rose Garden.

Dietrich answered proudly, that he intended to keep his money, arms, hands and feet, and those of his subjects also.

"And tell him," added Laurin, "that I send him my thanks and greeting for coming to my assistance, but that I am now free, and have entered into a bond of love and friendship with the King of Bern."

Both sides prepared for battle, but before a blow was struck, Laurin rode into his uncle's camp, and tried to make peace between Walberan and Dietrich. His uncle told him he was no better than a broken-spirited serf, and refused to listen to his words. So the fight began, and raged furiously for many hours. At length, late in the afternoon, Dietrich and Walberan met, and challenged each other to single combat. It was a terrible struggle—both kings were severely wounded, and it seemed to the onlookers as if both must die. Suddenly Laurin threw himself unarmed between their swords, flung his arms round King Walberan, and entreated him to make peace. Almost at the same moment Hildebrand did the same by the angry Dietrich, and after much expenditure of words, the peacemakers had their way.

So the fighting was changed to feasting, and the kings entered into a friendly alliance at the banquet that evening. The hero of Bern made a long speech in praise of Laurin, who had endangered his life in endeavouring to make peace, and to whom he therefore restored the free and independent rule over his kingdom and Rose Garden. When he had finished, Queen Virginal came forward, leading fair Künhild, and laid the hand of the maiden in that of Laurin, saying that she knew he would regard her reward of his faithfulness as the greatest he had that day received; for Künhild had promised to be his wife if her brother did not object. As no dissenting voice was heard, the marriage was celebrated there at once.

In the May-month of the following year, when the roses were again in bloom, the dwarfs put the finishing touches to a beautiful palace, which they had built in the Rose Garden. Many a herdsman and Alpine hunter has seen it; but to those who go in search of it from mere curiosity, it remains ever invisible.

To this day Laurin and Künhild show themselves at odd times in the valleys of Tyrol, and there are people yet alive who are reported to have had a distant glimpse of the wonderful Rose Garden.

CHAPTER V.

THE GREAT ROSE GARDEN AND ILSAN THE MONK.

DIETRICH WAS now a man in the prime of life—a perfect hero, and man of valour. The number of his comrades had much increased, and many doughty deeds had been done.

Once when the king was feasting with many of his comrades, he looked round the table with pride, and said he believed that no ruler on earth had such heroes about him, that no other had prospered so well as he with the help of his chosen comrades, and that none might be compared with them. The warriors shouted their approbation. One alone was silent. The king turned to him, and asked whether in all his journeys he had seen bolder warriors.

"That I have," cried Herbrand. "I have seen some that have not their match upon earth. It was at the good town of Worms, near the River Rhine, in the land of Burgundy. It is there that the great Rose Garden lies—five miles long by two and a half broad. The queen and her ladies tend it themselves, and twelve great warriors keep watch and ward lest any one enter the garden without the queen's permission. Whoever does so must fight with the guard, and no one yet, whether giant or warrior, has been able to withstand them."

"Let us go and pluck the roses that have been watered with the blood of heroes," cried Dietrich. "I think that my comrades and I will get the better of the guard."

"If you mean to try your luck," said Herbrand, "you must know that the victor will receive a kiss and a wreath of roses from lovely women."

"Ah, well," said the old master, "for the sake of a rose and a woman's kiss I would not risk a single hair of my head or beard. He who wishes to pluck roses or kiss women will find enough at Bern; he need not go to the Rhine to find them."

Trusty Eckehart and a few more of the comrades agreed with him, for well they knew what the Burgundian warriors were like. But Dietrich loudly declared that he was not going to fight for the sake of roses and kisses, but for honour and fame; and that if his comrades did not wish to go with him, he could go alone. Of course, they would not hear of that, and all who were present agreed to go. The names of those who thus adventured their lives were: Dietrich himself, Master Hildebrand, strong Wittich, Heime called the Grim, Wolfhart, the young heroes Siegestab and Amelung (or Omlung), Trusty Eckehart, and Hertnit, Prince of the Reussen; but they only numbered nine in all, and twelve were needed to meet the twelve watchmen of the garden. Hildebrand knew what was to be done. He said—

"Good Rüdiger of Bechelaren will not refuse to be the tenth; the eleventh must be brave Dietleib of Styria, and the twelfth my pious brother, the monk Ilsan."

They started forth at once to induce the chosen three to join them. They went first to Bechelaren, in the land of the Danube. Rüdiger received them hospitably, and at once consented to go

with them, but said that he must first get leave of absence from
Etzel, whose margrave he was. The heroes then went on to
Styria to visit Dietleib. They did not find him at home, but his
father Biterolf, who was there, earnestly entreated them to give
up the journey to the Rhine, because, he said, only a fool would
undertake a conflict for life or death with the world's bravest
warriors, for the sake of a rose and a kiss. But when they met the
young hero a short time after, they found him ready to go with
them. This settled they went on to Münchenzell, the monastery
to which Hildebrand's brother belonged. As soon as Ilsan heard
the object of their journey, he went straight to the abbot, and
asked leave to accompany the hero of Bern to the Rose Garden.
The abbot told him that such was scarcely a monkish request,
but Ilsan grew so angry, and so loudly affirmed that valiant
deeds were in his eyes as seemly for a monk as for any other
man, that the abbot quailed before him, and gave him leave to
go. So Ilsan donned his armour under his monkish dress, and
started with his friends. His heart beat high with joy that he was
again bound on one of Dietrich's adventures, while his brother
monks stood by and shook their heads, saying they feared it
would not end well, seeing it was no saintly quest, but a worldly.

The heroes went first to Bern, which was to be the general
meeting place. Margrave Rüdiger was the last to arrive, for he
had been detained by his visit to Etzel. Rüdiger was now sent on
before the others as ambassador to King Gibich at Worms, to
inform him of their intended invasion of the Rose Garden. The
Margrave was well known in the Rhineland, and was received as
an old friend by the king, who rejoiced to hear of his leader's
enterprise.

The garden was entered on the appointed day, and the warriors stood opposite each other ready for battle; twelve against
twelve, and yet always one against one. It was a terrible sight, for
many a hero fell dying amongst the roses, and watered them
with his heart's blood. When proud Wolfhart had slain his adversary he contemptuously refused the kiss offered him by a lovely
maiden, and contented himself with the garland of roses. The
monk, Ilsan, walked into the lists on foot, clad in his grey robes.
He jumped about among the roses with such strange agility that

his opponent thought he had a madman to deal with. But he soon found that his reverend foe was made of sterner metal than he supposed, for he lay vanquished, a wiser man, though wounded almost to the death. The victor received the wreath of roses on his tonsured head, but when he kissed the lovely maid who gave it him, she shrieked aloud, for his bristly beard had stung her rosy lips. Seeing this, he said with comical disgust,—

> "The maidens of Rhineland are fair to see,
> But far too tender to pleasure me."

Many other heroes received the prize of victory, while others were severely wounded. Peace was not concluded until sunset. The brave hero of Bern soon afterwards returned home, pleased with the result of his quest.

CHAPTER VI.

THE FAITHFULNESS OF DIETRICH.

DIETRICH LIVED in friendship with Etzel, king of the Huns, from the time Rüdiger first brought them together. When the hero came back from Burgundy, he had sent ambassadors to the king, and promised to help him if he was in any difficulty. It was not long before he was reminded of this promise.

The Margrave, who was known in all lands by the title of the good and gentle, came to Bern one day as he had often come before, for he was a welcome guest. On such occasions the warriors would talk over their past adventures, and tell tales of noble and doughty deeds. Rüdiger told amongst other things of his adventures in Spain, and how he had at last left that country, and taken service under King Etzel, who had always been a true friend to him since the beginning of their acquaintance. He went on to relate how King Etzel, powerful monarch as he then was, did not shun to speak of the hardships and homelessness of his early youth.

"Yes, truly," interrupted Master Hildebrand, "and I know as

much of his early youth as ever the great king himself. Once when Wilkinus was ruler of the Wilkinmen—"

"Ha! my great-grandfather!" cried Wittich. "What have you to say of him?"

"I only know," continued the master, "that he was a mighty chief, and that many kings were subject to him; amongst others, King Hertnit. After the death of Wilkinus, Hertnit rebelled against his son and heir, Nordian, and forced the latter to acknowledge him as his liege lord. The conquered king obtained the rule of Zealand in fief, and declared himself satisfied, although he had four gigantic sons, namely, Asperian, Edgar, Awentrod, and terrible Widolf of the club, who was always kept chained up, because he did so much destruction whenever he was in a rage. When great Hertnit died, he divided his kingdom amongst his three sons. Osantrix (Oserich) obtained the rule over the Wilkin-men, Waldemar that over the Reussen, and Ylias became jarl of the Greeks. The eldest of the three wooed beautiful Oda, daughter of Melias, king of the Huns. He won her by trickery and force, with the help of Nordian's four giant sons. Oda's father and husband became allies after the marriage, but they could not conquer the bold Frisians, who often made raids into the land of the Huns, and burnt, destroyed, or stole whatever they laid their hands on. For Melias was old and weak, and the Wilkin-men lived so far away that their help always arrived too late. The leader of these bold invaders was the mighty man of valour now known as King Etzel, or Attila as he is sometimes called. He was a son of the Frisian chieftain Osid, and after his father's death had to allow his brother Ortnit to succeed to the rule of Friesland, and himself go out into the wide world, with nothing but his armour and a good sword. But Frisians are a bold and warlike people. Many of them joined themselves to the young hero, and accompanied him in his viking raids into the neighbouring land of the Huns. When Melias died, the notables of the land elected their former enemy, bold Etzel, to be their king, and thus the robber chief and invader became the sovereign and protector of the country he had once laid waste."

"Yes," returned Rüdiger, "that is quite true, and there is more to tell. King Etzel wished to marry Erka (Herche or Helche), the beautiful daughter of Osantrix, chief of the Wilkin-men. I was sent as ambassador to her father, and was well received; but when I told the king the object of my mission, he grew wrathful, and said that he would never give his consent to such a marriage, for Etzel was not the rightful chief of the Huns; adding that the position was his by right of his wife, the daughter of Melias. He cared not when I threatened him with war; but desired me to go my way. Etzel invaded the country with his men; and when, after much fighting, a truce was at last agreed to, neither side had gained much advantage.

"A year later, I went back with a number of brave men, and had a strong castle built for me in the Falsterwood. This done, I stained my face, and otherwise disguised by a long beard, went again to visit Osantrix. I told him I was a faithful servant of the late King Melias, that I had been ill-treated and deprived of my lands by Etzel, and had therefore taken refuge with him. This story gained me his confidence, and having occasion to send his daughter Erka a message, he made me his ambassador. I told the maiden of Etzel's wooing, and how he wished to share his power and glory with her. At first she was very angry, but at last consented to marry him.

"One moonlight night, I brought horses to the gates of the fortress where she was shut up with her young sister; broke the bars, and carried off the princesses. We were pursued, but managed to reach the castle in the wood where my men were awaiting me. I had scarcely time to send a message to Etzel, when Osantrix came upon us with all his host. He laid siege to our stronghold; but we managed to defend ourselves till Etzel came with a great army, and forced the Wilkin-men to withdraw. Carried off one of the princes we know not where and Osantrix has even now collected a large army to invade our land and make slaves of our people. He is accompanied by Nordian's giant sons, who are the terror of our people. Now, noble Dietrich, Etzel thinks that if you will come and help him, he is sure of victory."

"Ah well; if my dear comrade Wildeber will go with me,"

cried Wittich, "I think that we two shall be able to reckon with the giants."

Dietrich promised his help, and ordered all preparations to be made for the campaign. The Bernese heroes arrived just in time, for the two armies were standing opposite each other in battle array. The fight began.

Dietrich and his men took up their position in the centre division. The Amelung banner, borne by Herbrand, floated proudly above their heads, and Wittich rushed foremost into the fray. He first encountered the grim giant Widolf, who gave him a blow on the helmet with his iron club. The dragon that formed the top of the helmet was bent by the terrible blow, and although Wieland's work did not break, the hero himself fell from his horse, and lay senseless on the ground. Over him rushed the men-at-arms in the wild *melée*. Heime alone drew rein. He stooped, and drew the sword Mimung out of Wittich's hand, for he held him to be dead. When the wild fight was over and done, the Wilkin-men retreated from the field, and the Huns pursued them, plundering where they could. Hertnit, nephew of Osantrix, reached the battle-field too late. He could not prevent his uncle's defeat, but he found Wittich, as yet scarcely recovered from his swoon, and took him prisoner.

The victors feasted at Susat, and rejoiced over their great deeds; but Dietrich was sad at heart, for he had lost sixty of his men; and worse than all, his friend and comrade, Wittich, was among the missing. In vain had they sought him on the battle-field. All wondered what had become of him. When the king of Bern, richly rewarded for his help by Etzel, made ready for his departure, Wildeber came to him, and asked for leave of absence, because he would not, could not, go home without Wittich. Dietrich willingly gave his consent, for he could not help the foolish hope springing up within his breast that perhaps Wittich might be yet alive, and that his friend might find him.

The next day Wildeber went out hunting, and slew a bear of unusual size. He skinned it, and went with the skin to Isung, the minstrel, and arranged with him a plan to free Wittich should he be a prisoner in the hands of Osantrix. Isung helped him to draw the skin over his armour, and fasten it up carefully; then led him

WITTICH AND THE PRINCE
IN A DUNGEON.

(After the painting by Adam Miller.)

The way is not a short one between Wittich, the hero, venturesome as he was powerful, heroic as he was skillful in swordsmanship, and Wittich, the captive, fretting away his life in a loathsome dungeon. But the events that brought him to this sorry condition concern powers preternatural and superhuman; a magic sword and Nordian giants, whose strength compensated their smaller wit. By these Wittich, bravest of his tribe, was vanquished and borne away to prison, there to repine until he discovered a fellow prisoner in the person of a prince, his king's (Etzel's) son, whose misery made the hero forget his own. The picture here reproduced is by a celebrated Danish artist who, as a pupil of the old school, has admirably represented a dungeon scene of the period.

in the guise of a dancing bear to the stronghold of the chief of the Wilkin-men.

Now wandering players and merry-andrews, of every sort, were welcome guests in all castles and cottages, so Isung and his bear were well received.

Osantrix laughed heartily at the marvelous agility of the creature in dancing and springing to the sound of the fiddle, and even Widolf, the grim giant, who was led about with a chain by his brother Awentrod, laughed for the first time in his life, making the halls shake with the sound. Suddenly it occurred to the king that it would enhance the sport to set his twelve boarhounds on the bear, to see how strong it was.

Isung vainly entreated the king to forbear the cruel sport, alleging that his tame bear was worth more to him than all the gold in the royal treasury; but Osantrix was not to be persuaded. The great dogs were loosed, and the barbarous sport began. To the astonishment of all, the boar-hounds were either worried or smitten to death by the bear.

Osantrix sprang angrily to his feet, and slashed at the creature's shoulder with his sword; but the steel armour under inside the bear-skin saved the hero's life. Another moment, and the bear had wrenched the sword from the king's hand, and split his head open. The second blow did to death grim Widolf, the third his brother Awentrod. Isung stood staunchly by his friend when the Wilkin-men sought to avenge their king. The courtiers, however, soon took flight in deadly fear of the player and his wild beast.

Wildeber now threw off the bear-skin, took the helmet off one of the giants, and fully armed, set out in search of Wittich. The heroes searched the palace. They found Wittich's good steed Skeming, and his armour; but neither him nor the sword Mimung could they discover.

At length they discovered him in a damp, dark dungeon, chained to a wall beside a youthful prince, and grown so pale and thin as to be hardly recognizable. Fresh air, food, and wine soon made a change in his appearance. He put on his armour, and sadly took another sword, saying that none could be as good as Mimung.

"Now let us begone," said Isung, "lest the Wilkin-men should come back."

So Wildeber and he helped themselves to horses from the royal stables, and the three heroes galloped away.

"Of a truth," cried King Etzel, when he heard their story, "you are bold men. You have done me good service, and have brought the war to an end unaided. The lord of Bern is richer than I, in that he has comrades who willingly venture their own lives to serve a brother-in-arms."

He kept the heroes for several days to recruit their strength, and then sent them home laden with rich gifts.

Dietrich was overjoyed to see his brave warriors again, and showed them honour in many ways; but noticing that trusty Wittich was silent, and had no appetite for wine or food, he asked him what ailed him. And Wittich answered that he sorrowed for the loss of Mimung, his father's best gift, and would go in search of it though he had to wander through every land.

"I have a notion that you need not take so long a journey," replied the king, "for I cannot help thinking that the sword Heime wears is as like Wieland's work as one drop of blood is like another."

The conversation was interrupted by the arrival of two warriors in rich armour, who had been sent by the Emperor Ermenrich, Dietrich's uncle, to tell the hero that Jarl Rimstein, his vassal in a great fief, had revolted against his authority. Ermenrich, therefore, entreated his nephew's aid, and Dietrich promised to help the emperor.

THE MARCH AGAINST RIMSTEIN.

BEFORE STARTING, Wittich said that he could not go to Rimstein without his sword, and Heime refused to give it up, alleging that it was his by right of war; but the king smoothed matters for the time by desiring Heime to lend it to his comrade during the campaign.

The warriors set out. The rebel jarl proved himself a tougher foe than had been expected, and even after weeks and months had passed, his castle seemed as impregnable as ever.

One moonlight night when Wittich was out alone, he met six warriors whom he knew, by the device upon their shields, to belong to the enemy. They fought, and Wittich slew their chief, his sword Mimung cutting him in two from the neck to the waist. The other five fled in terror, lest a like fate should befall them. On examining the dead man, Wittich found it was the jarl himself that he had slain, so he returned to the camp well pleased. Next morning he told Dietrich and his comrades what had chanced, and how the war was now at an end.

"He is indeed a bold warrior," said Heime sarcastically; "he has slain a weak old man, who could not defend himself a bit better than a woman. But now I must have Mimung back again, for I only lent it for this enterprise."

"Let me first try it on your head, false comrade," answered Wittich, indignantly. "You left your brother-in-arms to die in a strange land, and were traitor enough to rob him of his weapon of defense as well. You shall now pay the penalty of your meanness."

Heime drew his sword Nagelring, and a fight was imminent; but Dietrich thrust himself between the angry men, and commanded them on their allegiance to keep the peace.

Ermenrich rejoiced to hear of Wittich's deed, and that the war was at an end. He gave rich presents to Dietrich and his men, and asked the royal hero to give Wittich leave of absence, that he might marry fair Bolfriana, the emperor's ward, and undertake the government of her rich fief of Drachenfels (the "Trekanfil" of Norse legend). Dietrich was pleased at his comrade's good fortune, and at parting, he merely reminded him of his oath of fidelity, which the hero at once renewed.

Not long afterwards Wittich was married to Bolfriana, and was endowed by the emperor with the great fief of Drachenfels, which extends to Fritilaburg (Friedburg?), and far beyond the eastern mountains. So Wittich became a mighty chief, as he had told his father that he would. Heime also, when his father Studas died, went to Ermenrich's court to take the oath of allegiance. He received other lands from his imperial master, and, what he liked still better, much red gold besides.

CHAPTER VII.

THE HARLUNGS.

ERMENRICH HAD a great and mighty empire. His lands stretched out to the east and west, and many kings owed him fealty. His counsellors were wise and clear-headed men, whose advice was of the utmost use to him. Chief among these was Sibich, the marshal of the realm, who was helped in his arduous labours by Ribestein, the head of the royal household, and his constant companion. These men had always used their influence with the emperor to keep him true to his alliance with his nephew, the king of Bern, of whom, in his heart of hearts, his imperial highness was not a little jealous. But a great change was soon to take place in the policy pursued at Romaburg.

Sibich had a young and beautiful wife, of whom he was very fond. Now Ermenrich once sent him away on a long journey, and during his absence did him foul wrong. When the marshal returned, and heard from his weeping wife of the emperor's treachery, he was filled with wrath. At first, he snatched up a dagger to kill his foe, but restrained himself, for he had thought of a subtler mode of vengeance. He desired to make the emperor the murderer of every member of his family, to deprive him of all his allies, and finally have him assassinated. It was a plan worthy of the devil himself, and was carried out with great craft and intelligence.

Sibich's first step was to buy over Ribestein to his design, which he did for a large sum of money, avarice being the man's weak point. This done, Ribestein agreed to write letters to the emperor as if from the duke of Tuscany, the count of Ancona, the prince of Milan, and others, warning him that his son Friedrich was plotting against him.

The evil deed was easily accomplished, as Ribestein had

copies of all the coats of arms and seals used by the grandees of the empire. Ermenrich was naturally of a suspicious disposition, so he readily fell into the snare laid for him. He consulted Sibich as to what were best to be done, and the false counsellor advised him to send Prince Friedrich with a letter to Jarl Randolt, ostensibly to demand payment of the tribute the jarl owed, but really containing an order that the prince should be slain. The emperor did as he was advised, and Sibich took care that the deed should become generally known. A cry of horror went through the land, and Ermenrich was hated by all.

Reginbald, the second son, met his death in a different fashion: he went down in the rotten ship in which his father had sent him on a pretended mission to England.

One son alone remained, Randwer, the third and youngest, a high-spirited, handsome youth, in whom there was no guile. That helped him nothing, however. One day, in the innocence of his heart, he gave his young step-mother Swanhild a bunch of flowers, when they were out hunting with the whole court, and Ermenrich, whose mind had been poisoned by false Sibich, ordered Swanhild to be trampled under foot by horses, and Randwer to be hung. His commands were obeyed. He was now alone in the world, a childless old man.

"Well, Ribestein," said the marshal to his accomplice, "we are getting on very well. The emperor's only remaining heirs are the Harlungs, Imbreke and Fritele, who live at Breisach, on the Rhine, with their governor Eckehart; and then Dietrich of Bern. The Harlungs and the hero are both brother's children. You were not born and brought up in Romaburg, so I will tell you the story.

"Ermenrich's grandfather left two sons beside him—namely, Dietmar, the father of Dietrich, who received the kingdom of Lombardy, and Dieter, surnamed Harlung, who during his father's lifetime received the Breisgau and an enormous hoard of red gold. Now listen to this. If we can only get rid of the Harlungs and the hero of Bern—yes, open your eyes and ears as wide as you can—you and I can divide between us the inheritance of Ermenrich!"

Ribestein jumped at the proposal as a fish jumps out of the

water with joy on a bright day. He had never thought of such a thing before; but he quickly understood what was required of him, and set about the evil work at once.

The Harlungs were first brought under suspicion. Letters were shown to the emperor purporting to be from Imbreke, Fritele, and even from their governor Eckehart, addressed to different notables of the empire, and setting forth Ermenrich's crimes in the darkest colours. One of the letters contained the following passage: "Since our liege lord has, in his desperate wickedness, slain his own children, he must himself perish, and that on the highest gallows." The emperor was so angry when he read these words that he determined to collect an army, and march against his rebellious nephews.

The troops were called out without any one knowing against whom the campaign was to be made. They marched towards the Rhine till they reached Tralenburg, which belonged to the Harlungs and where the brothers then lived. Two horsemen kept watch by the river. When they saw armed men, they feared something was wrong, and, dismounting, swam with their horses across the river. They gave the alarm, and all was prepared for defense. Imbreke and Fritele knew the science of war; but they were still very young, and Eckehart, their governor, was detained at Breisach by business of the state. When the Harlungs saw their uncle's banner, they thought all danger was over; but soon found to their cost that it was a warlike and not a peaceful visit. Wittich and Heime were with the imperial army; but as soon as they learnt Ermenrich's plans they rode away to Breisach to warn the faithful Eckehart of what was going on. As they journeyed together, they became good friends again.

Tralenburg was at length reduced by fire and taken by storm. Without seeing his nephews, Ermenrich ordered a gallows to be erected, and the two brothers to be at once hung thereon. In those days the word of a mighty potentate was law, and the emperor was obeyed without remonstrance. Ermenrich now took possession of the Harlungs' land, and sent out men to search for the rich hoard the murdered princes had inherited from their father. It was at length found hidden in a cave. The

emperor rewarded his army richly, and kept the rest of the trea-
sure-trove for himself.

Meanwhile Heime had returned. He had come back intending
to reproach his liege lord with his evil deed, and to throw up his
fief. But on receiving a large share of the booty, he forgot his better purpose. He was entrusted with the care of taking the treasure
to Romaburg. When he saw the heap of red gold and precious
stones, he took care that a considerable portion of it should find its
way to Studa's grange, and not to Romaburg. Meanwhile curses
both loud and deep were uttered in every land against the
emperor. Eckehart brought the news of the Harlungs' fate to
Bern, and Dietrich's wrath burned when he heard it. He said the
time would surely come when he could demand expiation from
Ermenrich, and punish his evil counsellors Sibich and Ribestein.
The fiery young heroes Alphar and his brother Sigestab wished to
start at once alone with Eckehart to avenge the murder. But their
father Amelolt and Hildebrand persuaded them to wait.

"What is only put off may yet be done," said Alphar to his
brother, laying his hand upon his sword.

Somewhere about this time Sibich and Ribestein met to hold
counsel as to what they should do next.

"Another stone is out of the way," said Sibich; "now we must
try to find levers strong enough to move the great rock that
stands in our way."

The accomplices felt that they must be careful and not push matters too fast, for, in the first place, the emperor's own soul was darkened by the crimes he had committed, and whenever he was alone
he was haunted by the unsubstantial ghosts of those whose death
he had compassed,—and, in the second place, before declaring war
upon the hero of Bern, they felt it would be safer to gain over as
many as possible of his comrades to their side. But they were hurried on faster than they wished, for Ermenrich's uneasy conscience
would not let him rest—he must have excitement.

The first step taken was to demand tribute of Dietrich of
Bern. So Reinhold of Milan was sent into the land of the
Amelungs to levy the tribute. The messenger returned in a few
weeks' time with empty hands. He said that the notables had

flatly refused to pay what he demanded, for they had already paid it to the lord of Bern. And Dietrich had desired him to tell the murderer of the Harlungs to come himself and take the tribute, which would be paid him to the last mark at the spear's point and the sword's edge.

The emperor sent Heime to Bern to tell Dietrich that if he did not pay the tax, he would come in person and hang him on the highest gallows.

Heime was well received in Bern. Dietrich thought that he had come in memory of old times, but when he delivered the emperor's message, the hero asked him if he remembered his old oath of fidelity; to which Heime replied that he had served out his bond, that he was now a vassal of the emperor, who had given him land and gold, and to whom he therefore owed service. Therewith he took his leave.

Heime was not long gone, when Wittich appeared. He galloped up to the castle gate.

"Arm, comrades, arm!" he cried, "there is not a moment to lose. Ermenrich approaches with an innumerable army. I rode on before to warn you of his coming. Faithless Sibich intended to have taken you by surprise, and whoever falls into his hands is not far from death."

Dietrich reminded him of his oath, but like Heime he excused himself, and rode away.

The Norns appeared at this time to have thrown their darkest web over the head of the hero of Bern. One blow struck him after another. From Wittich he hastened to the sick queen Virginal. All night long he held her in his arms. In the morning she died, and grief for her loss prevented his acting with the quick determination usual to him. Master Hildebrand, however, was not idle. He had summoned all the vassals with their following from far and wide in the land of the Amelungs. And the night before the queen's death, many allied princes joined them; amongst the number, Berchtung of Pola (in Istria), and the king's faithful comrade, Dietleib of Styria, with all their men.

In the morning the old master called the king, and told him that the time was come to fight for his land and people. The hero of Bern made a mighty effort to master his grief. He pressed a last kiss on the pale lips of his dead wife, and passed away on his march to the great battle.

The emperor had already subdued the duke of Spoleto, and had advanced as far north as Milan. There he encamped, and not suspecting any surprise, he and his men all went to sleep. Meanwhile Dietrich had arrived within a short distance of his camp. While the others rested, Hildebrand rode forward to see what watch the enemy kept, and finding them unprepared, he advised an immediate onslaught.

The imperial forces were suddenly aroused by the battle cry, "Hey for Bern! Hey for the red lion!" They hastily got ready for the fray. The battle raged furiously. Dietrich and his followers were far outnumbered by the foe, but that only made them fight with the more desperation. And which of them could have failed to do his duty under such a leader!

Wolfhart cried, "If we *must* die, let each man throw his shield behind him, and take his sword in both hands."

He did as he said, and Sigestab and Eckehart followed his example.

Wittich and Heime fought bravely as of old, but they avoided their former chief, and were at length carried away in the general flight. For the imperial troops were routed by a flank movement made by Hildebrand.

Ermenrich went back to Romaburg in a very bad humor. He felt inclined to hang Sibich and Ribestein for leading him into a scrape, yet he refrained, as he hardly knew what he could have done without them.

Dietrich sent the treasure gained in Milan home to Bern under the charge of some of his comrades and Berchtung of Pola undertook to provide pack-horses on which to convey it. The convoy travelled by forced marches, but when they reached the lake of Garden, and saw the stars mirrored in its bosom, and heard the splashing of the waterfall, Amelolt thought, that being in the land of the Wolfings, they need no longer fear robbers, and might enjoy a little needful rest. The wearied men hailed his proposition with joy, and, after supping on the provisions in their wallets, soon fell asleep on the soft turf. Hildebrand with ten of his followers tried to keep awake, but they were so tired that the sound of the murmuring water acted on them like a lullaby, and soon they were sleeping as soundly as the rest.

At daybreak they were roughly wakened. Wild faces glared upon them, strong hands bound them, and scornful laughter echoed in their ears. Four of the warriors, who had sought to defend themselves sword in hand, were cut down. The others were all bound and carried away with the treasure.

They had not been prisoners long before the comrades saw that they had fallen into the hands of their deadly enemy—faithless Sibich. He had heard of their journey in charge of the treasure, and had brought his troops by sea to Garden, had lain in wait near the lake, and had then fallen upon the sleeping men. Thus it was that the brave heroes were conquered by cunning.

One warrior had escaped the common misfortune, and this was Dietleib, the hero of Styria. He was sleeping in a thicket a little apart from the rest, when Sibich's men fell on the camp. Hearing the noise, he sprang to his feet, slew several of the men-at-arms, mounted his horse and fled to Bern, a bearer of sad tidings. He found every one there in great anxiety. Ermenrich had again invaded the country, had taken Milan, Raben (Ravenna), and Mantua, and, worse than that, many of Dietrich's men had deserted him, and joined the enemy.

The warriors who preserved their faith, and were determined to die with their lord if needful, were few in number. A message was sent to Ermenrich that the hero of Bern was willing to exchange his prisoners of war for his brave comrades. The answer he received was, that he might do with his prisoners as he liked— the warriors the emperor had taken were all condemned to be hanged. This was the worst news Dietrich had ever heard.

Then the lady Ute, Hildebrand's high-hearted wife, arose, and, accompanied by other noble ladies, went to the enemy's camp and entered the presence of Ermenrich. She offered him in exchange for the prisoners Sibich had just made, all her jewels, and those of all the other women and maidens of Bern. Ermenrich told her harshly that what she offered him was his already, and that if the king wished his comrades to be set free, he and they must leave the country as beggars, on foot, and leading their horses.

Hildebrand's wife could not bear to hear that. She had fallen on her knees before the emperor; but now she rose, and told him proudly that the heroes of Bern and their wives knew how to die, but not how to leave their country in dishonour. The women left the camp in deep sorrow.

When Dietrich heard the bad news, he had a long struggle with himself. He had been victorious before with smaller numbers to support him, but victory was always uncertain, and how could he allow his dear old master, and noble Berchtung, brave Wolfhart, Amelolt, Sigeband, Helmschrot, and Lindholt, to die a shameful death? It was a hard struggle. At length he bowed his head to necessity. He consented to Ermenrich's terms.

On being set free from prison, his comrades received their horses and arms again, and then they, and other faithful souls, three and forty men in all, accompanied their lord on his sad journey. There was not a dry eye in Bern when the king went away, and even in foreign lands the fate of Dietrich and his comrades was spoken of with bated breath.

The heroes would not mount their horses when they had crossed the borders of the imperial domains, for the king walked on unheeding over the wild mountain roads. So the small band of brave men wandered through the beautiful Danubian land, and approached Bechelaren, where Margrave Rüdiger held court. There they received a brotherly welcome.

One day, when they had been some time at Bechelaren, Dietrich, who had been thinking of the contrast between his desolated home and the smiling land he saw before him, said, with a deep sigh, that everywhere around him was peace and unity, and he would like to remain there forever and forget his woes.

Wolfhart reproached him vehemently for wishing to forget his home, adding, "If that is the case, I shall go back and fight till my last drop of blood is shed."

"Not so fast, young hero," answered the Margrave, "King Etzel owes thanks for the help once granted him. I will go with you to the court at Susat, and am certain that he will help you to regain the land of the Amelungs."

CHAPTER VIII.

KING ETZEL, WALTER AND HILDEGUNDE.

WHEN ETZEL became king of the Huns, he was the mightiest of all chieftains, but his lust of power was not satisfied. He collected a great army, and falling upon the land of the Franks, demanded tribute with threats of devastation. The Frankish king was unprepared to defend himself, so he paid large sums of money, and gave as hostage for his good faith, the boy Hagen of Tronje (Tronege). His own son was too young, being yet in the cradle.

The Huns went on to Burgundy, where they also levied tribute, and received as hostage the king's daughter Hildegunde, a child of four years old. They were equally successful with King Alphar of Aquitaine, who paid them much red gold, and gave them his young son Walter as hostage.

Hagen and Walter early showed great warlike ability. They learnt from the Huns to ride, throw the spear, and fight after the German fashion, and few could equal them in manly sports. Hildegunde became very lovely, and was a great favourite with the queen. Time went on, and these young people all grew up. Helche advised her husband to marry Hagen and Walter to Hunnish maidens of high degree, so as to confirm them in their devotion to himself, and their adopted country; but the youths did not admire the beauties of that nation, whose blubber-lips did not provoke a kiss. Walter was more attracted by slender Hildegunde's rosy mouth, fair curls, and blue eyes, than by any of the daughters of the land; and he was more pleasing in her eyes than the bow-legged Hun whom the queen desired her to marry.

Meanwhile the Franks and Burgundians had thrown off the yoke of the Huns, and Etzel did not dare to enforce it in the then condition of affairs. Hagen one day found out what had chanced, and, according to one account, he made his escape to his own people, but, according to another, was sent home loaded with honours. But Etzel did his best to keep Walter with him, for he knew his bravery and worth.

Once when the king returned with his warriors from conquering an invading horde, he gave a great feast, and asked Hildegunde to sing him a song. the maiden complied, and sang about her old home and her mother, and how she trusted to return to them once more, when the hero came for whom she waited. Etzel did not take in the sense of her song, as she had expected; he had raised the wine-cup to his lips too often for that. But Queen Helche understood, and determined to watch Walter and the maiden, lest they should fly together.

Walter, too, had understood the meaning of the song, and soon found an opportunity of arranging matters with Hildegunde regarding their flight.

"Do not sleep to-night," he whispered one evening, "but slip into the treasure chamber, and take as much gold and silver as you can carry out of the seventh chest; it is part of the tribute money that your father and mine paid the Huns long ago. Put the money you have taken in two caskets, and bring them down to the hall. You will find me waiting for you at the gate with two saddled horses. We shall be gone a long time before the drunken Huns find out that we have escaped them."

They carried out Walter's plan in every particular, and made their way to Bechelaren first, then to the Rhine, and finally to the mountains of Wasgengau (Vosges), in the highest of which, the Wasgenstein, they found a cave with such a narrow entrance that one man could there defend himself against an army. Walter wished to rest awhile, for he had had but little sleep during their long and toilsome journey, so he asked the maiden to keep watch, lest a sudden attack should be made upon them. He had not been long asleep when Hildegunde saw the sheen of armour in the distance. She wakened the hero, telling him that the Huns were upon them.

"These are not Huns, but Burgundians," he answered, starting to his feet. And he found they were messengers sent by King

Gunther, to demand that the treasure should be given up to him. Walter offered to hand over a shield full of gold, but this was refused, and the fray began. But the assailants could only approach one at a time; so the hero, who had learnt from the Huns to throw the javelin, was able to kill them one after the other with these missiles, and, when they failed, with his sword. Hagen had come with Gunther's men, but he stood apart during the fight, siding with neither party; only when he saw his friends falling fast, his hand involuntarily sought his sword, but he did not draw it. He returned to the king, and advised him to try an ambush.

Next day, as Walter and Hildegunde were continuing their journey across the open country, they were set upon by two men in complete armour, who sprang out upon them from behind a clump of bushes. They were Hagen and King Gunther. Despairing of flight, Walter leaped off his horse, and they did the same. With wonderful agility he dodged, now to the right, now to the left, to avoid their blows; at length his sword cut through one of King Gunther's greaves, and the edges entered the bone of the leg. He stood over the fallen king, and was about to deal him a death-blow, when a stroke from Hagen disabled his sword-arm. He dropt the sword, but with his left hand drew his dagger, and plunged it into Hagen's eye. Seeing them all three disabled, Hildegunde came forward to propose a truce, and bound up all their wounds; after which she and Walter went on their way in peace. They arrived at Aquitaine without further adventure, and were there married. The young hero in later days always took part with the Burgundians and Ermenrich, as we saw before when Dietleib challenged him at Romaburg.

CHAPTER IX.

ETZEL AND DIETRICH AGAINST THE REUSSEN.

BUT NOW we must return to Dietrich and Etzel. When the hero of Bern desired Etzel's help in freeing the land of the Amelungs from the tyranny of the usurper, he found that it was impossible for the latter to grant it. His hands were already overfull with his own quarrels.

Waldemar, king of the Reussen, and brother of that Osantrix whom Etzel had formerly slain, and whose daughter he had married, now invaded his borders, and threatened to overrun the country. In truth, Etzel needed Dietrich's help, and the latter did not hesitate to grant it.

The war lasted a long time. Many men were slain, and much fair land was devastated before the invaders were forced to retire. Dietrich himself was so severely wounded that it was some time before he felt like himself again. There was one thing which happened during the war that saddened and shamed honest Margrave Rüdiger, and that was the remembrance of the way in which Etzel had on one occasion fled before Waldemar, thereby proving the latter the better man. Indeed every one felt that the defeat of the Reussen was owing more to the leadership and heroism of the hero of Bern than to any other cause.

Etzel pursued the enemy within their own borders, and forced them to pay him tribute.

Dietrich was held in high honour by the Huns, but they did not see the advantage of helping him to regain his own land, and he felt sad at heart. At last Queen Helche thought of a way to make him happy. She proposed to give him her beautiful niece Herrat to wife, and then they might rule together over the princess's fair land of Transylvania. Dietrich and Herrat made no objection to the marriage, which was soon afterwards celebrated. But Etzel erred in thinking that the hero of Born would ever be content to sink into the position of a vassal of the Hunnish empire. Neither he nor Herrat were made of such slight stuff, and Etzel was obliged after all to give the help he had before refused.

THE RAVEN-FIGHT (BATTLE OF RAVENNA).

"GOING BACK to Bern! Dietrich is going to Bern! We are to have a campaign in Lombardy," was the cry which rang through the land of the Huns.

Yes; Dietrich was really going back, accompanied by many brave comrades new and old, and at the head of a large army. Even Etzel's two sons, mere boys as they were, insisted on going too. The line of march lay through the great mountains and fair plains of Lombardy. Amelolt (Amelung) and Hildebrand, at the head of the Wölfings, stormed Garden, and took the fortress. But the old master had not time to stay and embrace the Lady Ute and his son Hadubrand, for they were not in the castle at the time, and he had to rejoin the army without delay. He came up with the rest at Padauwe (Padua), which Dietrich failed to subdue. The army, leaving Padauwe behind it, moved on to Bern, from which Dietrich heard that Ermenrich's men had been expelled by the citizens.

At length the hero was at home in his beloved Bern, where he was received with great rejoicings. He had not long to rest; for a few days after his arrival Alpher came, bringing a message from Duke Friedrich of Raben (Ravenna), that the Emperor Ermenrich was besieging his town, therefore he begged the hero's assistance. The Bernese forces made a rapid march, and arrived unexpectedly in the neighbourhood of the imperial army.

It was of no use to send out scouts. The foe lay hidden in every thicket. Dietrich asked his heroes which of them would undertake to gain the enemy's outpost, and immediately young Alphart, the Lady Ute's foster-son, declared himself ready. Others wished to have the duty; but he had spoken first, and it was given to him.

ALPHART'S DEATH.

THE YOUTHFUL hero rode on towards the dangerous outposts. Suddenly, spears and arrows rained round him, and fell rattling from helm and shield. But they did no harm, for his armour had been made by dwarfs. The enemy's leader rode up to him, and desired him to yield, saying that he might give him his sword without shame, for he was Duke Wölfing, and would return the weapon to Alphart when he was ransomed.

"What?" cried the hero, "are you Duke Wölfing, the only traitor of our race? You shall have your wages here to-day, and from
my hands."

The combat between the two men was short. Alphart slew his
opponent. Upon this, the duke's retainers hastened up to avenge
him, but the young hero killed half of them, and put the rest to
flight.

"A spirit from the nethermost hell has come to fight for
Dietrich," cried the men-at-arms. "It slew more than fifty of us
single-handed, and we ourselves hardly escaped with our lives."

"Do you not know that the hero of Bern is a son of the devil?"
was the answer; "and what is more natural than that a father
should come to his child's assistance? No mortal man can be
expected to fight with such a foe."

"I will go out and see if it be not made of flesh and blood,"
cried stout Wittich. "Even though it had all hell at its back, I
care not; I must have a turn with it."

He armed himself quickly, and caught up a sword without
noticing that it was not Mimung. Heime, whose life he had
saved a short time before, offered to go with him, and avenge
him should he fall.

Alphart recognised the men from a distance.

"Ye are two faithless comrades," he cried, "and have come to
meet your doom."

The combat between him and Wittich began forthwith, and
the latter soon perceived that he had not Mimung. He was twice
felled to the ground. In his sore distress, he called on his comrade to help him; but Heime hesitated, because it was considered dishonourable for two warriors to fight against one. When
Alphart, however, called upon Wittich to yield, if he would not
be slain on the spot, Heime sprang forward, and covered his
comrade with his shield, thus enabling him to get to his feet
again. After which both warriors attacked the young hero.

Alphart was as active on foot as he was strong of hand. He
felled Heime, but Wittich came to his help, and so the battle
went on. The three warriors bled from many wounds; but it was
Heime's hand that finally dealt the death-blow.

"Faithless comrades that ye are," sighed the dying Alphart, "the curse of your dishonourable deeds will follow you to the grave."

The conquerors left the place of combat in silence. They did not noise abroad the fame of their deed. Yet their armour was bloody, and they were sorely wounded. The men-at-arms whispered in mysterious tones:

"They have been fighting with that spirit from hell, have slain it, but have seen some terrible sight."

The news of Alphart's death was received with deep sorrow in the Bernese camp. Dietrich prepared to offer battle to the emperor on the following day, and made all necessary dispositions in case he fell in the fight.

THE BATTLE.

MASTER HILDEBRAND held watch. Not contented with keeping a distant look-out on the enemy's movements, he went to see with his own eyes what was passing within their lines. A thick mist covered the earth, and hid every object from view. Suddenly the old master and his companion, Eckehart, heard the tramp of a horse. They drew their swords, and waited. At the same moment the moon broke through the mist, and they recognised by its light Rinold of Milan, who, although one of Ermenrich's men, was at the same time a friend of theirs. They greeted each other heartily, and Rinold said that if he might advise Dietrich, he would counsel him to return to the land of the Huns, where he had made himself a home; for the emperor was too powerful to be overthrown.

After taking leave of their friend, Hildebrand looked about carefully, and discovered a path leading through a wood by which he could outflank the imperial forces unperceived. On his return to the camp, he arranged with Dietrich that he should take three divisions by this path, and fall upon the enemy at daybreak. Meantime, the king was to be ready to attack in front, the moment he heard Hildebrand's horn sound to the rear of the enemy.

No sooner had the sun risen than the battle began. Great

deeds of valour were done on either side. It were an endless task to tell of each hero's achievements. Among those who fell were the two young sons of Etzel, who showed themselves worthy of their name.

During the course of that day, Dietrich and Wittich met at last, and it was in this wise. Twilight was drawing on apace, when Wittich, led by his evil star, or by his companion, Rinold of Milan, went back to visit the outpost. Dietrich saw them go, and, remounting, galloped across the valley towards the height, and the other two turned to meet him. When Wittich saw the king riding towards him, his face distorted by the angry spirit that possessed him, and his breath issuing from his mouth like flames of fire, a terror he had never known before overmastered him. He turned his horse and fled, followed by Rinold.

"Halt, cowards, halt!" cried the king. "Two against one! surely ye are strong enough?"

"Halt, comrade!" said Rinold, "I cannot bear the shame of this."

Wittich turned; but no sooner did he see the terrible face and flaming breath of his old leader, than he fled once more, leaving Rinold alone to bear the brunt of the attack.

"Stop, traitor," shouted Dietrich. "You have the sword Mimung in your hand, with which you once conquered me at Bern, and do you now fear to stand?"

But Wittich, by encouraging words, and a free use of the spur, urged his noble steed to a yet swifter pace. The king did the same, and Falcon was even fleeter than Wittich's gallant charger. The surf might now be heard beating on the sea-shore. The fugitive warrior reached the strand. He could fly no farther. And behold, at the same moment, two white arms and a woman's head rose out of the waves.

"Wachilde—ancestress—save me—hide me from that spirit of hell," he cried, and took the terrible leap.

And Wachilde received him in her arms, and bore him to her crystal hall at the bottom of the sea. Dietrich did not hesitate to follow. The waters swept over him and his horse, but Falcon rose again and swam through the roaring surf to the shore. The king looked all about, but Wittich had vanished. He could see nothing but the foaming waves. Sadly the king returned to the camp, having found neither the vengeance nor the death he had sought.

The Huns declared that they would return home as soon as they had buried their princes with fitting honor. Dietrich heard their determination unmoved. He was thinking of those who had fallen. Master Hildebrand, on the other hand, did what he could to induce them to follow up the victory that they had gained the previous day; but it was labour lost. They had had enough of fighting at the battle of Ravenna.

Broken-hearted, Dietrich returned to King Etzel, by whom he was received with the greatest kindness, in spite of all that had come and gone. He sank into a state of sorrowful brooding and melancholy, until at length Herrat, his faithful wife, came to him, and spoke words of comfort and encouragement. And he roused from his dull woe, and started again for fair Lombardy, accompanied by the Queen.

CHAPTER X.

A STRANGE ADVENTURE.

THE KING, Queen, and the old master took leave of Etzel, who was too sad about the death of his boys to take much interest in their coming or going.

The travellers at length came to a wooded hill with a castle perched on the top. This castle belonged to a robber-knight named Elsung, who had always been an enemy of the Amelungs and Wölfings. The old master, who acted as guide, and led the way, bade the king be prepared. He did not speak a moment too soon, for Elsung at the same instant appeared, followed by some horsemen. The robber-knight drew rein, and haughtily demanded, as toll from travellers, their horses and armour, Hildebrand's long beard, and the beautiful woman who accompanied them.

"We need our horses and armour that we may fight in the land of the Amelungs," said Hildebrand, "and we cannot spare the woman, for she acts as our cook."

"Nay, then, you are Amelungs yourselves," cried Elsung, "and must each give me your right hand and left foot as ransom. If you refuse, I will have your heads as well, that I may avenge my father, whom Samson slew."

The heroes deigned no further answer. They paid another toll than that demanded with the points of their swords and spears, and with such hearty good will that Elsung's men were either slain, or else took to flight, and their lord himself was finally overthrown and bound.

As Hildebrand was about to tie the prisoner to a horse Elsung said:

"You are Ermenrich's men, so I will tell you the news that has just reached me. The brothers of the Lady Swanhilde, whom the emperor had trodden to death by horses, have fallen upon him and have cut off his hands and feet."

"Ha!" cried the hero of Bern, "do you bring such good news? Take your liberty in payment thereof."

The travellers now pursued their journey, and after meeting with several more adventures, at last arrived safely at Garden, where they were at first received with suspicion; but the Lady Ute recognised her husband the moment she saw him, and Hadubrand was introduced to his brave old father, whom he had not seen since his childhood.

TO BERN.

THE HERO of Bern was welcomed with the utmost joy by his people, and soon collected an army, which among its most cele-brated warriors numbered brave Lodwig and his son Konrad, faithful Eckehart and his comrade Hache. Nor was Heime wanting; he had done penance for his sins in a cloister, and now, hearing of Dietrich's return, hastened to him to renew his oath, death having released him from the fealty he had formerly owed to Ermenrich.

Dietrich's and Sibich's forces met. A terrible battle took place. Dietrich fought with heroic valour, sweeping down all before him. Eckehart and Hache sought untiringly for faithless Sibich, and at last recognised him among the fugitives, although he had cast from him all signs of the imperial dignity he had usurped. Eckehart seized him by the scruff of the neck, swung him before him on his horse, and galloped back to the camp.

"Remember the Harlungs," he cried, and immediately ordered a gallows to be erected.

Sibich entreated for life, bare life. He offered much red gold to have his death put off for even a short space, but—

"Remember the Harlungs," was the only answer he received.

And so the victory was won. The hero of Bern marched to Romaburg at the head of his army. He was everywhere met by the princes of the land of the Amelungs. They greeted him as their chief, and on his arrival at Romaburg he received the imperial crown.

THE PASSING OF DIETRICH.

HERRAT WAS a faithful wife and helpmeet. The old master and many of his other ancient friends were round him; but in the midst of his glory Dietrich could not forget the faithful comrades who had died in his service, the friends who had given him their all, and to whom he could no longer show either love or kindness.

His power was great. The empire was more extensive than it had ever been before, and peace reigned within its borders. Once, indeed, a giant had committed great devastations within the land, and Heime had sought him out, but only to be slain. Dietrich himself had then gone forth, and had conquered the monster. It was the last combat in which the aged hero ever took part.

His wife, noble Herrat, soon after fell sick and died. From that time forward his character seemed changed. He was gloomy and morose, and committed many actions for which no after repentance could atone. The only one of his former pleasures that gave him any happiness was that of hunting. When he heard the cheerful sound of the horns, his face would clear up, and a smile play on his lips, and he would once more look like the Dietrich his friends had known of yore. Once, when he was bathing in the river, a great stag with golden horns, wonderful to look upon, trotted slowly along the bank, and passed into the wood close by. He sprang out of the water, threw on his clothes, and called for horse and hounds. Before the servants could bring him what he desired, Dietrich perceived a coal-black steed come towards him neighing. Seizing his sword and darts, he hastily mounted the noble animal, and galloped after the stag. His servants followed with the fleetest horses in his stables, but could not come up with him. The hero rode on faster, and ever faster. His people waited weeks, months, and even years for his return, but all in vain. The mighty empire had no ruler. Bloody wars broke out in consequence. His subjects longed for his return, that his strong hand might rule the land again; but still he did not come. Wodan, his ancestor, had caught him up to himself, and had made him one of his wild huntsmen. Many a benighted traveller has seen him rushing past, mounted on his coal-black steed. The people of Lausitz and other parts of Germany talk of him as Dietherbernet, and see him in the Furious Host even to this day.

THE NIBELUNG STORY.

CHAPTER I.

SIEGFRIED'S YOUTH.

ONCE UPON a time there was a noble prince in the Netherlands called Siegfried (Sigfrit, Siegwart, or Sigurd). His father, Sigmund, was descended from the glorious race of the Wölfungs, who traced their lineage back to Wodan. His mother, Sigelinde, was of equally high birth. They both rejoiced in the early signs of strength and activity displayed by their son, and hoped that when grown to man's estate, his heroic deeds might gain him glory and renown.

The boy, however, soon became aware of his wonderful strength, and showed a haughty, unbending spirit. He would suffer no contradiction: he beat his playfellows black and blue when they displeased him, even those among them who were much bigger than he. The older he grew, the more he was hated by all the other boys, and the more anxious his parents became regarding his future.

At last Sigmund told the queen that he only knew of one way to bring the young rebel under rule, and that was to apprentice him to the smith, Mimer, who lived in the neighbouring forest, and who was a strong and wise man, and would teach the boy how to forge the weapons he should one day wield as a warrior. The queen gave her consent, so the father took the necessary steps.

When the smith heard the whole story, he declared himself ready to undertake the task assigned him, for he had a strong belief in the pacifying effects of hard work. Everything went well for a time. One year passed on after another, till the prince grew almost to man's estate. But labour in the smithy was irksome to him, and when his comrades set him right, he beat them, threw them down, and, on one occasion, went so far as to drag the best smith among them—Wieland—by the hair to his master's feet.

"This will not do at all," said Mimer; "come here and forge yourself a good sword."

Siegfried was quite ready to do so. He asked for the best iron and the heaviest hammer, which was such a weight that it took both hands to wield it. Mimer drew the strongest bar of iron out of the forge, glowing red, and laid it on the anvil. Siegfried swung the hammer with one hand, as though it had been a plaything; but when it came down upon the iron the blow was like a clap of thunder, the house shook to its foundation, the iron shivered into splinters, and the anvil sank a foot deep into the ground.

"This will never do," said the master as before; "we must try another plan, my boy, if you are to make yourself a suitable weapon! Go to the charcoal-burner in the pine wood, and fetch me as much of his charcoal as you can carry on your strong shoulders. Meanwhile I shall prepare the best iron to make you a sword, such as never yet was possessed by any warrior."

Siegfried was so pleased to hear this, that picking up the largest axe he could find, he set out into the forest. It was a beautiful spring day. The birds were singing, and the grass was studded with violets and forget-me-nots. He plucked a bunch of the flowers and stuck them in his leather cap, from a half-conscious feeling that they might perhaps bring him good luck. He went on further and further, till he reached the middle of a dark pine forest. Not a bird was to be seen; but the gloomy silence was broken by a gurgling, hissing, and roaring, that might easily have affrighted a less daring spirit. He soon found the reason of the noise. A dismal swamp lay before him, in which gigantic toads, snakes, and lind-worms were disporting themselves.

"I never saw so many horrible creatures in my life," said Siegfried; "but I will soon stop their music."

So saying, he picked up dead trees and threw them into the morass, till he had completely covered it. After which he hastened on to the charcoal-burner's house. Arrived there, he asked the man to give him fire that he might burn the monsters.

"Poor boy," said the charcoal-burner, "I am very sorry for you; but if you go back the way you came, the great dragon will come out of his cave and make but a single mouthful of you. Smith Mimer is a faithless man; he came here before you, and told me that he had roused the worm against you, because you were so unmanageable."

"Have no fear, good man," answered Siegfried; "I shall first slay the worm, and then the smith. But now give me the fire, that I may burn the poisonous brood."

The lad was soon back at the swamp. He set fire to the dry wood with which he had covered it, and let it blaze. The wind was favourable, and fanned the flames to a great fire, so that the creatures were all burnt up in a short space of time. The lad then went round the dismal swamp and found a small rivulet of hot fat issuing from it. He dipped his finger in it, and found, on withdrawing it, that it was covered with a horn-like skin. "Ah," he thought, "this would be useful in war." He therefore undressed, and bathed his whole body in the liquid fat, so that he was now covered with horn from head to foot, except in one place, between his shoulders, where a leaf had stuck to his skin. This he did not discover until later. He dressed himself again in his leather garments, and walked on, his club resting on his shoulder. Suddenly the dragon darted out upon him from its hiding place; but three good blows of his club slew the monster. He then went back to the smithy to take vengeance on the master smith and his comrade. At sight of him, the men fled affrighted into the forest, but the master awaited the youth's arrival. At first Mimer tried the effect of flattering words; but finding they were vain, he took to his sword. Siegfried then dealt him one mighty blow, and had no need to strike again.

Having done this, the lad went into the smithy, and with great patience and care forged himself a sword, whose blade he hardened in the blood of the lind-worm. Then he set out for his father's palace. The king sharply rebuked him for his evil deed in slaying the master smith, who was so good a subject, and so useful to the whole country. And the queen, in her turn, reproached him with many tears, for having stained his hands with innocent blood. Siegfried, sobered by his father's reproof, and softened by his mother's tears, did not try to excuse himself; but, falling at the queen's feet and hiding his face in his hands, he said the sight of her tears cut him to the heart, and for the future he vowed that his deeds should be those of a gentle knight. Then the hearts of the parents were comforted.

From that time forward Siegfried was changed. He listened to the advice of men of understanding, and strove to learn how to act wisely and well. Whenever he felt one of his old fits of passion coming over him, he thought of his mother's tears and his father's reproof, and conquered the evil spirit that threatened to master him. The expectations of the people were great respecting him; they were sure that in him their nation had found a new hero. And then, he was so handsome and graceful, that the women admired him as much for his looks as the men did for his prowess.

YOUNG SIEGFRIED SAILS TO ISENLAND.

HIS FATHER and mother were so proud of him that they longed for the day when his name and fame should be hailed with applause in every land.

The king at length deemed that the time was come to give Siegfried and his comrades, and many young nobles of his own and other lands, the sword and armour that marked a warrior. This investiture was in those days a ceremony of great importance, and took up the same place in a young man's life as the ceremony of knighthood in later times. The solemn investiture was succeeded by feats of arms and trials of skill. Siegfried was victorious in all, and, at the end of the day, the populace shouted: "Long live young Siegfried, our king; long may he and his worthy father rule over us!"

But he signed to them, and said, "I am not worthy of such high honour. I must first win a kingdom for myself. I will entreat my noble father to allow me to go out into the world, and seek my fortune."

When the warriors were all assembled at the feast in the royal hall, Siegfried did not take his place at the upper end of the table beside his father, but modestly seated himself among the young warriors who had still their names to make. Some of the party began to talk of distant Isenland, the kingdom of the beautiful and warlike Brunhild, who challenged all her wooers to do battle with her, thereby slaying many.

They talked of the land of the Nibelungs, learned in magic; of the Drachenstein, where a flying dragon, of fiendish aspect, had taken up its abode.

Others, again, talked of the lovely princess at Worms on the Rhine, who was carefully guarded by her three brothers and by her uncle, strong Hagen.

"Oh, how pleasant it must be to see such marvels, and to seek out adventures!" cried Siegfried, and approaching his father, he asked permission to go out and see the world.

The king understood his desire, for he had had an adventurous youth himself; and promised to let him go, provided his mother gave her consent.

It was pain and grief to the queen to part with her son, but she at last permitted him to go, and one fine morning he set out, dressed in a shining suit of armour, mounted on a swift horse, and bearing the sword which he himself had made. His spirits were high, and his heart full of hope, as is the case with every youth of spirit who goes out into the unknown world to seek his fortune.

He went northwards in the direction of Isenland. On reaching the sea-shore, he found a vessel ready to start, but the skipper feared a storm, and only set sail at Siegfried's entreaty. After a quick but tempestuous voyage, Siegfried landed, and went up to the palace.

Queen Brunhild received him in the great hall, where many warriors were assembled, each of whom had come determined to woo the lady by great feats of arms.

On the following day the warriors assembled in the lists, where Brunhild joined them before long. She was clad in full armour, and looked as haughty and as beautiful as Freyja, when she led the Valkyries of old to the battles of the heroes.

Siegfried gazed at her in astonishment. She was so much taller and nobler looking than any of the maidens in her train, who were armed equally with herself. He almost wished to join the ranks of the wooers, and win her hand. He raised a stone in sport, and flung it far beyond the lists; then, turning to the queen, took leave of her with all reverence, and returned again to his vessel, saying to himself:

"I could never love her, she is too like a man. That maiden must be shy and modest, gentle and kindly, who would gain the heart of a brave warrior so utterly that he would think nothing of spending his heart's blood in her service."

After a quick voyage, he resumed his journey by land, now through rich and well-cultivated plains, and again through desert lands, where wild beasts and robbers had their abode. He had many a hard fight by the way, and slew all manner of giants and monsters. The minstrels sang of his great deeds in cottage and castle, so that his name became known far and wide.

When he reached the land of the Nibelungs, the kings of that country, Schilbung and Nibelung by name, asked him to divide between them the treasure left them by their father Nibeling, for they could not agree as to what was a fair division. In payment for this service they offered him the good sword Balmung, which was the handiwork of dwarfs, and was tempered in dragon's blood. The hero divided the treasure with the utmost fairness, yet the brothers were not satisfied. They told him that they were sure he was keeping back the most valuable things for himself, and commanded twelve enormous giants to seize him, and confine him in the hollow mountain where the treasure was kept. The hero at once drew Balmung, and began slaying one giant after another. Then the royal magicians chanted their spells, and called up a thick mist; a storm arose, and the mountain trembled under repeated thunder claps. All in vain. The last of the giants fell, and finally the two brothers were slain; then the mist cleared away, and the sun shone full on the victorious warrior.

When the Nibelung people saw the wonders that had been done, they greeted Siegfried as their king. But even yet his difficulties were not at an end. An avenger had arisen: this was Alberich the dwarf. Well armed with enchanted weapons, he came up against the bold warrior. He was now visible, now invisible, according as he drew the cap of darkness over his helmet, or took it off. After a long struggle Siegfried overthrew him.

The dwarf was now in his power, but Siegfried could not kill a defenseless foe. Alberich was so touched with this generosity that he swore to be true to his victor: an oath he never broke. After this, no one disputed the hero's right to the land of the Nibelungs. He was recognised as king by the whole people, and also became possessed of all the treasures in the hollow mountain, and of Alberich's cap of darkness by reason of his victory over the dwarf.

When Siegfried had reduced the whole kingdom to order, and appointed proved men to be governors of the provinces, he chose out twelve noble warriors to be his trusty companions. The treasure furnished him with rings and chains of silver and gold with which to enrich his followers. The whole band looked like an assemblage of kings under the lead of some yet mightier chieftain.

He and his men now set out on their journey homewards, and reached the Netherlands without further adventure. The king and queen were overjoyed to see their son, of whom they had for a long time heard nothing but indistinct rumours. Siegfried remained at home for many days to rest and recover from his weariness. He often passed hours sitting at his mother's feet, as when he was a little boy, and telling her of his hopes and longings. His confidence and trust in her made her very happy. But when he stood before her in all the panoply of war, her heart beat high with pride that she had such a hero for a son.

Pleasant as it was to be at home again, Siegfried could not long be contented with idleness; his soul panted to be out in the battle of life, where alone a man preserves his strength of mind and body. He told his father that he wished to go to Worms, in the Rhineland, and try his fortune with the great warriors of Burgundy.

The king's face clouded when he heard this. "My son," he said, "do not go to Burgundy, for there dwell the boldest warriors in the whole world. No hero has as yet withstood them. There are grim Hagen, strong Ortewin of Metz, and King Gunther, with his brother Gernot. They all unite in guarding the lovely maiden Chriemhild, whom many a brave man has wooed, only to lose his life."

"Ha! That is a good story!" cried bold Siegfried. "These mighty warriors shall yield me their kingdom, and the lovely maid as well, if she be pleasing in my eyes. With my twelve Nibelungs at my back, I have no fears about the fighting."

The king's remonstrances and the queen's entreaties were alike in vain. They were obliged to consent to their son's undertaking this adventure.

CHAPTER II.

SIEGFRIED IN BURGUNDY.

THE LOVELY maiden Chriemhild, who lived in the land of Burgundy, was the daughter of King Dankrat and his wife, the Lady Ute. Her father had long been dead; but his three sons, Gunther, Gernot and the boy Giselher, nicknamed "The Child," regarded their beautiful sister as the costliest pearl in their crown. The royal brothers were surrounded by brave warriors, to whom fear was unknown. First among these was grim Hagen of Tronje, un-beautiful of face, and one-eyed, but known and feared both in the land of the Teuts and in that of the Latins. He enjoyed great honour for another reason, that he was the uncle of the kings. After him came his brother, the marshal Dankwart; Ortewin of Metz; the Margraves Gere and Eckewart; Rumolt, the chief cook; Volker of Alzeyen, the faithful minstrel; Sindolt, the cup-bearer; and Hunolt, the steward. These and many other brave men, too numerous to mention, served the kings, and guarded their interests.

Young Chriemhild lived very much alone. She loved to wander about the garden and under the shady trees, and hated all

sights and sounds of war. Her brothers once persuaded her to go
out hunting with them; but a roe-deer fell dead at her horse's
feet, and the sight so distressed her, that she went straight home
and could never be induced to go out hunting again.

One day the queen entered her daughter's room at an early
hour, and seeing her look sad and troubled, she asked what ailed
her.

Chriemhild answered: "I dreamed that I had brought up a
noble falcon, and had grown very fond of it; but once, when I let
it fly up among the cliffs, two eagles attacked and killed it before
my very eyes."

"My child," said the mother gravely, "the falcon is some noble
warrior, whom you will learn to love with all your heart; and the
eagles are two false men, who will seek to compass his death by
cunning. May God give you strength and wisdom to turn their
plans to naught!"

"Mother!" said Chriemhild, "do not speak to me of men. I
fear to go amongst them. If there were no men on the earth,
there would be no more wars or bloodshed."

"Who knows?" answered he mother, laughing. "Women often
shed more blood, and cut deeper with their tongues, than any
man with his sword. But the time will come when you will learn
to love some hero, and will become his wife and chief admirer."

"Never," cried the maiden in a voice of horror. "Mother, you
terrify me even more than my dream."

Ute and Chriemhild went down to the garden. They had not
been there long when they heard the sound of horses prancing
in the court, and horns blowing. The queen went to see what
was going on, and soon came back to tell her daughter of the
arrival of some strange warriors in shining armour, and mounted
on beautiful horses. She asked the girl to come and help her to
receive the guests. But Chriemhild refused to do so, and Ute
returned to the palace alone. Meanwhile Gunther and his
brothers had heard of the coming of the strangers. No one knew
who they were, so Hagen was sent for, and he at once recognised Siegfried. He further advised his nephew to receive the
hero and his men with all honour, and to enter into friendly
alliance with them.

Gunther resolved to follow Hagen's counsel; but Siegfried said that he had come to prove to his own satisfaction whether the Burgundian warriors were as great in battle as he had always heard. He offered them the Nibelung realm and treasure as the prize of victory, and said that for his own part he was ready to defend himself against double or threefold the number of his own party, if the kings of Burgundy would venture their kingdom against him. Bold Ortewin and other Burgundian heroes answered that it was not their habit to fight strange warriors for aught else than their armour and horses. And King Gernot came forward and said,—

"Lord Siegfried, we want neither your goods nor your blood; I rather desire to receive you as an honoured guest, and become your friend and ally, if you will also be ours." So saying, he held out his hand, which Siegfried clasped in his, as he replied:

"God be my witness that I will be your faithful friend and ally, and if you ever come to see me, I shall greet you as honoured comrades."

The Nibelungs then followed their hosts into the banqueting hall, where many a toast was drunk to the success of the new alliance.

Siegfried enjoyed his stay in the land of roses and vineyards. The days passed happily in hunting and jousting; but a great longing to see fair Chriemhild soon took possession of him, and grew stronger every day, for he was always hearing of her sweetness, modesty and gentleness—qualities that had ever pleased him best in women.

Chriemhild had also heard of him; but the only time she ever saw him was once when curiosity led her to peep out of a high window, when he was jousting in the court below. He seemed to her like the white god Balder, of whose beauty and glory her forefathers had told many a tale. At that very moment, he looked up, and she shrank away, fearing lest he had seen her; but he had not. Chriemhild could not understand herself. She hoped that he would stay at Worms—she, who had never before cared who came or went.

An embassy from Daneland and Saxonland arrived at Worms. The kings Lüdegast and Lüdeger declared war against Burgundy,

if the kings of Burgundy did not at once pay them tribute, as in
olden times.

The tribute was refused, and the Burgundian army was called
out. Siegfried and his men joined King Gunther's forces. The
armies met. The Danes and Saxons numbered forty thousand;
the Burgundian forces were much fewer. Each side fought
bravely, but Siegfried's performances were perhaps more wonderful than any other man's. He took King Lüdegast prisoner,
and brought him sorely wounded into camp; handed him over
to the care of servants, and returned to the battle. The fight
raged on for hours. Grim Hagen was always in the front rank,
and near him were Volker, Sindolt and Hunolt. Siegfried fought
by their side, always keeping the king of Saxony in sight. At
length he reached Lüdeger, and swung his sword over his head.
Then the Saxon king exclaimed,—

"Ha, Siegfried of the Netherlands, the devil has given me into
your hands. I acknowledge myself your prisoner."

The battle was at an end, and the victors, covered with glory
and laden with booty, set out on their return to the Rhine. They
were received at Worms with great joy, and Siegfried's name was
in every mouth. King Gunther prepared a feast of victory, which
was to take place some weeks later, so that the wounded warriors might be well enough to take part in it. Lüdeger and
Lüdegast offered a large ransom for their liberty. While the
Burgundians were debating what sum it would be proper to
demand, Siegfried exclaimed:

"A king's head is neither to be bought nor ransomed for gold,
silver, or precious stones. It can only be won in love through
well-doing. Let the imprisoned kings go free, provided they
promise Burgundy their help in war."

When the days of feasting were over, the guests all took their
leave, and the Nibelung hero was about to do the same. But
Gunther, acting on Ortewin's advice, begged him to tarry a little
longer, for the women, and more especially his sister,
Chriemhild, wished to show him their gratitude. The hero's face
lighted up with pleasure, while he answered that in that case he
would stay. When the king went to the women to tell them what
he wished them to do, he felt at the bottom of his heart a little

fear lest his sister should refuse; but, though she blushed, she consented to do his will.

At the time appointed, she entered the hall at Lady Ute's side; and as she entered, her eyes and Siegfried's met. She said a few words to him with her usual gentle courtesy, and his heart beat with a feeling he had never known before. No one in the crowd noticed the look that had passed between them except Queen Ute, who rejoiced to see it, for she loved them both. She contrived that the hero should sit next to her daughter at the feast, and that he should afterwards join them in the garden, while the other warriors sat over their wine.

CHAPTER III.

THE DRAGONSTONE.

SIEGFRIED RETURNED to his lodging that evening feeling happier than he had ever done before. Early next morning, he rode out into the wood to hunt; but his thoughts were so full of Chriemhild that he let the game pass by unheeded. Coming back empty-handed in the afternoon he found both town and palace in great confusion. Warriors and citizens were shouting and crowding in every open place. Queen Ute was weeping and wringing her hands. Siegfried heard broken fragments of conversation; but no one answered his questions. At length he entered the great hall, where he found Hagen, and asked him the meaning of the disturbance, and whether some dreadful thing had happened.

"That it has," replied Hagen; "it could not be worse; but what is to be, must be, and as men said in the olden time, 'what the Norns have ordained must needs be best.' Hearken, Siegfried. When we were in the tiltyard this morning, we were startled by hearing a rushing noise in the air, and the brightness of the sun was darkened as if the wolf Skol were devouring it. The thing of terror that approached was a flying-dragon, of shape so monstrous, that there is none like it in all the realm of Hel. As it flew over our heads, we flung spears at it, but they bounced off its horny skin like reeds. Next moment we heard a cry, and saw that the monster had caught up sweet Chriemhild from her seat in the garden, and was bearing her off through the air so rapidly that both were soon out of sight."

"And none of you went in pursuit!" shouted the Nibelung hero, "cowards that you are!"

"Are you mad?" asked Hagen, unmoved. "Are you a bird, that you can fly through wind and cloud?"

"I shall seek out the monster," said Siegfried quietly; "if I have to wander through the whole world and Hel's realm itself, I shall find the maiden, or—my death."

He hastened away, mounted his horse, and rode by unknown paths, leading he knew not whither. A ferryman set him across the Rhine, and then he wandered about among the bare mountains, but found no trace of the dragon's abode. At length he reached a dark and trackless pine forest. The boughs of the trees hung so low that he had to dismount, and lead his horse by the bridle. As night came on, he threw himself under a tree, utterly exhausted, leaving his steed to graze at will.

At midnight he heard the tramp of a horse's hoofs, and, looking up, saw a faint red light approaching. The rider was a little dwarf. On his head was a golden crown, the point of which was formed of a shining carbuncle. The hero asked the dwarf to show him the way out of the forest, and the little creature answered that he was glad they had met, for no one knew the forest better than he; adding, that he was the dwarf-king Eugel, who lived in the mountains hard by with his brothers, and thousands more of their race.

"As for you," he continued, "I know that you are Siegfried of the Netherlands. I have often seen you when I have been going about the world with my cap of darkness on. You could never have got out of the wild wood without my help, but would infallibly have found your grave at the Drachenstein, where the terrible giant Kuperan and the great dragon have taken up their abode."

On hearing this, Siegfried shouted aloud for joy, and promised the dwarf a rich reward, even to the whole Nibelung hoard, if he would lead him to the Drachenstein. This Eugel refused to do, fearing for the hero's life; but when Siegfried threatened to slay him, and at the same time seized him by the waist and shook him till his crown fell off, he promised to obey. He replaced his crown and rode on first through the dark forest. At daybreak they reached their destination.

"Knock at that door," said the little king. "It is there that Kuperan lives. If you are hero enough to slay the giant, I and mine will serve you, for now we are entirely in the power of that monster."

Having thus spoken, he donned his cap of darkness, and vanished.

Siegfried knocked at the door, at first gently, then louder and louder, at the same time shouting to Kuperan to give him the keys of the Drachenstein. Suddenly the door sprang open, the giant rushed out in a tremendous passion, and asked in a thundering voice what Siegfried meant by disturbing his morning's sleep. With these words he hit out at the warrior with the pole he had in his hands, which was taller than any of the three tops, and every blow of which rang like a castle bell. Siegfried sprang aside to avoid the pole, and then the battle began. The giant swung his pole with such good will that trees and rocks came rattling down, but he never succeeded in touching his agile foe. At length, holding his weapon in both hands, he brought it down on the ground with such terrible force that it clove the earth three fathoms deep. As he stooped to draw it out, the hero sprang upon him and gave him three deep wounds. The giant, howling with pain, slunk into his dwelling, and slammed the door behind him. Siegfried battered at the iron door, but could not move it. He sought to force an opening with his good sword, and succeeded in cutting some holes and crannies. He peeped into the inner room, and saw the giant binding up his wounds, and then arming himself in a suit of mail, that glistened like the sun when mirrored in the sea. In another minute Kuperan came forth, and the combat was renewed. After a long struggle, Siegfried had the best of it, and the giant begged for his life, swearing to be a true comrade and helper in the hero's fight with the dragon, who could not be overcome without his aid. Upon this Siegfried gave Kuperan his hand in friendship, bound up his wounds, and promised on his side to be his faithful comrade; but as he entered the cavern first, the false giant hit him so hard a blow on his helmet that he fell sense-less to the ground. Eugel, who was watching all that passed, unseen, came up at the same moment and flung his cap of dark-ness over the hero. While the monster thought he had vanished through enchantment, and felt about for him outside, Siegfried recovered from his swoon, sprang to his feet, and tearing off the cap of darkness, cut down the giant with the first blow. He once more forgave the traitor, but forced him to go on before.

Faithless Kuperan again tried to murder the hero at the entrance of the Drachenstein, and Siegfried would not have again forgiven him if he had not needed his help to save the maiden. The giant now brought out the key, unlocked the door, and led the hero through many passages into a vaulted chamber, in which a soft twilight reigned. Looking round, Siegfried saw her whom he sought, looking pale and wan, but very beautiful. He called her name, and hastened to her. He even dared to clasp her in his arms; he felt that she returned his kiss, and the consciousness that he was loved made him feel so strong that he could have fought all the powers of hell for her sweet sake. Chriemhild wept bitterly, and entreated him to be gone before the dragon came back; but Siegfried asked for nothing better than to come face to face with the monster, hew him in pieces, and save the princess. The giant now told them that a sword was hidden in the Drachenstein, so fashioned that it could cut through the scales of a dragon. Siegfried set out to fetch it, accompanied by Kuperan and Chriemhild. Siegfried saw the hilt of a sword on a ledge of rock just blow the edge of the beetling cliff. He stooped to pick it up, and at the same moment the monster seized him, and strove to fling him over. A terrible struggle began, in which the bandages came off the giant's wounds, his blood streamed down, his strength failed him, and Siegfried flung him into the depths below. A loud laugh of joy was heard, and the victor, turning, saw King Eugel, who thanked him heartily for having delivered the dwarfs from their cruel task-master. At his command a number of mannikins appeared, bearing food and wine to refresh the brave warrior after his exertions. He was much in need of food, for he had not tasted a mouthful for two days. The dishes Chriemhild placed before him, and the wine she gave him, tasted better than anything he had ever eaten or drunk before.

All at once a rushing sound was heard in the air, and a howl of rage, so terrible, that all the dwarfs hid themselves in any crannies of the rock that they could find, and the hero and maiden were startled out of their momentary feeling of security. Chriemhild entreated, prayed her lover to conceal himself; but he was a stranger to fear, and refused to fly. The monster approached like a storm-cloud, preceded by flames of fire. It came nearer and nearer, dark, mysterious, gruesome. The mountain trembled, and the little dwarfs, hiding in the fissures of the rock, feared to be crushed to death. At Siegfried's request, Chriemhild withdrew into the vaulted chamber. And now the dragon fell upon the hero, tore away his shield with its claws, and tried to seize him in its great teeth. The warrior knew how to act; he sprang aside, until the fiery breath that issued from the dragon's yawning jaws had cooled. Then he renewed his attack, now on the right, now on the left of the monster, taking care to avoid its claws.

All at once he felt himself encircled by the dragon's tail. He made a marvellous spring, freed himself, and sought to attack the creature in front, where it was undefended by scales. Upon this, the dragon caught him so tight within its curling tail that he could not free himself. In sore distress he seized his good sword Balmung in both hands, and gave so hard a blow that the rocks trembled; but his object was attained. The tail was cut off, and rolled thundering over the edge of the cliff. A second blow, as hard as the first, divided the monster in two. 'Tis true, the jaws still snapped at the hero, but he, with the last effort of his strength, flung the pieces over the cliff. Having done this, he fell back exhausted and half stifled by the poisonous breath with which the dragon had so long surrounded him. When he came to himself he found Chriemhild's arms around him, and the dwarfs busily engaged burning herbs and sprinkling essences to do away with the baneful effect of the fetid odours with which the place was impregnated.

The dwarfs now led the hero and the maiden into their underground kingdom, where a feast was prepared for them. While they rested, Eugel told them that the dragon had formerly been a man of handsome figure and face, but that a mighty enchantress, whom he had deserted, changed him into a dragon, under which form he was to remain for the rest of his life, unless a pure maiden should consent to marry him within six years.

The dwarfs offered the warrior his choice of all their treasures. He took certain things from them, placed them on his horse beside Chriemhild, and, accompanied by Eugel, set out on his return to Worms. When they reached the edge of the wild forest, the dwarf-king looked at him sadly, and said:

"You must know, bold warrior, that your life will be short, but glorious. You will fall by the envy of your own kindred. But your fame will last through all ages, and your name will be held in honour by the bards of every nation as long as the human race exists on the earth."

Eugel then took leave of him, and returned to his home in the forest. When Siegfried and Chriemhild came down to the banks of the Rhine, the hero took the treasure that the dwarf had given him, and sunk it in the deep waters of the river.

"What is the use of gold to me?" he said. "My life is to be short, but glorious! Hide it in thy bosom, mighty river; may it gild thy waves and make them gleam more brightly in the sunlight! Gold does the devil's work in the hands of the children of men; it sharpens the assassin's dagger to strike some unsuspecting heart—perhaps mine. But as yet I live in the light of day. I will rejoice in my glory, and in my love for the sweetest maiden on the face of the earth."

He then rejoined Chriemhild, and called the ferryman to take them across the Rhine, after which they pursued their way to Worms, and were received there with great rejoicing.

Siegfried took the first opportunity when he found Gunther alone to ask him for his sister's hand, and the king answered:

"I will give her to you with all my heart, if you will first help me to win a high-born and most heroic woman to be my wife. I mean Brunhild, the proud queen of Isenland, for whose sweet sake many a wooer has already gone to his death."

"I know her well," replied Siegfried, "and have seen how she bears herself in the fray. She fights bravely and well, yet I do not fear but that she will find her master in you and me. You will do well to prepare for an early start, that we may get back before the end of summer."

Queen Ute and her daughter feared the result of the adventure, but Siegfried told them to be of good courage. He promised to stand by Gunther in life and death,—even the proud queen of Isenland would scarcely prove so hard an antagonist as the monster of the Drachenstein. The king proposed to take a thousand warriors in his train, but Siegfried dissuaded him; and when at last they started, the party of adventurers consisted of Gunther, grim Hagen, Dankwart and himself.

CHAPTER IV.

THE WOOING OF BRUNHILD.

AFTER A favourable voyage they arrived at Isenstein, and rode up to the palace. Servants hastened to meet them and take their armour and horses. Hagen was at first unwilling to give up his horse and armour, but he yielded when Siegfried told him that such was the law and custom at Isenstein. The warriors entered the hall where Brunhild awaited them, clad in her royal robes. She greeted her guests with courtesy, and told the Nibelung hero how glad she was to see him again, as she had been told of his great deeds of valour; adding that she supposed he had come to enter the lists. Siegfried then informed her that he had only come as the comrade of King Gunther, his lord, who desired to try his fortune, and who was well worthy of the high prize of victory.

"This is news to me!" said the queen, "I always thought you were your own man, and owed no allegiance to another."

Then, turning to King Gunther, she told him that she had also heard of his great deeds, and asked him who were the warriors that bore him company. Gunther answered with many thanks for her kind reception, and explained who and what his companions were. Brunhild laughed and asked whether he intended to fight aided by his three comrades.

"No, I alone am to fight," answered the king; "I alone compete for the great prize."

"Very well," said the lady, "the lists are open, prepare to do your best."

The warriors were led into the castle court, where a wide space was enclosed for the combat. The queen's serving-men surrounded it, well armed. One of these proclaimed in a loud voice:

"If any nobly-born warrior ventures to play the three-fold play with the queen, and gains the victory, she and her kingdom shall be his; but if he is conquered, his head and wealth belong to her."

Four grooms now dragged a great stone into the lists, which the combatants were to "put" (throw). It was as large and heavy as a millstone. Three other men brought in the huge broadsword which the maiden was accustomed to fling.

"If the woman can play with such a thing as that," said Hagen, "she is the devil's bride. No son of man can win her!"

"If we only had our weapons," cried Dankwart, "neither the king nor we need lose our lives."

"Be of good courage, King Gunther," said Siegfried, "I will fetch my cap of darkness from the ship, and will help you without any one seeing that I do so."

He hastened away whilst all eyes were fixed upon the queen, who now entered the court, surrounded by her ladies, and clad in full armour.

"Is it right, noble queen," said Hagen, "that your men should be armed, while we remain defenseless?"

"Bring the warriors their armour," commanded Brunhild. Then turning to Hagen, she continued: "But, for all that, you must lose your lives here. If I conquer Gunther, as I have hitherto conquered all who have entered the lists with me, your heads will fall under the axe of yonder man."

The heroes looked in the direction in which she pointed, and perceived a man clad in blood-red garments standing without the barrier holding a sharp axe in his hand.

The trial of strength began.

Brunhild went up to the stone, lifted it in both hands, and flung it the length of six fathoms. After which she leapt forward with one spring as light as a bird, making the point of her foot touch the stone. This feat was greeted with applause. Then came a silence as of death. Gunther advanced. Aided by Siegfried's strength, he lifted the stone, weighed it in one hand and flung it a full fathom farther than the queen. It was a stronger hand than his that helped him both in this and in the leap that followed, which carried him beyond the stone.

In the first feat of strength, he was thus indisputably the conqueror.

Then Brunhild rose with flashing eyes, and seized the heavy spear with its sharp steel point.

"Now look to yourself, proud king," she cried, and flung the weapon with such force that it crashed through his shield, and would have laid him prostrate had not Siegfried come to his aid by turning the point towards the edge of the shield instead of the centre. Then tearing it out of the broken shield, he turned the weapon so that the blunt end pointed at the queen, and guiding Gunther's hand, Siegfried launched it at her. And immediately Brunhild fell backwards, her chain armour rattling with the force of her fall.

The combat was at an end, the victory won. Brunhild rose. She stood calmly before the people, accepting her fate; but whoever could have read her heart would have seen it full of shame, anger, and a wild thirst for vengeance. The notables of Isenland were summoned to appear at Isenstein within three days to take the oath of allegiance to Gunther. Brunhild begged the Burgundian warriors to remain her guests during that time. She asked where the Nibelung hero was, and when he stepped forward and said that he had been busied about the ship and the sailors, she called him a faithless servant for not having been by while his master played so dangerous a game.

A great feast was made in the hall. Many ladies were present, but the queen remained in her own apartments. Gunther's feelings were very mixed. He was ashamed not to have won the victory single-handed, and yet he was pleased at having gained his object. Hagen drained many a cup of wine, and watched the laughing warriors around with a grim look on his stern face. When the heroes of the Rhine were taken to their common chamber, Hagen advised them to see that their weapons were at

hand, because he feared the queen was nursing some treacherous plan against them. Bold Siegfried answered that he would at
once set out for the land of the Nibelungs, and return with an
army of good men and true. He made his way to the ship unperceived in the darkness, and set sail for his own kingdom. Arrived
there, he went straight to the dwarf Alberich who guarded the
treasure, and desired him to call out a thousand well-armed
men to go with him to Isenland. His commands were obeyed in
an incredibly short time, and he and his troops set out to join his
friends. On the third morning, he landed in front of the palace,
to the great joy of the Burgundians. The queen, on the other
hand, was anxious, not knowing what the arrival of so large a
force might mean. But Gunther comforted her by explaining
that Siegfried had brought over a band of his Nibelungs to do
honour to him, the king.

During the next few days everything was arranged for the
proper government of Isenland, and when Brunhild at length
took leave of her people and her mother's brother, who had been
appointed governor, there was hardly a dry eye to be seen. The
queen herself was not happy, for she felt sure she would never
see her home again; but Gunther would not let her lose time,
being anxious to get back to Worms to celebrate his marriage.

When the travellers arrived in Burgundy, they were received
with great joy by every one. the Lady Ute welcomed Brunhild
as a daughter, and Chriemhild kissed her, and promised to be a
faithful sister to her. So the two maidens stood side by side: the
one, grand, beautiful, and mysterious as a starlight night; the
other, sweet, gentle, and lovely as a May morning. None looking
at them could say which was the fairer. But Siegfried had no
doubt. He never moved from Chriemhild's side till they reached
the castle.

That evening Gunther asked Siegfried and Chriemhild if they
were still of the same mind as before, and, finding that they
were, announced that he would make preparations for a double
wedding on the following day.

Brunhild sat at the feast that evening by Gunther's side, pale
and cold as marble, while Chriemhild sat smiling and whisper-
ing between her mother and her lover.

"King of Burgundy," said Brunhild, at last, "I cannot understand why you gave your sister in marriage to one of your vassals. She ought to be the wife of a great king."

"Say not so," answered Gunther; "Siegfried is as much a king
as I am. He is king of the Nibelungs, and after the death of his
father Sigmund, the whole Netherlands will belong to him."

"It is a strange story," she said; "he told me himself that he
was your man."

"I will explain it all to you another time," replied Gunther;
"we'll say no more about it just now."

The double wedding took place next day. When the ceremony
was over, the old queen showed her daughter-in-law all her possessions, and gave up to her all authority in the house.

"Ah, mother Ute," said the young wife, "the Burgundians are
rich in wealth and great in power; but they are poor in wisdom
and weak in action, otherwise King Gunther never would have
come to Isenland."

Without waiting for an answer, she turned and left the room.

The feast was at an end, twilight had long fallen, and the
guests all sought their beds. Gunther and his queen went to
their private apartments. When he would have followed her into
her room, she barred the way, saying,—

"This is no place for you; you can find a more fitting room
elsewhere in the palace. If I permitted you to enter, I should
lose my great strength."

At first he tried entreaties, then threats, and lastly force. They
wrestled together, but she very soon mastered him, bound him
hand and foot, and left him lying outside the door. He did not
sleep much that night.

Next morning, before the household was stirring, the proud
queen loosed her husband's bonds, desired him to hold his
peace, and to respect her will in future. Gunther was sad at
heart the whole day long; he looked at his wife with a feeling
that was almost horror, and often left the feast to walk alone in
the garden. Siegfried met him there, and asked what ailed him.
When he heard the strange story, he cried:

"Be comforted, dear comrade; we have conquered this proud
woman before, and I think we shall get the better of her again.

I will follow you to-night, hidden under my cap of darkness, when you take the queen to her room. Blow out the candles and let me take your place. Then she shall have an opportunity of trying her great strength against me."

"Ah, good comrade," said Gunther, "I fear for your life. We did ill to bring her from Isenland to the sunny banks of the Rhine. She is a demon, as Hagen says, and has her marvellous strength from her dear friends the devils."

"Well," said Siegfried, "and even if a demon has taken up his abode in her heart, it shall go hard but we'll get the better of him. I shall be with you to-night in my cap of darkness."

The kings returned to the feast, Siegfried looking as cheerful as ever, while Gunther was bowed down by manifold cares and anxieties. At midnight Gunther led Brunhild to her room, blew out the candles, and immediately Siegfried took his place. The wrestling began, Brunhild pushed him between the wall and a cupboard, and tried to bind him with her girdle. She squeezed his hands till the blood spirited from under his nails. Such a wrestling match was never seen between a man and a maid. He used all his hero-might, and pressed her into a corner of the room with such force, that, shivering and moaning, she entreated him not to kill her, and she would be an obedient wife. No sooner did Siegfried hear this than he slipped softly away, leaving Gunther alone with the queen.

The wedding festivities lasted eight days longer; then the guests took leave of their host, and went home with many rich gifts. Siegfried and his wife also made ready for their departure. The hero refused to take any dowry with his wife, for, in his opinion, the Nibelung treasure was wealth enough.

It was on a beautiful day that the travellers reached the Netherlands. King Sigmund and Queen Sigelinde came out to meet them, and received them with great joy. An assembly of the people was summoned to meet, and after a short speech from the throne, the old king and queen placed their crowns on the heads of Siegfried and Chriemhild. The people shouted, "Long live our young king and queen! May they reign as long and as happily as their forerunners!"

It seemed as if the people's wish were to be realized, for years passed on, and all went well with the royal family. Queen Sigelinde had the great joy of holding a grandson in her arms. The child received the name of Gunther, in honour of his uncle in the distant Rhineland. And King Gunther, who had a son born about the same time, called the infant Siegfried. Not long after this the old queen was taken ill and died. This made a break in their domestic happiness; but still there was peace in the realm, and along its borders.

Chapter V.

Treason and Death.

Eight years, or thereabouts, had come and gone, when messengers arrived from Burgundy inviting Siegfried and Chriemhild to a great feast. They accepted the invitation, and Sigmund determined to accompany them to Worms.

Brunhild had said one day to her husband, "King Gunther, why does your brother-in-law Siegfried never come to our court like the other vassals? I should like to see both him and your sister Chriemhild. Pray send, and command their presence at court."

"I told you before," answered Gunther, somewhat nettled, "that my brother-in-law is as mighty a king as I. He rules over the Nibelungs and the Netherlands."

"How strange!" she replied. "You cannot deny that he called himself your man when he was in Isenland."

"Oh! he only said that to help me in my wooing," said Gunther, feeling uncomfortable.

"You only say that," was her answer, "to make your sister seem to have a higher rank. But however that may be, I should very much like to see them both at our court."

"Very well," he answered kindly, "I will send messengers to invite them to the Midsummer feast, and they will not refuse to come."

He went away, and did as he had said. Brunhild remained alone, plunged in thought.

"There he goes," she muttered. "The man that conquered the once heroic maiden, who thought herself strong enough to brave the battle like the Valkyries of old. And he, what is he but a weak reed, moved hither and thither by every breath of wind that blows? How much greater Siegfried is! He is a hero with the world at his feet. But then a vassal! To be sure, none such could dare to raise his eyes to the queen of Isenland. Had he done so, she must have scorned him, and would scorn him to this very hour."

Siegfried and his party came to Worms at the appointed time. There was no end to the feasting, tilting and minstrelsy. Old Sigmund renewed his youth again, and delighted to talk of old days with the Lady Ute, whom he had known as a child. The young queens were always together, at church, or at the feast, or else in the gallery overlooking the tilt-yard. The only amusement to which Chriemhild did not accompany her sister-in-law was the chase.

One day when they were sitting together in the gallery watching the feats of agility and skill shown by the warriors, she said in the joy of her heart:

"Is not my Siegfried glorious among warriors, like a moon among the pale stars of night? He is a royal hero."

"He is well deserving of your praise," replied Brunhild, "but still he must yield the first place to my husband."

"Of a truth," answered Chriemhild, "my brother is a bold warrior, but he does not equal my husband in feats of arms."

"Why," said Brunhild, "did not he win the prize at Isenstein, while Siegfried remained with the ship?"

"Do you mean to accuse the Nibelung hero, the dragon-queller, of cowardice?" cried the young wife indignantly.

"He cannot stand so high as the king of Burgundy," answered Brunhild, "for he is not his own man, but owes fealty to my husband."

"You lie, proud woman!" exclaimed Chriemhild, her face flushing with anger, "you lie most insolently. My brother would never have let me marry a man who was not free. Siegfried owes no man allegiance, neither for Nibelungland nor yet for Netherland. The first kingdom he conquered with his own right hand, the other is his inheritance; and I, his queen, may hold my head as high as you."

"Try it, chatterer! I shall always walk into church before you."

With these words Brunhild left the gallery. Chriemhild felt both hurt and angry. It was the first grief that had ever befallen her, and she could not get over it. She went to her rooms, put on her costliest garments and the jewels that had come out of the Nibelung treasure; then, followed by her ladies and serving-men, she walked to the minister. Brunhild was already there with her train. She would have passed the proud woman silently, but the latter exclaimed:

"Your husband is my husband's man, so wait here, and let your queen go first."

"Better for you had you held your peace," said Chriemhild. "A paramour go before a king's wife, indeed!"

"Are you mad?" asked Brunhild. "What do you mean?"

"I will tell you what I mean," replied Chriemhild, "when I come out of church;" and passing before her enemy, she went into the house of God.

The proud queen stood still, weeping, at the entrance door. Shame and anger struggled at her breast, and she could scarcely wait till the end of the service. At length the door opened, and Chriemhild appeared.

"Now," exclaimed Brunhild, "stop and explain what you meant by your insulting words, you wife of a bondsman."

"Wife of a bondsman?" repeated Chriemhild, as though she had not heard the other words. "Do you recognise the gold ring on my hand shaped like a serpent?"

"It is mine," said Brunhild. "Now I know who stole it from me."

"Well," continued Chriemhild, "maybe you also remember the silken girdle I wear round my waist, with its gold buckles and precious stones. My husband gained both the rings and the girdle that night, when he, not Gunther, conquered you."

Chriemhild went her way with the air of a hero on the day of his greatest victory. The proud queen remained standing where her sister-in-law had left her, her head bowed with shame. She sent for her husband, and when he came, told him how she had been insulted. And Gunther promised to ask Siegfried if he had any knowledge of what had taken place. He received his brother-in-law in the royal hall, and in the presence of many of his bravest warriors. He told him what had chanced, and immediately the Nibelung hero declared, in all good truth, that he had never spoken of dishonour and of the queen in the same breath; adding that too much weight should not be laid on the words that women spoke in anger. He then offered to clear himself by a solemn oath. But Gunther interrupted him, saying he knew him of old, and that his word was as good as his bond.

"Hearken, then, ye men of Burgundy," said the hero; "you see that I am pronounced innocent of causing the humiliations your queen as endured, and indeed I have always regarded her as a modest woman, and a good wife. And now, dear comrade Gunther, chide your wife as I shall chide mine for what they have this day done, that we may never again be brought to dispeace by their idle chatter."

He then turned and left the hall; but many a Burgundian felt that their queen had suffered a cruel wrong.

Next day Brunhild began to make preparations for her departure to Isenland. The king and his brothers entreated her to stay; but she sat silent and immovable as a stone figure.

"We cannot let you go," cried the king. "We will at any cost expiate my sister's thoughtless speech. What price do you demand?"

She rose, looked round the circle of warriors, and said in a hoarse and hollow voice:

"Blood!"

The Burgundians started, and stared at each other, none daring to speak. She continued in the same tone:

"Not all the waters of the Rhine could wash the stain from my honour. The heart's blood of yonder man alone can do it."

The uneasiness of the warriors increased; but Hagen said:

"Are the bold Burgundians grown weak with age? Have they become children again? I will explain the matter. Our queen demands the heart's blood of Siegfried. Ha! The words seem to terrify you!"

The Burgundians exchanged whispers about Siegfried's

strength, how it were certain death to fight with him, and more-
over, that he was innocent of all blame in the matter.

Then grim Hagen turned to Brunhild, and said, "Lady, it was
against my advice that Gunther went to woo you in Isenland;
but now that you are our queen, your honour shall be safe in our
hands. I will satisfy your desire."

"But," exclaimed young Giselher, "it is not the way in
Burgundy to return evil for good. Siegfried has always been true
to us, and I, at least, will not be false to him."

Hagen tried to persuade Volker, the minstrel, to help him in
the work of assassination, for Siegfried was not a man they could
attack openly. But Volker refused. Ortwin offered himself in his
stead, saying that the mere fact of Siegfried having given the
ring and girdle to his wife was an insult to the queen of
Burgundy, and must therefore be revenged.

Gunther here broke in passionately, "Such a murder would
cast dishonour on all Burgundy, and it is my duty as the king to
prevent it."

"Lord of the Rhine," cried Brunhild, rising from her seat, "I
give you three days to think of it. After that, I either go to
Isenland, or have my revenge." With these words she left the
room.

"No weapon can hurt him," said the Margrave Gere, "for he
has bathed in dragon's blood, and is only vulnerable in one
place, on which a lime-leaf fell when he was doing it."

"If he guesses what we are after," added Sindolt, "he and his
thousand Nibelungs will conquer the kingdom."

"I will do it by cunning," said the grim Hagen.

The king could not make up his mind one way or the other.
He would—and would not. And when the warriors separated,
nothing was settled. Three days later, when Gunther saw that
the queen's mind was fully made up, he consented with a sigh to
let his uncle Hagen try his plan.

About this time heralds came from Lüdegast and Lüdeger to
declare war against Burgundy. Siegfried at once promised to
help his brothers-in-law to defend the country. The ladies were
all busy preparing the jerkins their husbands were to wear. One
day when Chriemhild was thus employed, Hagen entered her

room. He bade her be of good cheer, because the hero having bathed in dragon's blood was invulnerable.

"Good friend," she answered sadly, "my Siegfried is so bold that he often pushes into the midst of the enemy, and, in such a case, he might easily be wounded in his only vulnerable point."

Hagen begged her to embroider a little cross upon his jerkin to mark the place, so that he might always cover it with his shield. She promised to do so, and immediately worked a little cross with silver thread upon the garment. Her anxiety was needless, for the next day fresh messengers came to say that the kings had changed their minds regarding war, and were now determined to be true to their old alliance. Soon after this Gunther made preparations for a great hunt to be given in honour of the continued peace. On the morning on which it was to be held, Chriemhild entreated her husband to remain at home. She had had such terrible dreams the night before, that she feared for his life. He laughed at her, and then kissed her, saying that a bad dream would be a foolish reason for keeping away from the hunt.

"Besides that, be comforted, dear wife. What harm can happen to me? I shall be amongst faithful friends and comrades all day long. I shall take Balmung and a sharp spear with me, and I should like to see him who would dare withstand me."

He kissed her again, and hastened away. She ran to the window, and watched him until he disappeared from sight. The morning passed very pleasantly, and then the warriors sat down to their mid-day meal, which was spread out on the grass. There was food in plenty, but the wine ran short. Hagen explained that he had sent the wine on to another place, thinking it was there they should have dined; but he told his friends of a cool spring under a lime-tree not far off, and offered to run a race there with Siegfried. The latter laughingly accepted the challenge, adding that he would carry his sword and hunting-tackle, while Hagen went empty-handed, that the race might be more equal. The two warriors ran across the meadow ground towards the linden, and, as they ran, the field flowers tried to stop bold Siegfried, the branches of the trees beckoned him to go back, and the birds in the linden sang sadly as though they would say,

"Turn back, noble hero, the traitor is behind you." But Siegfried did not understand the language of the flowers, trees and birds. He trusted his friend as himself.

"Here we are at last," he cried to the panting Hagen. "Here is the clear spring; see how the water sparkles. Let us rest under the cool shade of the linden, until the king comes up, for he must have the first draught."

He laid aside his sword and other weapons, and threw himself on the flowery grass.

"How dull you look," he continued to Hagen, "and yet it is such a bright and beautiful day, and we have had such good sport this morning. Ah, here are the others. Come, Gunther, we are waiting for you. You must have the first draught."

Gunther stooped and drank of the fresh, clear water of the spring, then Siegfried followed him, saying with a laugh:

"I intend to have a real good drink. But do not fear, noble friends, I shall leave you plenty. This spring is like mankind: one part goes down into the earth, and another comes up into the light of day, but it never ends."

"Very true," said Hagen; "what matters one life more or less?"

The Nibelung hero bent over the well and drank thirstily, and as he did so, Hagen caught up his spear and plunged it into his back, in the exact spot where Chriemhild had embroidered the silver cross on his jerkin. He did it with such force, that the point of the weapon went through his back and came out at his chest. The wounded man sprang to his feet, and not finding his sword where he had put it, for it had been removed by one of the conspirators, seized his shield and struck the murderer to the ground. More he could not do. He sank back helplessly amongst the flowers, which were dyed red with his blood. The silver stream was also reddened, and all the sky was crimson with the light of the setting sun. It seemed as if nature were blushing for the evil deed that had just been done.

Once more the hero feebly raised his beautiful head, and said, looking round upon the Burgundians:

"Ye murderous hounds, what harm did I ever do you? Had I known of your treachery, ye had all lain dead at my feet. A devil from hell must have tempted you to do this foul deed. None of you ventured to meet me in open battle, and so you fixed upon Hagen to do the cowardly deed. Your names will be known until the latest times as those of cowardly traitors. And now, King Gunther, dishonoured as you are through this ill-deed, and weak of will, listen to the words of a dying man. Protect my wife, she is your sister, protect my poor wife from Hagen."

These were the last words of the royal hero.

The warriors stood silently around him, their hearts filled with sorrow and repentance. Gunther at length said:

"We will tell the people, who all loved the dead man, that he was murdered by robbers. Chriemhild will never then hold us to blame."

"Nay," said Hagen, "that may not be. I will not deny what my own cunning and my own hand have done. Our queen has now the expiation that she demanded, and your honour required. Burgundy is safe from all enemies, for no man was ever Siegfried's equal, or ever will be. What do I care for the complaints of a people or for the tears of a woman? Let us make a bier of branches, that the dead warrior may be borne to Worms thereon. Ha! here is Balmung, his good sword; to-day it shall do its old master a last service, and its new master a first."

When the bier was made, the hunting party set out for Worms in very different fashion from that in which they had started in the morning. They did not arrive until late at night. It almost seemed as though the dead hero inspired both warriors and serving-men with terror. None of them would carry him up the staircase. Hagen called them cowardly loons, and raising the body on his shoulders, carried it up, and laid it outside Chriemhild's door. Next morning early the queen got up, and made ready to go to the sanctuary. She called a chamberlain, and he, seeing a dead man whom he did not recognise in the half-light, lying in the passage, told his mistress. She shrieked aloud:

"It is Siegfried! Hagen has murdered him at Brunhild's command!"

The servants brought lights, and they saw that she had spoken truth. She threw herself on her husband's body, and with her tears washed his face clear of the blood stains that marred it. There he lay before her, pale, cold, and motionless; never, never again should she hear his voice,—never again. The word rhymed in her ears and seemed to madden her. She would willingly have died with him, and have gone down to the grave; or, as her fore-fathers believed, have rejoined him in Freyja's halls.

Old Sigmund, on hearing the news, uttered no word, but his heart seemed broken. He kissed his son's wounds, as though he hoped thereby to recall him to life. Suddenly he started to his feet, and the old spirit awoke me in his heart.

"Murder! Vengeance!" he cried. "Up, Nibelungs, up, and avenge your hero."

He hastened into the court, and the Nibelungs, hearing his words, crowded round him in full armour. The old man received a sword and coat of mail from them, but his trembling hands were too weak to hold them, and next moment he had sank unconscious on the ground. The Burgundians were awaiting the assault with arms in their hands, and grim Hagen was bringing up new forces to help those already there.

The Nibelungs retired, gnashing their teeth.

On the third day after this, the bier was taken to the sanctuary to be blessed by the priest. The populace crowded into the church, that they might give a last look at the dead hero, who had done so much for Burgundy. Chriemhild stood by the uncovered coffin, which was adorned with gold and precious stones. Her eyes were tearless, but all could read her sorrow in her face and bearing. A veiled woman passed close by amongst the crowd. Chriemhild alone recognised her.

"Go, murderess," she cried, "do not approach him, lest the very dead should bear witness against you."

The Unknown vanished in the crowd.

The Burgundian warriors now came to view the corpse, as custom demanded. When Hagen came up, the wounds of the dead man opened, and his blood flowed forth in a warm stream, as at the hour of the murder.

"Do not stand there, assassin," cried Chriemhild; "do you not see how the dead bears witness against you?"

The bold warrior remained where he was.

"I do not deny what my hand has done. I only acted as I was bound to act by my fealty to my liege lord and his queen."

If Chriemhild had had a sword in her hand, and had been possessed of a man's strength, Hagen had scarcely quitted the sanctuary alive.

Many gifts were made to the poor in honour of the dead hero, who was buried on the fourth day. The grave-chamber was richly decorated, and over it rose a high mound. Chriemhild followed the coffin to its quiet resting place. There the lid was opened once more at her command. She kissed and wept over the pale face of her husband. Her women at length had to bear her away, for she would have remained there forever. Hagen was standing without, grim and unmoved as ever, and said with his usual fatalism, "What has happened, must needs have happened. The will of the Norns must be done." The queen did not hear him. She did not see how Gunther, Gernot, and many of the other warriors tried to hide their grief and repentance. Her thoughts were all with the dead.

Sigmund and the Nibelungs prepared to return home. They wanted to take Chriemhild with them, to guard her from the false Burgundians, but she would not leave her husband's grave, and only begged the old king and the Margrave Eckewart to take care of her little son, and bring him up to be like his father. For she said he was an orphan, fatherless, and perhaps motherless. She had only one wish, which she whispered in the old man's ear—the wish of vengeance. Sigmund took leave of none but the Lady Ute, who mourned for Siegfried as if he had been a son of her own, and of Giselher, the youngest of the brothers. Then he set out for the Netherlands.

Time passed on, and it almost seemed as though Chriemhild had grown content, and had become reconciled to her brothers. Grim Hagen alone seemed to fill her with horror, and Brunhild she also avoided. She, one day, told her brother that she wished the Nibelung treasure to be brought up to Worms, as it was her private property. Gunther rejoiced at this proof of her renewed confidence in him, and at once consented to send for it. Alberich delivered the treasure to the messengers without hesitation and at length it arrived at Worms. The queen made generous gifts to the people, and whenever she found a brave warrior who possessed but few worldly goods, she would provide him with all that was necessary for his calling, and with daily pay besides. So that she gradually became complete mistress of a small army, which grew daily larger, and more powerful.

Hagen warned the kings of this; he told them that the Lady Chriemhild meditated vengeance. He did not care for his own life, he said, but the fair land of Burgundy must not fall into her hands. The only way that he could see of preventing this consummation would be for the kings to take the Nibelung treasure under their own care. The brothers would not consent. Gernot said that enough harm had been done to their sister already without heaping small indignities on her. Once, when his liege lords were absent, Hagen, who had always considered that prevention was better than cure, called his men together, and fell upon the warders who had charge of the Nibelung treasure. He carried off all that remained of it, and sank it in the deep waters of the Rhine. It was of little use that the kings heard of his ill-deed on their return; it was of little use that Chriemhild made indignant complaint; the deed was done, and could not be undone.

"If you were not our uncle," said Gunther and Gernot, "this should have cost you your life."

A short time afterwards, Hagen showed his nephews the place in the Rhine where he had hidden the treasure, and made them swear that none of them would betray its hiding place as long as one of them was alive. Chriemhild was sad and sorrowful as before; she always sat with her mother, and embroidered tapestry in which she depicted the scene of Balder's death, and showed how he was cruelly slain by his brother Höder, and how Nanna died of a broken heart, and shared her husband's bier. But in Balder every one recognised the features of her hero, and in Nanna her own; while Höder had the features, garments and murderous weapon of grim Hagen. She often held the needle suspended in her fingers, and sat watching the picture thoughtfully. When the Lady Ute asked her on such occasions, "What are you thinking of, my child?" she would answer, "I was thinking of Hagen."

CHAPTER VI.

KING ETZEL'S WOOING.

SOME WELCOME guests arrived at Worms. Margrave Rüdiger of Bechelaren, surnamed "the Good," came with some of his warriors to the Burgundian court. Gunther, Gernot and Hagen were old acquaintances of his, and he had often held young Giselher on his knees as a child. Now that he came to the house of mourning, his gentle, noble spirit had such an effect on Chriemhild that she would sometimes accompany her mother to the hall, and listen to the Margrave with a gentle smile, such as had not been seen on her face since her hero's death. But if Brunhild or Hagen entered, she would go away at once.

Days and weeks passed on, and at last Gunther said to his guest that he fancied the Margrave had not come merely for the pleasure of renewing an old acquaintance, but had something on his mind. Then Rüdiger answered:

"Well, King Gunther, I will tell you what brings me here. You know that good Queen Helche, the faithful helpmeet of my liege lord King Etzel, died some years ago, and that her sons were slain in battle by Wittich. The king of the Huns has long sat lonely in the wide halls of Etzelburg, but he has now made up his mind to marry again. He consulted me on the subject and I advised him to try and win the hand of the noble Lady Chriemhild, your sister and the window of heroic Siegfried. If you will give your consent to the match, I am empowered to say that she shall be queen of the Huns."

"She is no longer under my charge," was the answer; "she is queen of the Nibelungs, and of the Netherlands, and I fear that she will not be willing to marry again."

"I will take her the good news," said Giselher, "and mother Ute will advise her to do as we wish."

The young warrior immediately rose, and went to the women's apartment. He found his sister busied as usual with her embroidery. He told her that it was time she should give up grieving so much for her dead husband, and reminded her that she was still young, and might yet be happy. Then he told her what Rüdiger had related of Etzel's court, its greatness and its glory, and finally told her of Etzel's wooing. But Chriemhild answered with solemn firmness, that she would not leave the grave-mound in which all she loved was buried.

Then mother Ute spoke. "If you will be Etzel's queen, my child, you will be the most powerful of women."

"Most powerful of women," repeated the daughter thoughtfully. "Look, Giselher," she went on, pointing to her embroidery, "you know whom that hero is intended to represent?"

He shook his head and she added, "It is Vale, the Avenger, of whom our fathers said that he revenged Balder, and sent dark Höder to his own place."

"These are old wives' stories that are forgotten now," answered Giselher. "Let us speak of him in whose name good Rüdiger is come to woo you."

"Yes—but what if it were to be fulfilled?" she said, "perhaps— ask the Margrave to come to me, that I may hear his wooing myself."

Giselher left the room, and the Lady Ute went out also, leaving Chriemhild alone, as she requested.

"Siegfried," said the young queen, "it is for your sake that I leave your resting-place, from whence you have so often come to me, in waking and in sleep, and pointed to your wounds— those gaping, bleeding wounds, that will never close until it is granted me to send grim Höder down to dark Hel."

Rüdiger appeared, and in courteous fashion wooed the queen in his master's name; but not till he had promised, in the name of the god Irmin, that she should have men to fight her battles when she needed them, did she consent to go to the land of the wild Huns, and to become Etzel's wife.

The Burgundians all rejoiced when Rüdiger told them the good news,—the three royal brothers especially, for now, they thought, their sister would again be happy. But Hagen came to them, and said,—

"What are you thinking of, that you thus call the lightning down on our heads? Do not give your sister to the king of the Huns. Between the widow of Siegfried and us, such friendship alone can exist as that between fire and water. Either must the one be quenched, or the other fly off in steam. It is a childish action to supply one's enemy with a sword to cut off one's head." But the brothers refused to listen to his warnings. Preparations now went on apace for the journey to Etzelburg. Ambassadors were sent to the Nibelungs and to the Netherlands to tell them of the queen's contemplated marriage. They returned with a numerous company of warriors and servants. At length all was ready, the kings went with their sister as far as the Danube, where they took leave of her, and Margrave Rüdiger took their place as leader of the travelling party. At the borders of the land King Etzel with a large following awaited the queen's arrival. His face lighted up with pleasure when he saw the pale beautiful countenance of the Lady Chriemhild. He told her that she should have full power over his treasures and his lands,- -that, in short, she should be his queen. She answered that she would be a faithful and obedient wife, but that her love was buried with Siegfried. The king paid no attention to the last words. He made sure of winning her love through kindness and affection. And so they went on together to Etzelburg. The marriage festivities lasted a fortnight, and were celebrated in the usual way.

Chriemhild took little part in the rejoicings. She did all that she had to do, thinking of Siegfried the while. Now, amongst the warriors present, there was one who was famed for his unusual strength, bold Dietrich of Bern. His thoughts were far away in the beautiful land of the Amelungs, which his uncle Ermenrich had taken from him by guile and force. He longed to return to his own people, and win the victory for them; but Etzel would not give him the necessary help. Sometimes, as he sat grave and sad in the great hall, while other men were laughing and talking, the queen would go to him, and tell him of Hagen's foul deed. He understood that she wished to woo him to vengeance, but he was silent, for he neither could nor would raise his sword against the Burgundian warriors who had been his faithful comrades in the olden time.

Months and years passed on; a little boy was born to the royal pair. He was the image of his mother and received the name of Ortlieb. The king and country rejoiced equally in the birth of an heir to the throne. For his son's sake, Etzel loved his wife more

than he had ever done before, and would have given her anything she chose to ask; but she cared for nothing; she remained
grave, quiet, thoughtful about her duties, but sparing of her
words. Even her little boy, carefully as she tended him, did not
bring her happiness. She was never seen to smile even on him.
The wound that her first husband's death had dealt her would
not heal. The spirit of vengeance, rising out of the abyss, never
ceased to whisper in her ears, "Blood for blood, murder for
murder," and her ears were open to its cry.

CHAPTER VII.

THE BURGUNDIANS VISIT HUNLAND.

ONE DAY when the king was playing with little Ortlieb, and
speaking to his mother, he said how much he wished that the
child should one day be a hero like Siegfried. She nearly
shrieked when she heard the name, but forcing herself to be
quiet, begged her husband to invite her brothers and their
friends to come on a visit to the land of the Huns. It was the first
request that she had ever made, and so King Etzel was overjoyed to hear it. He despatched the minstrels Swemmeling and
Wörbeling, with four and twenty noble warriors, to invite the
Burgundian kings to the Midsummer festival. And Chriemhild
sent a special message to her mother, begging her to come too.
In spite of Hagen's remonstrances, the three kings accepted
Etzel's invitation.

Hagen prepared for the journey as though they were setting
out on a campaign, and not to a feast. The Lady Ute would have
liked to go, but her age and infirmities hindered her taking so
long a journey. Brunhild also remained at home, for she had no
desire to see her enemy's good fortune; besides, she had long
given up caring for festivals; she only cared to spend her time
near Siegfried's grave-mound.

"The Nibelungs are going to visit the Huns," said the common people, as they watched King Etzel's visitors crossing the
Rhine; for, ever since the treasure had come into the country,

the kings and their followers had been called Nibelungs, after the unknown land.

The travelers rode for twelve days through the Black Forest and many waste places, till they reached the Danube. At the borders of Bavaria neither inn nor ferryman was to be found. While the rest made preparations to encamp for the night, Hagen went deeper into the inhospitable land, and came to a spring that ran into a small lake. There he saw some women bathing in the clear water, and at once knew that they were swan-maidens. Seeing him, they swam away, but he got possession of their feather garments, which obliged them to speak to him.

"Give us back our garments," said one of them, "and I will tell you of the future."

He promised to do as she desired, if she would tell him how their journey should end. She then prophesied pleasant things to him, and the hero gave back all the swan-garments. No sooner had he done this, than another of the maidens informed him that her sister had spoken words of guile, for that, far from the happy ending she had foretold, the priests alone of all that numerous company should ever see the Rhine again; as for the warriors, they should all die by the sword, if they did not at once return home. Hagen answered that he was ready to defend himself and his kings, and then asked how to cross the river. The swan-maidens directed him where he should find a ferryman, and then flew away.

Hagen followed the advice given him, and brought his company down to the ferry. The boatman turned out to be an old enemy, so after a hand-to-hand encounter, he was slain, and Hagen took his place. When they were half way across the river Hagen flung the priest, who accompanied them, overboard, that at least one portion of the swan-maiden's prophecy might come to nought. But he had miscalculated in this instance; the priest's floating garments upheld him on the turbulent waters, and the current drove him back to the shore.

"The holy man has the devil's own luck," said the grim warrior. "I care not, however. What must be, will be, as the Norns used to say."

The travellers pursued their journey rather more rapidly than before. At length, after meeting with several adventures, they arrived at Margrave Rüdiger's castle, where they met with a hearty reception from their old friend and his wife. During their visit to Bechelaren Giselher fell in love with fair Dietelinde, the only daughter of the house, and wooed her through his brother. So, according to old custom, the youth and the maiden were called to appear before the whole company in the great hall of the castle, and say whether they were willing to be man and wife. Giselher did not hesitate for a moment. His "yes" was loud and clear. But fair Dietelinde blushed, and looked down, and her whispered "yes" was only obtained in response to a second demand. Then Giselher clasped her in his arms, and gave her the kiss of betrothal. The bond was therefore sealed for life.

The Burgundians, or Nibelungs as they were generally called, remained at Bechelaren for many days, and when they went away, their host pressed all manner of costly gifts upon them. Hagen refused to receive anything in the way of ornament, and only begged for a strong shield that hung on the wall amongst other pieces of armour.

"It is Nudung's shield, and he, our only son, was slain by faithless Wittich," said the Margravine; "take it, noble hero, and may it guard you well."

The travellers continued their journey, and arrived at the land of the Huns, on the borders of which they were met by Dietrich and many other warriors. Accompanied by these and by Rüdiger they at length arrived at Etzelburg. The queen came down to meet them in the castle court. She greeted the kings, and kissed young Giselher, but scarcely seemed to see the warriors who accompanied them. Hagen was angry, and said,—

"When one comes as an invited guest, one is accustomed to hear one's host at least say 'Welcome.' This praiseworthy custom does not seem to obtain in the land of the Huns."

"Lord Hagen of Tronje," said Chriemhild, "have you done anything to gain such greeting? Have you, perchance, brought me some of the stolen Nibelung treasure?"

"It lies deep sunk in the Rhine," replied the warrior, "and there it will remain till the end of time. But had I known that you desired a gift, I am rich enough to have brought you one."

"I can do without it," said the queen, "I too am rich; I only thought you might perhaps have desired to restore to me my own again."

"I find my shield, helmet, sharp sword, and coat of mail a heavy enough weight to carry," replied the hero, "but I promise to try and bring you the devil. *He* has much rich treasure."

"I do not need your gifts," cried the queen, "nor do I desire them. You have served me ill enough in time past with your murderous and thievish hand. I have not yet requited you for what you have already done for me."

She turned away in anger, and calling her men-at-arms around her, promised to reward whoever avenged Siegfried's death.

The queen then asked her brothers to divest themselves of their armour, as it was not customary to appear in the panoply of war before King Etzel. Hagen at once advised them not to do so, warning them of the consequences in plain terms.

Chriemhild exclaimed that she would give much to know whose advice he was following in this matter; then the Amelung hero came forward, and boldly avowed that it was he who had given this counsel, for he knew well the devilish plots that were being contrived in the palace. The queen only answered him with an angry look, and at once retired to her apartments.

While the kings talked together in the friendliest fashion, the Hunnish warriors looked askance at the Burgundians. Hagen, desirous of showing that he felt no fear, asked one of his comrades to go with him to the inner court to await the coming of the queen. His familiar friend, Volker the minstrel, declared himself ready. They seated themselves on a bench near the queen's hall. As they sat there —Hagen with his good sword Balmung laid across his knees—Chriemhild came down the steps, and asked him why he had hated her so, and why he had slain the noble Siegfried.

"Well," he said, "I never denied that I did it. The queen of Burgundy was insulted for his sake, and the royal house dishonoured. The shame had to be washed out with blood, and as the hero was too strong to attack in the open field, he had to be slain by cunning. Any one may blame me, any one may strive to avenge

the deed, I am not afraid. I have no cap of darkness, and am easily to be found."

Then Chriemhild turned to her serving-men and desired
them to slay the slanderer of their queen, and the treacherous
murderer of Siegfried. But the two brave men were so terrible
to look upon, that none of the Huns dared touch them, although
the queen offered them much gold. They then went their way,
and the queen returned to her apartments, blushing with
shame.

A message now came from King Etzel begging the Burgundians
to visit him in his palace. They accepted the invitation, and he
greeted them like old friends. After having welcomed the
heroes, he said that he should very much like to know who the
two warriors were that looked so brave, and stood so close
together.

"They are Volker the minstrel, and my uncle Hagen of Tronje"
replied King Gunther.

"What, Hagen!" cried Etzel. "So we have met again at last, old
friend, and I can tell you to your face that you have not belied
the promise of your youth. But you are much changed in your
looks from what you were in the old days when I was proud of
your brave deeds in my service, and set you free, to return to
Burgundy. You have lost an eye since then, your hair is mixed
with grey, and your face has grown so rugged that you might
alarm the boldest warrior when you swing your broadsword."

"Who can tell," replied the hero, "how soon I may have to do
it again?"

"Never in the land of the Huns," answered the king; "you, like
all Burgundians, are a favoured guest."

The evening passed quietly, and it was nearly midnight before
the Burgundians were led to the great hall, where couches were
spread for them with down cushions covered with gold embroidery. They agreed with Hagen that it would be well to keep
watch during the night for fear of surprise, and that each man
should place his weapons where he could get them at a
moment's notice.

Hagen and Volker kept guard. They had been seated for some
time in silence, when all at once the minstrel saw helmets and

shields glancing in the starlight. He pointed them out to his companion, who knew that they were the queen's men, and needed no telling to inform him on what errand they were come. The minstrel wanted to spring out upon them, but Hagen prevented him, because some of the enemy might then have slipped into the hall, and perhaps murdered their sleeping friends. So peace was preserved for the time; and at dawn the Burgundians marched to the sanctuary to keep the solemn Midsummer festival. King Etzel appeared with his train, and asked, in astonishment, why they wore their armour. But they answered that such was their custom, not thinking it well to tell him what had happened during the night.

After the service was over, a great repast was served, which was in turn succeeded by games, dances, music, and other entertainments. In all feats of arms and trials of skill in the lists, the Nibelungs showed themselves better men than the Huns. At length the games appeared to be over, and the warriors desired to rest after their exertions. As they were leaving the scene of contest, a prince of the Huns presented himself in shining armour, and offered to try his skill against the strangers, who, he alleged, had hitherto only measured their strength with the common people, and not with the princes. Bold Volker caught his spear more firmly in his hand, and turned to accept the challenge. His thrust was so shrewd that he wounded the Hun severely, and a cry of "Murder, down with the murderer!" arose on every side. A free fight would have begun in another minute, had not King Etzel thrown himself between the belligerents, and threatened death to any of his people who hurt one of his guests. Peace was then outwardly restored; but the sullen glances each side cast on the other, showed the angry turmoil in every heart.

That evening Etzel brought his little son Ortlieb into the hall, that he might present him to his guests. The warriors all admired the handsome, frank-mannered child, and told the father that they did so; but Hagen said he did not think the boy would live to grow up, he looked so delicate.

This speech of Hagen's increased the bad feelings of the Huns towards the Burgundians tenfold; but no one betrayed his thoughts. A little later a great noise was heard in the court without—shouts, the clang of armour, howls and cries.

THE FIRST BLOOD. BLÖDELIN AND DANKWART.

BEFORE THE warriors went to the feast that evening, Queen Chriemhild had spoken privately to the hero of Bern. She promised him Etzel's help in regaining his kingdom, if he would do her one service—if he would avenge Siegfried's death. But he told her that he could not, for the Burgundian warriors were old friends and comrades of his; besides, he reminded her, that they had come to Etzelburg in all good faith and loyalty. A few minutes after Dietrich had left her sad and hopeless, Blödelin, Etzel's brother, came in, and told the queen of what had happened that afternoon in the tilting ground. Seeing how hot his anger was, Chriemhild thought she might perhaps succeed in gaining him over to her cause. She therefore told him of the unavenged death of Siegfried, and promised him a rich treasure of silver and gold if he would do her will. But he refused, from fear of Etzel's anger. Upon which the wise woman offered him a margravate in addition, with lands and towers, and the hand of a beautiful maiden of her court, whom he had long wooed, and wooed in vain. These promises gained him to her will. He told her that he would cause a quarrel to spring up between the men on either side, and if Hagen came to try and settle matters, he would have him overpowered and carried to the queen in bonds.

Chriemhild then retired to her chamber, which was pervaded by a soft light, the curtains of Indian silk keeping off the rays of the sun. As she sat there thinking, the words that her mother had once spoken rushed into her memory. "Women often strike deeper wounds and shed more blood with their tongues than men with their swords." She would have started up, and recalled Blödelin; but at the same moment she saw, as distinctly as if it had really been there, Siegfried's bier with the dead warrior stretched upon it. She saw him raise himself, and stretch out his arms to her; but when she started forward to meet him, there was nothing but empty air. She determined now to go on to the bitter end. Whether her vengeance brought about the death of her little son, and of King Etzel; whether it brought about the destruction of the kingdom, she did not care. She could die, and die willingly, if only she had the murderer's life.

Meantime, Blödelin was making his preparations. His men were rejoiced to hear the news he brought them, and followed him joyously to the hall, where Dankwart the Marshal, Hagen's brother, had charge over the serving-men. The hero rose from his seat to greet the prince, who exclaimed:

"Prepare to die. The queen demands a bloody atonement for the death of the great Siegfried."

"But why should I have to expiate a murder of which I knew nothing?"

"That cannot be helped," said the Hun; "my men's swords cannot return unstained to their sheaths."

"Then I am sorry that I gave you words of peace. I shall now give you your answer with cold steel."

With that he drew his sword, and swung it so lustily at the warrior's neck that his head fell to the ground at one blow.

Wild shrieks and shouts of vengeance arose, and all prepared to take part in the fight that had become inevitable. Dankwart made his way fighting to the hall, his armour bespattered with blood; but the defenseless serving-men were slain to a man.

"Up, brother Hagen!" he cried, "save me from the faithless Huns. Lord Blödelin attacked both me and the servants, in order to avenge Siegfried's death. I slew him, but the servants are all dead, and I alone am escaped out of the traitorous toils that the Huns have laid for us."

THE SLAUGHTER.

THE FIGHT recommenced in the banqueting hall, in spite of all King Gunther's efforts to smooth matters over, and during the struggle the little Prince Ortlieb, the sole hope of Etzel's house, was killed. At length Hagen, Dankwart and Volker succeeded in locking and bolting the doors of the hall.

Etzel and the queen sat full of anxious care during the *melée*.

Dietrich and Rüdiger, neither of whom took part in the fight, were also grave and sad. At length the hero of Bern exclaimed.

"Listen to me, Nibelungs. Hearken to my words, ye friends of Burgundy. Grant me a truce that I and my men and Margrave Rüdiger may go away unharmed."

King Gunther recognised Dietrich's voice, and said: "If any of my warriors has done harm to you or yours, noble hero of Bern, I shall take your cause into my own hands."

"No one has done me harm," replied the warrior; "all that I request is that you should let us go freely."

"What is the good of such requesting?" cried hot-headed Wolfhart; "we have sharp keys to unlock the doors with, even if a thousand such as these Nibelungs tried to keep them shut."

"Hush! hush! foolish comrade," said Dietrich; "there was but little sense in that speech of yours."

King Gunther then commanded his people to open the door, and much to the wrath of the Burgundians, Dietrich passed through their ranks with Chriemhild leaning on one arm and King Etzel on the other, and followed by his six hundred warriors. After them came Rüdiger with four hundred men. Giselher said to the Margrave:

"Greet your daughter from me, and say to her that I shall think of her even in death."

Many of the Huns tried to escape with King Etzel, but Volker cut them down as they strove to pass the door.

No sooner were Dietrich and Rüdiger safely gone than the horrible carnage recommenced. The Burgundian swords had no rest, until all the Huns were lying dead or dying on the floor. After that the Nibelungs rested awhile from their labours, but Hagen speedily called them to be up and doing, and fling the corpses out, lest they should be in the way in any renewed attack. He was at once obeyed. The dead and wounded Huns were one and all flung into the court below.

Volker and Hagen now guarded the entrance, lest the enemy should unexpectedly break in.

While Etzel wrung his hands, and moaned over the slaughter of so many good men and true, Chriemhild offered a shield full of gold and jewels to whoever slew her deadly foe, Hagen of

Tronje. Of all who heard her one alone came forward and said that he would try and do her will. And he was Count Iring of Daneland, Haward's man.

He went forward boldly and performed prodigies of valour, but at length was beaten back, and fell dead under Chriemhild's window.

Haward and Irnfried of Düringen (Thuringia) determined to avenge bold Iring, so they called out their men and went to the attack. The fight began at the door, where Irnfried fell under the minstrel's sword, and immediately afterwards Haward was slain by the hero of Tronje. But still the men of Daneland and Düringen fought on unheeding, and Hagen exclaimed,—

"Give place. Let them go through the door, out of which they shall never come back alive. Volker shall play them a slumber-song to which our swords can beat the accompaniment."

So the Nibelungs opened their ranks, and the men of Daneland and Düringen entered the blood-stained hall. Once more the battle began. Many a brave Burgundian fell to rise no more; but not one of their enemies escaped alive.

THE PARLEY AND THE FIRE.

SILENCE FELL on the palace. The Nibelung warriors laid down their shields and heavy armour, that they might better rest from their labours, while Hagen and Volker kept watch by the door. During this time of quiet, the Burgundians tried to make peace. They reminded King Etzel that they had come to his land at his own invitation, and relying on his good faith, only to meet with treachery from him and his. But Etzel demanded that the Burgundians should acknowledge him their feudal superior. Then Giselher turned to his sister and asked what harm he had ever done her that she should behave in such a way. And even the women, who were weeping for their husbands and sons, bore him witness that all his life had been spent in doing good to others. Chriemhild was touched by his appeal, and told him that he, Gunther and Gernot should go free with all their warriors and men-at-arms, if only they would give up the murderer Hagen, that she might punish him as he deserved. But with one voice the Nibelungs refused terms which were dishonourable in their eyes.

Enraged at the boldness of her foes, the queen called upon the Huns to make one more assault, and drive them out of the house. Again the bitter strife began. Chriemhild knew no more compassion. She commanded her servants to set fire to the upper part of the house, which was built of wood, and soon the flames were seen spreading over the whole roof, which at length fell with a crash. A wild wail of human creatures in their last agony accompanied the fall. After that the queen retired to her own apartment, and standing at the window overlooking the house where her brothers and their friends must have been burnt, thought sadly and half remorsefully over the past. Only half remorsefully, for she felt her heart as full of hatred to Hagen as it ever had been.

Meanwhile the Nibelungs had not perished in the flames, as Chriemhild fondly imagined. The great vaulted hall in which they had entrenched themselves was too strongly built to have suffered much from the fire in the wooden upper story; though the Burgundians were for a long time as if shut up in an oven, the heat was so terrific; they yet escaped with their lives; and Hagen made them slake their intolerable thirst by drinking the blood of their fallen enemies.

When the Huns at length came to look for their charred bodies, they were not a little surprised to find themselves confronted by six hundred brave and utterly undaunted warriors.

SLAUGHTER AGAIN.—THE LORD OF BECHELAREN.

THE QUEEN heard with astonishment that the Nibelungs were still alive and armed for a new fight. While she pondered what it were best to do, one of the Hunnish notables told her that she should apply for help, either to the Margrave of Bechelaren, who had received so many benefits from the king, or to Dietrich of Bern, who had enjoyed Etzel's hospitality so long as a fugitive. Chriemhild thought the advice good, and at once sent off a message to Rüdiger.

The noble Margrave immediately obeyed the queen's summons. Etzel explained to him the true position of affairs, and reminding him of all the honours that had been heaped upon him, told him the time was come to prove his gratitude. He must punish the Nibelungs for the great scath they had wrought to the royal house and to the land of the Huns.

"My liege," said the good old hero sadly, "all that you have said is true, and I am ready to do you any service, however dangerous, but do not ask that I should break the faith I swore to them when they stayed with me at Bechelaren, before I led them to Etzelburg at your command. They trusted me utterly, and young Giselher chose my daughter to be his wife, and to share the Burgundian throne. Methinks it were an ill deed to raise my hand against them that trusted me."

When the king reminded him of his oath of allegiance, he continued,—

"Take back my castles and towns, the wealth that you have given me, and the possessions I have won for myself. I will go penniless into the wide world with my wife and child, and what is my best wealth, Honour and Truth."

"Nay, noble Margrave, but you cannot do so," replied the queen, "if you fail in obedience. Think of the time when you came to Burgundy to woo me for Etzel. I feared to go alone amongst the barbarous Huns, where I had not a friend or helper, and you swore to me with a solemn oath that you would help me against every adversary, except your liege lord. Your sworn faith to me is older than that which you promised to the Nibelungs. If you break your oath to me, you are dishonoured."

Rüdiger stood in silent thought before the queen. At length he said,—

"Take my head. I shall not even tremble when the executioner's sword touches me. But do not force me to do what my conscience disallows."

The conversation lasted a good while longer. At length Rüdiger with a heavy heart consented to obey the king and queen.

The Nibelungs stood by the window looking out for help. On seeing the noble Margrave approach with his men, Giselher exclaimed joyfully that all was not lost, that they should see

Bechelaren and the Rhine again. When Rüdiger came close to the door he explained his errand. Gunther reminded him of the friendship they had sworn, and Rüdiger answered sadly that the oath he had sworn to Etzel's wife forced him now to fight her battle. And so they took fair leave of each other, as noble friends forced to fight against their will. Once more the blood of the Nibelungs and their opponents stained the great hall. The heat of battle raged anew in every heart, and many men were slain. Amongst the number were Rüdiger and Gernot. At length the men of Bechelaren were conquered, and slain to the very last man. Two hundred Nibelungs also fell before the victory was gained.

The heroes were silent in the wide hall. They heard the sound of voices in the court without. The queen's voice was raised in indignation, as she accused the Margrave Rüdiger of playing the false traitor and making peace with the Nibelungs. Volker's anger was aroused at this unjust suspicion. Leaning out of the window, he told her not to vex herself on that score, nor accuse a good man falsely, for the hero of Bechelaren had died serving her. He then commanded the Margrave's body to be shown at the window, so that the king and queen and all the Huns should see it. Etzel uttered a loud cry of horror, and cursed the hand that had done the deed. He called for his sword, that he might himself lead the band of avengers, but he forebore to unsheath it when he saw that terrible pair (Hagen and Volker) still guarding the threshold.

Chriemhild stood looking on with folded arms. She was beautiful as ever, but it was now the beauty of a fallen angel. She shed a few tears for the loss of her old friend Rüdiger. Perhaps also because she feared that he was her last ally. She may likewise have pondered whether by any means she might yet attain her end. But be that as it may, the next events were unexpected by her as by every one else.

DIETRICH AND HIS AMELUNGS.

ONE OF Dietrich's men heard what had happened. He hastened to his master and told him the strange tale. Dietrich refused to believe it, and sent Helfrich to the palace to find out the truth.

On hearing the news of Rüdiger's death confirmed, the hero of Bern sent his old master Hildebrand to ask the Nibelungs why they had done this evil deed.

The master would have gone unarmed upon this errand, but Wolfhart cried out upon the folly of appearing as a lamb in the presence of wolves. The master thought the advice good and put his armour on. When he was on the way, he saw that all Dietrich's men were following him well-armed, under Wolfhart's guidance. He desired his quick-tempered nephew to go back, but the latter refused point-blank, saying that he could not let his uncle go alone; and the other warriors, one and all, declined to leave him. When the small band of five hundred brave men came in front of the house the Nibelungs were defending, Master Hildebrand lowered his shield, and asked if it were true that good Margrave Rüdiger was dead. Hagen answered that they wished it were untrue, but it could not be helped, for he had been slain in unavoidable fight. The Amelungs mourned aloud for their friend. Wolfhart would have avenged him on the spot, but the master held him back, threatening him with Dietrich's anger if he thrust himself into the quarrel. Then, turning to the Nibelungs, he demanded in the name of the hero of Bern that the Margrave's body should be handed over to them, that they might give him honourable burial. King Gunther replied that it was a good and worthy desire on their part, and one that ought to be gratified. Wolfhart called to them to make haste and bring out the body, upon which Volker said that they were too tired to do more work, so the Amelungs might come in and fetch it.

One word led to another, till Wolfhart lost his temper altogether, and rushed forward, followed by the Amelungs, shouting as with one voice their ancient war-cry. Master Hildebrand, drawn on in the general rush, was found in a foremost place when the battle began. The tired Nibelungs and the brave Amelungs— men who had formerly fought side by side in the great battle of Ravenna, and on many other fields—were now engaged in hand-to-hand conflict for life and death. Here was strong Sigestap, duke of Bern, there brave Helfrich, there the bold heroes Wolfwin, Wolfbrand, Helmnot, Ritschart, and others, all burning to avenge the death of Rüdiger. The confusion was so great that often those who wished to meet could not find each other. Thus Volker and Wolfhart were kept apart; the minstrel fell upon Sigestap, who had slain many of the Burgundians, and gave him his death-blow, only to meet Hildebrand a little later and himself to fall under his hand. Dankwart was slain by Helfrich; Wolfhart did many a deed of valour, until Giselher attacked him. After a tremendous struggle, the young king thrust him through the breast, but even then, though in mortal agony, he grasped his sword in both hands, and slew his adversary.

Old Hildebrand saw his nephew fall, and hastened to him. He lifted him in his arms, and tried to bear him from that hall of doom; but he was too heavy. The wounded hero opened his eyes once more, and said in a faint voice,—

"Uncle, tell our friends not to weep for me, for I have met my death at the hands of a brave king, as he has at mine. My wild blood has grown calm and still, and I am ready to sleep peacefully like a tired child."

These were the last words of the wildest, hottest warrior in Dietrich's train. Like Wolfhart, all the other comrades of the hero of Bern, save Hildebrand alone, lay stretched on the bloody floor; and with them all the Burgundians, except Hagen and King Gunther.

"Come now, Master Hildebrand," cried a rough voice, "you owe me satisfaction for the death of my comrade Volker."

It was Hagen that spoke. The master defended himself bravely; but the hero of Tronje was strong and determined, and Balmung was sharp. One terrible blow cut through Hildebrand's coat of mail, and the blood flowed freely from his side.

THE END OF THE NIBELUNGS.

WHEN THE old man felt the wound, and looked in the grim, rugged countenance of his antagonist, for the first time in all his long life fear took possession of him, and covering his back with his shield, he fled like a coward.

With shattered armour, and red with his own blood, and that of others, the old man came before his master. Dietrich asked whether he had fought with the Nibelungs, and why he was so wet with blood. Then Hildebrand told how the Burgundians had slain the good Rüdiger, and had declined to give up his body for burial.

The hero of Bern was so saddened by these tidings, that he asked no further questions; he begged the old man to command his comrades to arm themselves at once.

"Whom shall I command?" asked the master.

"The swordsmen of Bern are all here. You, my lord, and I, are all that remain of them; and of the Nibelungs, Hagen and King Gunther are the only ones alive."

At first Dietrich did not understand, and when he did, he mourned aloud for his friends and comrades.

"How could my brave men have fallen under the swords of these tired warriors? Who will now help me to regain the land of the Amelungs?"

So he cried in his sore distress. But soon, mastering his emotion, the hero prepared to avenge his fallen friends, and, accompanied by the master, went full-armed to the house where Hagen and Gunther awaited their fate with undaunted courage.

Hagen and Hildebrand exchanged so many scornful words when they met, that Dietrich chid them for a couple of old women, and demanded that the combat should at once begin. Hagen sprang forward without delay. Balmung was as sharp as ever it had been, and the hero of Bern had much trouble to defend himself; but the hand that wielded the sword was weary, and less nimble than of yore. Dietrich seeing this, made a sudden spring upon Hagen, threw him down and bound him fast. Then he bore his prisoner into the presence of Chriemhild, and recommended him to her mercy, saying that he was the boldest and bravest warrior in the whole world. He only noticed the thanks and praise she gave him for his doughty deed, and did not mark the gleam in her eyes, nor rightly interpret the flush that rose to her cheeks. He hastened away to the last battle with King Gunther.

Chriemhild had gained her end; that end to which she had waded through rivers of noble blood. Hagen read his fate in her eyes; but he never flinched: he would not give her that dear satisfaction. She wondered whether she could make him confess where he had hidden the Nibelung treasure. She spoke to him kindly, and promised to let him go safely home, if he would only tell her of the hiding place. The hero seemed touched by her gentleness, and said that he would willingly tell her, but that he had sworn to keep the secret as long as one of the three kings of Burgundy was alive.

She promised him again that she would keep her word, if he did her will; and then had him taken away to sure watch and ward.

"Lies, lies, all lies," he said to himself, as his gaolers led him away."

The hero of Bern soon afterwards appeared with King Gunther as a prisoner; the latter was at once taken to a separate dungeon. Chriemhild considered what was now to be done. Siegfried's murderers were now in her hands, both the man who had done the deed, and the king who had condoned it.

She felt a few qualms of conscience when she thought that Gunther was, after all, her brother; but she soon stifled them, and calmly pursued the path she had marked out for herself. King Gunther's head was cut off by her orders, and laid at Hagen's feet to convince him that now the last king of Burgundy was dead.

The hero thrust away the head contemptuously. "It was not thou," he said, "to whom I swore allegiance, and whose crown I strove to keep free from stain. The royal house of Burgundy, to which I belonged, is wasted, and its glory overthrown. Of what worth to me is the span of life that remains?"

That night Chriemhild had a happy dream. She thought that Siegfried stood before her as she had seen him; that he stretched out his arms to her in love and gratitude; and then vanished slowly in the grey dawn.

Next morning Chriemhild seated herself beside King Etzel in all her robes of state. The hero of Tronje was brought before her, a prisoner, and in bonds. She questioned him again as to the hiding-place of the treasure. Raising his head, he answered with all his former boldness:

"You are mistaken, woman, if you think that you have my mind in your power, that you have tamed me entirely. The kings are all dead now, Gunther, Gernot, Giselher; now none but God and I know where the treasure was sunk in the deep waters of the Rhine, and from me you shall never learn where you may seek with any hope of finding."

Chriemhild silently came down from the throne, and picked up the good sword Balmung that lay beside Hagen's armour.

"You took good care of the gold you stole from me," she said, "but another thing that you stole I have in my hands at this moment. My noble husband Siegfried wore this sword when last I saw him, before he fell under your murderous hand. I will now try whether it be strong enough to avenge its master."

She had drawn the sword from its sheath, and now swung it with both hands, and with such force that the head was cut from the body, and fell at the feet of old Hildebrand.

A cry of horror echoed through the hall, then all was still. Chriemhild thrust the bloody weapon back into its sheath, and said,—

"This blood may never be washed from the blade. Balmung must be taken to Worms as it is, and laid in Siegfried's grave. Perhaps he may then learn that his wife loved him faithfully and punished his murderer. Two things alone make up my life: Love and Revenge. My work is done."

"Strange," said Hildebrand, staring at the hero's dis-severed head, "that the bravest warrior in all the world should have been slain by a woman! But although he wronged me much of late, I will yet avenge him."

So saying, the old master drew his sword, and gave the queen her death-blow. Etzel shrieked out, and threw himself on his knees beside his wife. She was deadly pale, and had only strength to gasp rather than speak,—

"Let none touch the master for this," she said, and they were her last words.

CHAPTER VIII.

THE NIBELUNG'S LAMENT.

GREAT AS was the misfortune that had come upon the people and the royal house, the burial of the dead had yet to be seen to

WOTAN ENCIRCLES BRUNNHILDE WITH FLAMES.

(After a painting by K. Dielitz.)

Brunnhilde, a name that is spelled many ways, was a Valkyrie maiden, daughter of Wotan and Erda, who for disobedience was divested of her divinity and kissed into a charmed sleep. In order to prevent intrusion upon her sanctity Wotan covered her with a shield and then caused a wall of flames to burn perpetually around her. This charmed circle was, nevertheless, passed by Siegfried, who awakened and won her for a bride. By other versions of the story, Brünnhilde is represented as a queen of Iceland, an intrepid warrior, and vindictive as she was bold. The tale as herein told reveals how she became wife to Gunther, king of Burgundy, and through jealousy induced Hagen to assassinate Siegfried after he had married Gudrun.

as speedily as possible. King Etzel was too full of his own grief to attend to business of any kind, so Dietrich and Hildebrand gave all necessary orders, and themselves helped in the sad work.

All the dead were buried with every honour, save and except the hero of Tronje, who was forgotten. The grave-mounds were filled and closed, before the old master remembered the brave warrior, whose headless trunk still lay in the audience-hall. Hildebrand ordered that he should receive instant burial. So a separate grave was prepared for him, and there he was laid with all his armour, except the good sword Balmung, which was to be taken to Siegfried's grave, according to Chriemhild's wish. Many of the Huns went with the funeral procession; they neither wept nor made moan for the dead man whose strong right hand had brought so much evil on their native land. Next spring lovely flowers decked the other grave-mounds, while on Hagen's this-tles and thorns alone were to be seen, in the midst of which a venomous adder had found his home. All who had gone near enough to the snake to examine it carefully, maintained that it had only one eye like the hero of Tronje, and were firmly con-vinced that it was the form his spirit had taken.

AT BECHELAREN.

DIETRICH AND Hildebrand sent news to Bechelaren and to Worms of all that had occurred. They chose the noble minstrel Swemmeling as their ambassador, for they knew that he was tender-hearted, and would break the news as gently as possible.

The Margravine and her daughter sat by an open window, watching the clouds that rose in the east. Godelinde felt strangely anxious, a presentiment of evil overpowered her, and she could not resist telling her daughter.

She said that she feared evil news was coming, for she had dreamed the night before that Queen Helche had appeared to her, surrounded by the Burgundians, and many other warriors in full armour. "The queen," added Godelinde, "said that she wished all these heroes to go with her. She took your father and

Giselher by the hand, and led them away, the others following. I wished to join the procession, but she signed to me to go back. Then they all vanished in a grey mist, out of which a hill seemed to rise like—"

She was interrupted by sounds of arrival. It was the procession of mourners who had come under Swemmeling's guidance. The Margravine recognised Rüdiger's horse and armour, and the meaning of her dream was clear to her. But in the midst of all her grief, she tried to keep up, that she might comfort her daughter, who sat at her side, pale with terror.

The minstrel joined the ladies. The Margravine rose to meet him, and said it was needless for him to tell his tale, for she knew what had happened. A few moments later, they were able to listen to what Swemmeling had to say; so they asked him how the noble Rüdiger had met with his death. He took up his harp, and sang a song of the heroes who had kept their faith, and had conquered in the battle of life. He told how they come to the realms of Woden and Freyja, how they float over earth and sea, and how they speak to their friends in the breath of the wind and in the rustling of the leaves, and thus bring them comfort in their sorrow.

After that he gave them all the details of what had occurred at Etzelburg. On the following day Swemmeling had to continue his journey. A few weeks after his departure, the Margravine died of grief, and Dietelinde was left alone. She remained alone for a long time, but when Dietrich reconquered the land of the Amelungs, he took the orphan from Bechelaren, and brought her to his wife, the noble Herrat, at whose court she won the love of a bold warrior, whom she afterwards married.

Swemmeling made his way to Worms as rapidly as he could.

AT WORMS

MEANWHILE THINGS were going on very quietly at Worms. Queen Ute would sit spinning by the hour together, humming many a weird ditty, but seldom speaking. Queen Brunhild would sit by her side embroidering the death of Balder, which she copied from old patterns. Curiously enough, the white god was not like the pattern, but rather resembled Siegfried.

"Look, mother Ute," she said. "Is it not strange that, in spite of all my efforts, the picture will resemble Siegfried, as he looked that day when he rode out hunting for the last time. It is a sad story, and reminds me of an old legend that I used to hear in my childhood, in Isenland, in which a murder was committed for the sake of possessing a magic sword. It seems to me that when Hagen comes back, I must get him to give me Siegfried's sword, Balmung, that I may restore it to the dead hero. Otherwise I fear that Burgundy will suffer as Isenland suffered through the theft of that other sword."

"Neither Hagen nor any of the others will ever return to this house, on which the sin of bloodshed rests, as yet unexpiated," said mother Ute; and, breaking off, she began to hum one of her strange, weird ditties, which was so gruesome that none could listen to it without a shiver. About this time Swemmeling arrived, and told the queens of the journey to the land of the Huns, of the friendly reception the Burgundians had met with from King Etzel, and then of the quarrel, the battle, and its fatal results. No plaints, no weeping, no questions, interrupted the minstrel's tale. When he came to an end, the Lady Ute said:

"It is a sad tale, very, very sad, but it could not have been otherwise, for much heroic blood was needed to wash away the curse of murder from this house."

Neither did Brunhild weep. She made all necessary arrangements for the comfort of her guests. She asked that the good sword Balmung should be given to her, and looking at the bloodstains on the shining blade, she said:

"Grim Hagen stole this weapon out of Siegfried's grave. I will take it back to the hero, now that it has been dipped in the blood of his murderer, that he may rest in peace."

She went to the grave-mound with the sword, and did not return that day, nor during the night. When they sought her, they found her lying dead beside Siegfried's coffin, on which she had laid Balmung.

The Lady Ute went on spinning for many a day, and as she spun, she hummed a song of the snake-queen who murdered her own brood.

The Burgundian nobles, and all the people, mourned for their royal house and the fallen heroes. But when feuds arose in the kingdom, they united, and raised the young son of Gunther and Brunhild to the throne, appointing brave men to act as guardians for the king so long as he remained a child.

THE HEGELING LEGEND.

CHAPTER I.

HAGEN.

ZEALOUSLY STROVE the knights in tilt and tournament to uphold their country's honour before Sigeband their king, when he held the Midsummer feast at his high castle Balian in Ireland. Sweetly the minstrels sang the praise of warlike deeds; and eagerly did boys of noble birth contend in games of hurling the spear and shooting with the bow. But evermore did little Hagen, the king's son, bear him best in the gentle strife; and the heart of his mother, the Lady Ute, was pleased.

One days the boys were amusing themselves by throwing their spears at a target. Having thrown them all, they ran forward to get their weapons again, the prince among the rest. As he could run faster than his companions, he reached the target first, and was busy pulling out his spear, when an old man called to the children to run back and hide themselves, for danger was approaching. He pointed up at the sky, crying, "A griffin!"

The Lady Ute looked and saw a dark spot in the sky. It seemed too small to be dangerous. But it approached with the swiftness of an arrow, and the nearer it came the bigger it grew. All could now hear the noise made by its wings, and the sound resembled the rushing of the storm. The other boys fled in terror, but Hagen stood his ground nobly, and flung his spear with all his childish strength at the great bird. The weapon grazed its feathers harmlessly, and, at the same moment, it swooped down upon the child and bore him off in its talons.

So the feasting and mirth that had reigned at Castle Balian were turned into mourning, for the heir to the kingdom was gone. There was no hope of rescue; for though many a hero would willingly have fought with the griffin, its flight was so swift that no one could see where it was gone. Years passed on, and the king and queen had no news of their boy.

The griffin carried Hagen over land and sea to its nest, which it had built on a rock rising out of the water. It gave the boy to its young ones to eat, and then flew away in search of new booty. The little griffins fell upon the child, and prepared to devour him, but he made ready for his defense, thrust back their bills with all his strength, and caught the birds by the throat, striving to throttle them. At length one of the griffins, which was old enough to fly, caught him up, and carried him to the branch of a tree, that it might enjoy the sweet morsel alone. The bough was too weak to bear their united weight; it bent, broke, and the monster fell with the boy into a thicket of thorns beneath. The griffin fluttered away, and Hagen crept deeper into the thicket, unheeding the thorns. At length he reached a dark cave, where he sank down utterly exhausted. When he came to his senses, he saw a little girl about his own age standing a little way off and looking at him in astonishment. He raised himself on his elbow to see her better, upon which she fled to a greater distance, and no wonder, his appearance was so frightful. He was dirty, wounded, and bleeding, and his clothes hung about him in rags. He limped and crept as well as he could after the girl, and found that she had taken refuge in a large cave with two companions. They all shrieked when they saw him, for they thought he was either a wicked dwarf or a merman, who had followed them to devour them; but when he told them that he was a prince who had been carried off by the griffin, and had only escaped from the monster as by a miracle, they were comforted, and shared their scanty fare with him.

After that they told him their story, which was much the same as his own. He found that the girl he had first seen was called Hilde, and that she was an Indian princess; the second was Hildburg of Portugal; and the third came from Isenland. The maidens nursed their young companion with such care that his wounds were soon healed. When he was well again, he went out to provide the needful food, and ventured deeper into the land than the maidens had ever done. He made himself a bow and arrows, the latter of which he tipped with fish-bones, and brought home small game of all kinds. As the children had no fire, they were obliged to eat their food raw, but they became all the stronger and hardier for that, and when Hagen was twelve years old he was almost a man in size.

Meanwhile the young griffins were grown up, and were able to go out in search of food for themselves, so that the boy could no longer wander about as freely and fearlessly as before. Nevertheless, one evening he ventured down to the shore, and crept under an overhanging rock which hid him from view. He looked out at the foaming waves and the wild sea, which now looked dark as night, and again was lighted up by the vivid flashes of lightning that burst from the storm-clouds. He listened fearlessly to the loud peals of thunder, the howling of the wind, and the sound of the frantic waves dashing against the rocks. But suddenly he caught sight of a boat, struggling in unequal conflict with the elements, and his heart was filled with hope and fear; of hope because thoughts of home and his parents were awakened in his breast; of fear, because the boat seemed too weak to live on such a sea. Then he saw it drive upon a point of rock. There was one shriek of agony, and ship and crew were swallowed in the waves. The storm raged on, until morning came, and seemed with its soft light to calm the fury of the winds. On the strand were scattered pieces of the wreck, and the corpses of the luckless mariners. Hagen was going to sally out in hopes of picking up something useful, when he was stopped by hearing the whirr of griffin's wings, and knew that the great birds had come down to the shore, having scented the prey. While the monsters were busied with their meal, the boy crept out of his hiding-place in search of something to eat. But he only found drift-wood, and a drowned man in full armour, with sword and bow, and a quiverful of sharp-pointed arrows. He could have shouted for joy, for now he had arms, such as he used to see at his father's court. Quickly he donned the coat of mail, covered his head with the helmet, girded the sword to his side, picked up the steel bow and the arrows. It was high time, for at this moment one of the griffins swooped down upon him. He drew his bow with all his strength and the arrow struck his enemy in the breast, bringing it down with fluttering wings. It fell at his feet, dead. A second monster shared its fate, and now the three other birds attacked him all at once; but he slew them all with his sword. He took the heads of the dead monsters to his friends in the cave, who had passed a wakeful night in anxiety for him. Great was their joy when they found that the griffins were dead. They accompanied their hero to the place of his victory, they helped him to throw the great birds into the sea, and then, true to pious custom, they assisted him to heap up a mound over the dead warrior whose weapons had helped Hagen to victory. Vainly did they seek for provisions among the wreckage; but they found a well-preserved box with flint and steel, which enabled them to make a fire. So they were now able to enjoy a well-dressed meal, which after their former privations seemed a perfect banquet.

Hagen went out hunting much more frequently than before, and slew bears, wolves, panthers and other wild beasts. Once, however, he met with a curious creature. It was covered with shining scales, its eyes glowed like red-hot coals, and horrible grinders gleamed in its blood-red jaws.

He aimed a sharp arrow at its back; but the point glanced off the glittering scales, and the monster turned upon the lad. A second arrow was likewise without effect. Hagen now drew his sword; but all his efforts were useless, and he only escaped the terrible claws by his marvellous agility. When he was almost exhausted by the long struggle, he at length saw his opportunity, and plunged his weapon into the great jaws. Overcome with fatigue, he seated himself on the still heaving body of the creature. He longed for a few drops of water to quench his thirst, and as none was near, he eagerly drank of the blood that streamed from the monster's wounds. Scarcely had he done this than his weakness vanished, and an unaccustomed sense of power took possession of him. He sprang to his feet, longing to put his new strength to the test. He would not have hesitated to fight all the griffins and giants in the world. He drew his sword, and slew a bear with one stroke. In like manner he killed two panthers, and a huge wolf. He was covered with blood from head to foot, and looked so ferocious carrying the bear on his shoulders, that he frightened the maidens in the cave; but he regained his accustomed manner when he had seen the gentle Hilde.

Many years came and went. Hagen and his three friends had enough to eat and drink and were clothed in the skins of wild beasts. Although they were very happy together, they longed to return to the haunts of men, and often cast anxious looks over the sea in hopes of seeing some ship approach. At length one morning, when the three maidens were standing on the shore, a white sail appeared on the horizon, and came gradually nearer and nearer. They lighted a fire, and called Hagen, who joined them fully armed. Their signals were seen from the ship, and a boat was sent out, which soon approached the shore. The helmsman uttered a cry of astonishment when he saw their strange dress, and asked if they were human beings or water-sprites.

"We are poor unfortunate people," said Hagen; "take us with you, for God's sake."

So the sailors took them to the ship, and they were soon on board. The captain looked at them in amazement, and Hagen, in answer to his questions, told their whole story. When he spoke of his father Sigeband, the powerful king of Balian, the captain exclaimed:

"What! you can kill griffins like flies! Still you are a lucky catch for me, for I am that Count of Garadie to whom your father has done so much injury. You shall now be hostage till a proper sum of money is paid to me. Here, men, put this young fellow in chains, and steer for Garadin."

Scarcely had the Count said these words when Hagen fell into a Berserker rage. He flung the sailors, who would have laid hold of him, into the sea; then, drawing his sword, he rushed upon the master of the vessel, when a soft hand was laid upon his arm. He turned round furiously, but at the sight of Hilde's gentle, lovely face, his terrible anger vanished. Hilde spoke gentle words of conciliation, and Hagen listened. Then, turning to the Count, he promised to make all matters right between him and the king, if he would at once steer for Balian. The captain agreed to do so, and steered for Ireland. Favourable winds swelled the sails, and ten days later the walls and towers of Balian hove in sight. Naturally his parents did not at first recognise Hagen; but great was their rejoicing when they found who he was. A firm peace was concluded with the Count of Garadie, and the three maidens were received with all honour and courtesy.

Hagen did not long remain quietly at home in his father's house. He wished to see something of the world, and to gain both name and fame.

Time passed on, and Hagen, who was known far and wide for his great deeds, was appointed to rule the land in his old father's place. When urged by his mother to choose a wife, now that he had settled down after his wanderings, he wooed fair Hilde, the sweet companion of his childhood, and soon afterwards married her.

Queen Ute lived to hold a grandchild in her arms, who was called Hilde after her mother; but soon after that she and Sigeband died, leaving their son to rule alone.

The Princess Hilde grew up beautiful, and many wooers came to Balian to ask for her hand in marriage. But Hagen would receive no man as a son-in-law without first fighting with him, declaring that he would never give his daughter to one that was not stronger than himself. Whoever ventured to try conclusions with him had the worst of it. Wild Hagen, the terror of kings, became also the terror of wooers, and before long, he really had his house to himself.

CHAPTER II.

HETTEL THE HEGELING AND HIS HEROES.

NOW ABOUT this time King Hettel the Hegeling lived at Castle Matelane in Denmark. He was a bold warrior, and Nordland, Friesland and Dietmarsch owed him allegiance. Many princely heroes were about his throne. Chief among them was his kinsman, old Wate, who bore rule in Sturmland, and was famous for his doughty deeds of war. Not less celebrated were the minstrels Horand and Frute, both powerful lords in Denmark. Then

came Irold the Swift from Friesland, and Morung of Nifland;
bold warriors both, and ever ready to help their liege lord.

One evening, at the feast, Morung of Nifland advised King
Hettel to seek a wife, and said that Hilde, the Irish princess, was
the best maid for him to woo, for she was famous in all lands for
her beauty and virtue. And Horand answered, that the lady was
justly praised, but that wild Hagen, her father, would permit no
man to woo her, and that many a noble warrior had met his
death in fighting with him for her hand.

The king was much taken with what he heard of fair Hilde,
and greatly desired to raise her to the Hegeling throne. He asked
who would undertake the wooing for him. The courtiers advised
him to make old Wate his ambassador, and although the lord of
Sturmland had no desire to go on such errand, yet he promised
to set out, and said that if Horand and Frute would accompany
him he had no doubt the wooing would be successful.

The three warriors, joined by Irold of Nordland, prepared to
set out on their journey. They took a small fleet of ships laden
with costly wares, and a thousand armed men, and started on
their mission.

After a long voyage they reached Balian, where Wild Hagen
held his court.

Their arrival was greeted with the utmost amazement, for no
one in Ireland had ever seen such splendour before. The masts
of the Danish ships were of shining cypress-wood, the sails of
purple silk, and the anchors of silver. Sailors in rich garments
bore foreign wares from distant lands out of the ships, and
spread them before the astonished multitude. The captains
offered rich articles for sale, explaining that they were merchants, and had come to Balian on a trading expedition.

When King Hagen heard what was going on at the wharf, he
and Queen Hilde went down to the ships to see what was to be
seen. Then Frute at once came forward, and, drawing him
aside, explained that they were not really merchants, but fugitives, who desired to be protected from their king, Hettel the
Hegeling.

Hagen laughed when he heard this, for he had long wished to
try his strength in single combat with the Danish king. So he told

the warriors to be of good courage, and to come up to the palace with him. The strangers accepted the invitation. They gave the king and queen rich presents of garments and precious stones. Indeed, their riches seemed so inexhaustible, that Hagen would willingly have kept them in the country, and given them houses and lands. But they pleaded that they had left their wives and children in Hegelingland, where they hoped one day to return.

They all met in the banqueting-hall, and the strangers were presented to the princess. Wate alone spoke little, and often looked out towards the sea.

"Go, Hilde," whispered the queen, "and greet the foreign lord with a kiss."

The girl started with fear, for the hero of Sturmland was a full head taller than any of his comrades, and was a stern-featured man, with a large hooked nose, bald head, and long grey beard.

"What are you looking at, Lord Wate?" said the queen. "Do you see fairer women on the shore than here in the hall?"

"I am looking at my ship," answered the hero, "for a storm is coming on."

Then the princess smiled and said:

"Are you not happy with us, noble warrior, or do you always wish to be out among storms and fighting?"

"Lady," said Wate, "I never learned to talk sweet talk with women, or to dance with girls. I only care for the dancing of the stormy waves and for the din of battle, when the Norns sing of conquest or a glorious death."

This was the speech of the stern old man. But the other warriors talked of the lovely land of the Hegelings, of its castles and granges, and of the minstrels and knights who served their ladies in all honour and modesty. After this they took leave of their hosts and retired. The next day passed, as was usual on such occasions, in jousting, feasting and minstrelsy.

Horand used to sing, early in the morning and in the late evening, before the queen and her daughter, who were both delighted with his voice and his songs. Once, when he was alone with the princess, he sang about a great king who fell sick with love for a beautiful maiden named Hilde. The princess felt that there was something hidden behind the song. So she asked at length who the king was that cared for her. Upon which the minstrel showed her a portrait of King Hettel, and told her of her father's stern cruelty to all noble warriors who came to Balian to woo the princess. He told her also on what secret mission he and his friends had come, and entreated her to come with them to Hegelingland, where the king was waiting eagerly for her arrival. Once there, he continued, he would sing to her every day, and so would King Hettel, who knew far more beautiful songs than he.

Hilde promised that she would ask her father's permission to go down to the ships and look at the strangely beautiful stuffs and jewels on board.

What she promised she did.

One day the men of Hegeling came before King Hagen, and said that they had good news from their home. Their king had found that they had been falsely accused, and had therefore restored them to his favour. They wished now to take leave of Hagen and return to their own land. The king was displeased to think of losing his guests, and yet they should not go without rich gifts.

"Sire," said Frute the Wise, "we are so rich that we cannot well accept either silver or gold; but if you would show us a kindness, come on board our galleys with the queen and her ladies, and look at our treasures."

Wild Hagen shook his head, but his daughter and the queen wished so much to go that he at length gave away.

At the appointed hour, when the sails were spread and the ships were ready for departure, the king, queen, princess, and their ladies appeared upon the strand. Boats were ready to take them to the ships. Fair Hilde and her maid sprang quickly into a boat steered by Horand. But when Hagen and his armed followers were about to get into another boat, Wate, Frute and Irold thrust them back and pushed off from land. The wild chieftain immediately caught up his spear, and rushed into the sea till the waves dashed over his head. Spears were hurled on either side, but Horand brought the princess safely to the ship. Hagen ran along the shore and called despairingly for ships and men to pursue the traitors; but the Irish boats were not ready for sea, and even at that moment the sails of the Hegelings were disappearing in the distance.

The voyage lasted many days and many nights. Fair Hilde wept much for her father and mother, but Horand sang to her, now of great deeds, and now of love, till she was comforted. At length they reached the coast, where King Hettel awaited them. He came down to meet them, and soon gained fair Hilde's heart. On the following morning they prepared to go to Matelane. But when they were about to start, they saw white clouds appear on the western horizon, which, as they came nearer, were discovered to be ships forming a great fleet, and from the topmast of each ship floated the banner of the cross. The Hegelings took it to be a fleet of crusaders going out against the unbelieving Wilkin-men or Reussen; but very soon a flag was hoisted bearing the arms of Hagen, a tiger, and then they knew that the enemy was approaching.

King Hettel and old Wate drew out their men in battle array on the strand. The old man laughed loud for joy that he was really to have a passage of arms with the warlike Irish king. The other princes advanced with their men to prevent the enemy's landing. The warriors were all of good cheer; but fair Hilde, who looked down from the battlements of the castle on the turmoil below, wrung her hands with grief that she should be the cause of bloodshed.

The galleys cast anchor, and boats were put off filled with armed men. The battle began, and so firm was the resistance made to their landing that the boatmen could not approach the shore. Then wild Hagen flung himself into the water and fought his way to land, followed by his bravest men. His blows were so terrible that he carried all before him, and even Hettel fell wounded to the ground, and was with difficulty borne away from the field. Old Wate now came forward, and he and Hagen had a hand-to-hand encounter. Each fought like a lion, and neither gave way in the least before the other, although both were severely wounded.

At length King Hettel, his head bandaged, and looking pale from loss of blood, forced his way through the throng of combatants with Hilde leaning on his arm. He threw his arms round Wate, while she did the same to her father, and entreated them both to make peace for her sake.

Wild Hagen was touched by his daughter's words. He clasped her in his arms, and then held out his hand, first to Hettel, and then to the grim old hero of Sturmland.

Now that the battle was over, Wate went about binding the wounds of all whom he found, whether of Irish or Hegeling birth, with some healing herb, of whose virtues he was well aware. In the evening there was a great feast, and next morning the warriors all went to Matelane, where the marriage was to take place. A ship was sent to bring good Queen Hilde to her daughter's wedding, which was celebrated in the cathedral, with all pomp and circumstance.

CHAPTER III.

GUDRÛN.

KING HETTEL and fair Hilde lived happily at Matelane, and the men of Hegeling, Friesland and Dietmarsch were faithful subjects, out of love and gratitude for the justice and protection afforded them by their liege lord. Two children were born to the royal pair, Ortwin and Gudrûn (pronounced Goodroon), both of whom were strong and blooming as Nordland roses. As the boy grew older, he was given into the charge of the hero of Sturmland, that he might learn all that it became him to know from the greatest warrior in the land. Gudrûn remained at home with her parents, and was instructed by her mother, both by precept and example, in all woman's work and knowledge. So she grew up, and became celebrated in every land for her beauty, her gentleness and her wisdom.

Many noble princes came to woo her while she was yet very young. Among them was the proud Moorish king, Siegfried, gigantic in height, and brown of hue. With many kings for tributaries, he felt himself so great that he feared no refusal. Queen Hilde, however, thought the hero too arbitrary in his manners, and ignorant of the proper way to treat women. Hettel was of the same opinion; so he told the wooer that the maiden was to young to be able to conduct a royal household. The Moorish king returned to his distant realm in great anger and disgust. But before leaving Matelane, he had bribed some faithless men with gold to keep him informed of all that went on in the land of the Hegelings.

Now, at this time, King Ludwig ruled over Normandy and the neighbouring lands. He was a great and warlike king. His son, Hartmut, was like his father in character, and helped him in his wars. When the latter heard of Gudrûn he determined to woo her for his wife. King Ludwig thought it a mistake, because the maiden's grandfather, Hagen, had once been his feudal superior, and had never forgiven him for having freed Normandy from the Irish yoke; also he believed that Queen Hilde had inherited her father's temper. The Lady Gerlind, Ludwig's queen, was of a different opinion: she thought that Hartmut was worthy of the noblest wife in Christendom, and that, if they only set about the matter in the right way, his offer would be accepted. The young warrior was pleased with his mother's counsel, so ambassadors were sent out to the Hegeling court, bearing rich presents. Queen Hilde accepted the gifts with gracious courtesy, thanked the ambassadors for bringing them, and added that she supposed the lord of Normandy wished to pay off an old debt which he owed her father as his liege lord. The warriors were kindly treated, although the king and queen heard their message with displeasure, and said that the husband of their daughter must be of higher birth than the lord of Normandy. The ambassadors, seeing that no good would come of their further stay, returned to Ludwig with their evil tidings.

The Norman king was not much surprised at the result of the embassy; but the Lady Gerlind, whose ancestors had been powerful kings, chafed under the affront, and advised her son to avenge the insult with his sword. But the young prince had thought of another plan. He possessed strongholds and granges in Scotland. So he determined to go a-wooing himself in Scottish garb, accompanied by a large train of attendants. He was a hero, learned in all knightly duties, tall, manly, and strikingly handsome. He was accustomed to ladies' smiles, and to meet with kindness from women wherever he went; so he never for a moment doubted his power of winning the love of the

Princess Gudrûn. The ships were manned, a favourable wind filled the sails, but soon fell again, and the voyage was a very slow one.

Meanwhile another suitor had arrived at Matelane. This was bold Herwig, lord of Zealand. He was a brave warrior, celebrated in many a victory; a faithful friend and loyal foe. Fair curls surrounded his face, and his blue eyes shone with intelligence.

The maiden and he soon learned to understand each other, and before a word of love was spoken, each knew the other's feelings.

When Hartmut arrived, in the guise of a Scottish prince, he soon discovered what was going on.

A favourable chance led Hartmut to the garden one day, and there he found Gudrûn alone. He told her of his love, and at the same time explained who he was. She was startled, but soon recovering herself, answered that she cared for someone else. She further told him to beware how he betrayed his identity, for her father and mother regarded King Ludwig as a vassal, and his life would be in danger if they knew his name and quality. The word vassal brought an angry flush to the young hero's cheeks; he did not, however, betray his feelings, but took leave of the maid in seemly fashion, and, after saying farewell to the king and queen, set sail for his own land.

Herwig lingered on at the palace in the hope that he might find some opportunity of seeing and speaking to the princess alone. But, whether by accident, or because the queen prevented it, he never found his opportunity. So he went boldly to the king, and made a formal offer for Gudrûn's hand. Hettel listened to him calmly, and told him that the maiden was too young to marry. This, however, was merely an excuse, for he really thought the king of Zealand was too poor a match for his peerless daughter.

Herwig found no rest at home. He assembled his forces, and prepared to invade the land of the Hegelings. His army only consisted of three thousand warriors, but they were one and all tried men of valour, on whom he could rely. Hettel was totally unprepared for the invasion. His heroes were at their own homes, or scattered abroad; but he collected what men he could, and went out against the foe. Soon the clang of arms sounded on the strand, and the battle began. It raged fiercely for a long time. At length Queen Hilde, taking Gudrûn with her, and followed by her ladies, descended to the place of combat, and spoke so wisely that she soon induced the men to put up their weapons, and make peace. Hettel was so much pleased with the boldness and valour displayed by Herwig, that he consented to receive him as his son-in-law, but stipulated that the marriage should not take place for a year.

Herwig spent some time at Matelane in company with certain other warriors, and at midsummer, young Ortwin and several of his friends received their swords at the hands of old Wate of Sturmland, who bade them act in all things so as to be soon worthy of the honour of knighthood. At the jousts that followed the young men's prowess gladdened their teacher's heart. But the rejoicings came to a sudden end through the arrival of some wounded men from Zealand, who brought news that the Moorish king, Siegfried, had fallen upon the island, and was laying the country waste.

Hettel determined to send troops to help Herwig against the Moors; but the king of Zealand would not wait until they could be summoned; he set out at once, saying that they could follow; he would meantime go and show his people that he had not deserted them.

Herwig landed in a small bay. His heart was wrung when he saw the devastation caused by the cruel Moor, and knew that he was not strong enough to offer him battle. But he was not idle for all that. He and his three thousand followers separated into companies, cut off isolated bands of freebooters, and harassed the enemy as much as they could. So matters went on days and weeks. At length the Hegeling fleet arrived with Hettel and his heroes. A great battle was fought by sea and land, and although the Moors suffered terrible loss, both in men and ships, it was by no means a decisive battle. Siegfried knew that he had now no hope of winning the victory in open war, but still he trusted to the chapter of accidents to get him out of his difficulties. And he did not hope in vain.

Whilst King Hettel and his heroes were fighting in Zealand, Hartmut, with a large Norman army, had fallen upon the land of the Hegelings. Ludwig had accompanied his son. Together they had stormed the palace at the head of their men, had taken it, and carried away the Princess Gudrûn and her maidens, amongst whom was Hildburg, granddaughter of that Hildburg whom Hagen found on the griffin's strand.

The first messenger who brought the news of the Norman invasion was soon followed by a second, with tidings of the storming of the castle, and the carrying off of Gudrûn. The first thought in every mind was to set off in pursuit of the robbers; King Hettel sent to offer terms to Siegfried, telling him at the same time of what had chanced, and the Moorish king immediately offered to help to rescue the princess; so an alliance was concluded between Hettel, Herwig and Siegfried without more ado.

This being settled, they turned their attention to the ships; but great was their despair when they found that most of them had been burnt in the fight, and of those that remained very few were seaworthy. Herwig and his men would have started alone in the few vessels that remained, but Irolt the Frisian stopped them, by drawing their attention to a fleet that was already approaching the shore. The masts and flags of the coming ships all bore the sign of the cross, and on deck were figures in long grey garments, with the staff of peace in their hands.

"They are pilgrims going to the Holy Sepulchre," said Horand the minstrel.

The pilgrims disembarked and pitched their tents on the strand, to enjoy a little rest after their long and toilsome voyage.

"Necessity knows no law," said Wate. "These pious men must put off their journey for a little. They have plenty of time to do their penance in. Let us borrow their vessels and provisions. If we return, we can reward them richly for the enforced loan."

Horand and Frute warned their friends that such a deed would surely bring its punishment. The pilgrims raised their hands in piteous entreaty. All in vain. King Hettel decided to take the ships, and Wate and Herwig voted with him.

So the heroes sailed over the high seas in pursuit of the Normans, in ships that bore the cross as their pennon.

After many days' sail they saw before them a low flat island, called the Wölpensand, and on it a great army was encamped, upon whose banners was depicted a raven with widespread wings, the ensign of the Normans. They were able to get quite close to the land, thanks to the pilgrims' ships, before their real character was discovered. But no sooner had King Hettel landed than the Normans sprang to their feet, and shouting their battle-cry, stood ready to defend themselves.

The battle began. Lances and arrows filled the air, and many a deed of desperate valor was done on both sides. Darkness alone put an end to the fight. The victory was undecided. It was a dark and cloudy night, and the flickering watch-fires alone threw any light upon the scene. Then it was that King Hettel challenged Ludwig to single combat, telling him that he should always regard him as a coward if he did not at once arm for the fray. Ludwig accepted the challenge, and came out to meet the king. Many a savage blow did the heroes exchange before Ludwig at length gave his adversary his death-wound. Seeing their leader fall, the Hegelings rushed forward shouting their battle-cry, and a general engagement took place in the darkness. None could tell friend from foe, and many a brave warrior fell under his comrade's spears. The leaders on either side ordered the horns to blow the recall, and the two armies took up their position at a greater distance from each other than before. Knowing the vengeance the Hegelings would take on the following day, the Normans thought prudence the better part of valour, and set sail for home under cover of the night, taking their prisoners with them; for they were on their way home from Hegelingland.

At daybreak, old Wate called his men to be up and doing. Great was the astonishment of all when they found their enemy flown. Wate and Herwig were keen to follow the Normans without loss of time, but Frute and Morung advised them to be prudent. They reminded them of the numbers of men they had lost, and advised that they should go home, and wait till the young men, who were growing up, should be old enough to bear arms.

The wisdom of this advice was recognised by all. Herwig alone felt indignant, but he was powerless to act unaided, so he returned to Zealand to work for his people, until the time should come to renew the expedition.

Queen Hilde was sad at heart when she saw the Hegelings return vanished, and without either her husband or daughter. But what could she do? She was only a weak woman, unable to wield a sword, to avenge Hettel or to save Gudrûn.

Horand, Morung and Irolt mourned the dead king with her, but old Wate chid them for weakness, and bade them rouse themselves, and teach the youth of the land all warlike accomplishments, to the end that they might win the day when the time for vengeance should come.

CHAPTER IV.

QUEEN GERLIND.

MEANWHILE THE Norman fleet had reached its destination. Queen Gerlind, her gentle daughter Ortrûn, their ladies, and many of the citizens of Cassian went down to the harbour to welcome the heroes home. After they had greeted the kings, Ortrûn hastened to sad Gudrûn's side, and, embracing her, told her to be of good courage. Gudrûn was touched by the maiden's kindness, though it could not stop her tears; but when Queen Gerlind would have kissed her, she recoiled from her touch, for the sharp-featured woman with the bold, glittering eyes seemed to her a spiteful snake, ready to dart on his prey and crush it in his coils.

"Eh, pretty puppet," said the offended queen. "What, so shy? But you'll soon grow tame under my training." She would have said more, but Hartmut interposed, saying that Gudrûn was to be his wife when the days of mourning for her father were over. He then offered the princess his arm, and sorely against her will she had to enter the palace side by side with him. Some of the townsfolk, watching her, said, "How beautiful she is!" to which others made answer, "But how sad!"

Days and weeks passed on. Hartmut did his best to win fair Gudrûn's love, but all his efforts were vain. One day he asked her why she would not love him, and she replied that he was a great and noble warrior, well worthy of a woman's love, but she was betrothed to Herwig, and would never break her troth. Queen Gerlind was not of so patient a disposition as her son; she was determined to break Gudrûn's proud spirit, and force her to consent to marry Hartmut. At first she tried soft words and flattering speeches, but finding these of no avail, she had recourse to sterner measures, though she waited till her son had left home on a warlike expedition. Before going he confided Gudrûn to his mother's care, telling her she might "try to tame the wild bird" in any fashion she liked, that was not inconsistent with the maiden's royal dignity.

No sooner was Hartmut gone than Queen Gerlind set to work. She made Gudrûn dress like a servant, and then set her and her maidens to cook and sweep, and do all the hardest work in the palace. Gudrûn bore her wrongs in patient silence. Her soft hands were blistered with scrubbing pots and pans, and doing other kitchen work, with which she was busied from early morning till late at night. The queen would sometimes ask her viciously if she would not rather wear the Norman crown than continue to slave in that manner, but she answered gently that she would keep her troth.

So she did all that was given her to do through the hot summer days, and in the icy cold of winter, without uttering a single murmur at her hard fate.

Year after year she lived this wretched life. At length Hartmut came home victorious from his wars. He greeted his father, mother and sister with warm affection, and then looked around for Gudrûn. When he saw her dressed in coarse clothing and doing hard work he was very angry with his mother for her ill-treatment of the girl. He begged Gudrûn to forgive what was past and gone, and grant him her love, trying to rouse her ambition by dwelling on the wealth and greatness of the kingdom he offered to share with her. But Gudrûn answered that a noble-minded woman could love but once, and never again. So he left her, but took care to protect her from Gerlind's malice.

Gudrûn was restored to her former position, and slept that night in her old room. Next morning, when she awoke, she found the princess Ortrûn, whom she had not seen for a long time, bending over her. The two girls spent the summer together, and learnt to love each other warmly. As autumn came in, Gudrûn thought that her friend looked graver and sadder than her wont, and asked her the reason of the change. Ortrûn then confessed that as Gudrûn had not given way to Hartmut's entreaties, but remained obdurate as ever, Gerlind intended to separate her daughter from the Hegeling princess.

While the two girls were talking, Hartmut joined them, and said:

"Lady Gudrûn, the warrior to whom you plighted your troth is not worthy of your love, otherwise he would not have allowed so many years to pass without coming in search of you at the head of his men. He has forgotten you, and is most likely married to another."

"You do not know him, noble hero," answered Gudrûn; "death alone, which looses all bonds, could separate us."

"What if he has fallen in battle, or has died of some illness?" asked the young king.

"Then he shall find me faithful when I join him where there is no more parting," replied the princess, with a look of courageous resolve.

So Hartmut took leave of her, and again went away to try and forget her amid the excitement of battle.

When he was gone, Queen Gerlind once more deposed Gudrûn from her high estate, and sent her to wash the clothes, making her work from early morning till late at night, and threatening her with the rod if she were lazy; but the princess worked too hard to give her an excuse for inflicting this last indignity.

More years passed on, and at length Hartmut returned victorious as at first. He spoke to Gudrûn, but found her faithful as ever to Herwig.

Gerlind, after this, was harder than ever to Gudrûn. The other Hegeling maidens were given lighter tasks than she. They had to spin and card flax and wool, while their beloved mistress had to wash the clothes all the cold winter through, and often, on her return from the shore, she sank into an exhausted sleep

on her straw pallet, without having the strength first to take off
her wet garments. At last matters came to such a pass that her
cousin Hildburg could hold her peace no longer, and asked the
queen how she dared treat a princess with such cruelty and disrespect. Upon which Gerlind set her to join her mistress in her
work.

This was just what Hildburg wanted. Her great desire was to
be with her mistress, to cheer and comfort her, and lighten her
toil. Still Gudrûn had often to go down to the shore alone when
Hildburg was busy at the castle. On one of these occasions she
saw a swan come swimming over the sea.

"O swan, had I thy wings, I would soar into the sky and hie me
to my home."

While she spoke the swan dived into the sea, and in its place
up came a mermaid:

"O heart long tried and true, thy grief shall pass away: thy
lover and thy kindred live, and lo, they hasten to thy rescue."

So saying the mermaid dived, and again the white swan
floated on the wave. He spread is wings and rose in the air, flew
three times around the princess, and sang:

> "True love on the earth may yet be found,
>   True hearts that never roam;
>   Lo, through the breakers' foam
> 'Tis thy warrior's bark o'er the wave doth bound,
>   To lead his true-love home."

It was well for Gudrûn that she had this secret hope to support her, for Gerlind's cruelty grew daily more intolerable. The
princess and Hildburg were forced to wash the clothes on the
seashore, dressed in simple linen shifts, and without shoes.
When they begged for shoes, the cold was so terrible, their
taskmistress gave them insulting words, and threatened to
scourge them with thorns if their day's work were not finished
by evening. Trembling with cold in the cutting east wind, and
their beautiful hair blowing about their faces, they worked on
busily. Suddenly they saw a boat gliding swiftly along the shore,
rowed by two warriors in full armour. The maidens, ashamed of

their insufficient clothing, would have fled, but the men called to them to stop, and tell them what castle that was on the height above. When they added that they would throw the linen into the sea unless they received an answer, the girls came back, and as they did so, Gudrûn whispered:—

"See, it is Herwig. I know him well, but he—he has forgotten me."

And in good truth the hero was unaware that his long-lost bride stood there before him; but no sooner had she pushed her fluttering hair back from her face, than he recognised her, hastened to her, and clasped her in his arms. When the other warrior opened his visor, Gudrûn exclaimed, "Ortwin!" and threw herself into her brother's arms.

Then Ortwin turned to her companion, and said, taking her hand in his:

"It is you, Hildburg! Do not be ashamed to confess that you and I have long loved each other, and would have been openly betrothed years ago, had not the Normans carried you off."

They then exchanged the kiss of betrothal.

Herwig wished to take the two girls away with them at once, but Ortwin would not consent. He said they must come openly on the morrow for Gudrûn and Hildburg, who should never run away secretly from their captors.

The two girls stood on the shore watching the boat as long as it was in sight. At length Hildburg in startled accents begged her friend to help her finish the washing. But Gudrûn answered proudly that the days of her slavery were over, and, so saying, she cast one garment after another into the sea, and with a smile watched them as they floated away on the waves; but poor Hildburg tremblingly remembered that they were still in the power of the Norman queen.

When they reached the castle, Gerlind came down to meet them, asking why they were so early, and what they had done with the linen. Gudrûn answered that the work was too hard for them, and that she had thrown the clothes into the sea, where Queen Gerlind's men might find them yet, if she did not delay too long in sending out boats. The queen was dumb with astonishment when she heard the gentle, patient Gudrûn speak to her in such a manner; but soon recovering herself, she called her bond-women to fetch thorny rods, and beat the maidens for their insolence. The women hastened to do as they were desired; but Gudrûn called them to stop, telling them to touch her at their peril, for she would be their queen on the morrow.

"And you will really marry Hartmut?" asked Gerlind joyfully. "I fear there is some trick in this."

"Bring the king here," said Gudrûn; "I would speak with him."

The queen went thoughtfully to her son, and said:—

"Hartmut, that obstinate girl has given in at last, and has consented to be your wife, but . . ."

"No 'but,'" cried the hero, "she consents!—mother, I must hear her say so with her own lips," and he hastened from the room.

When he saw Gudrûn he would have clasped her in his arms, but she signed to him not to approach her, telling him that she could not listen to him in the abode of her misery; but that next morning, in the full light of day, and in presence of all the warriors, she would receive, and give the bridal ring. Hartmut now gave orders that Gudrûn should be provided with all that was necessary for the comfort and well-being of the future queen, and that her maidens should be restored to her.

His orders were fulfilled. The princess and Hildburg kept their secret well. It was not till the Hegeling maidens were all safe in their sleeping chamber that they heard of the arrival of Ortwin and Herwig.

CHAPTER V.

BATTLE AND VICTORY.

BEFORE DAY-BREAK one of the maidens stationed herself at the window, and gazed anxiously over the sea. After some time she saw vessels full of armed men approaching the shore; and with difficulty restraining a cry of joy she wakened her mistress and told her the good news. Not long after the alarm was given from the tower, where the sleepy watchman had just awakened.

Queen Gerlind had her wits about her more than anyone else. She did not need to be told who the enemy were, and had given the requisite orders to the garrison before Ludwig's and Hartmut's eyes were well open. But when the kings were ready, they countermanded her orders, and instead of defending the castle, marched out to meet the foe in spite of all her warnings and entreaties.

Each party moved forward to meet the other in close array, and no sooner had they met than the battle began. Ortwin and Hartmut fought hand to hand, and Ortwin had surely been overthrown had not bold Horand struck up the Norman's spear. But he too was unable to withstand the king, for being severely wounded he was soon afterwards carried to the rear by his men. Meantime Herwig and Ludwig had met, and after a terrible combat the latter was slain.

"The king is dead," cried his men, and they fled incontinently, pursued by the victor, strong Irolt, and Siegfried the Moor. The old hero of Sturmland pressed the advantage. His sword-arm was never still for a moment, and he was always in the front rank. When the terrified Normans fled to the castle they found, to their horror, that he was close behind them. They only closed the great gate just in time to prevent the enemy's entrance, but Wate was not to be deterred. He shouted to his men to bring up ladders and storming tackle, meaning to scale the wall.

Hartmut, ignorant of his father's death, had continued to fight bravely till he saw that the Normans were flying. He then retreated slowly to the castle with his immediate followers. Looking up at the battlements, he saw Queen Gerlind giving a man a naked sword, and pointing with fierce earnestness to the women's apartments in the castle. He knew his mother, and feared that she was telling the man to go and murder the Hegeling women, so he exclaimed in a loud voice of command:

"Coward! If you raise your hand to murder any woman, I will have you hung before sunset."

The man let the sword fall to the ground, and slunk away. At this moment Hartmut, to his intense amazement, caught sight of old Wate at the castle gate. He looked round for help but Ludwig was nowhere to be seen; on every side waved the banners of the Hegelings and their allies, and their foremost men were fast closing round him and his little band. Hartmut was too brave to fly; he prepared to defend himself to the last. The lord of Sturmland now came forward to attack him; and although he fought desperately, it had gone ill with him if Herwig had not thrown himself in the old warrior's way, and pleaded for his rival's life. In the heat of the conflict, Wate did not notice who it was that addressed him; he brought down one of his sledge-hammer blows on Herwig's helmet, and the king of Zealand was stretched upon the ground beside many a dead and dying Norman. This mistake restored the wild lord of Sturmland to his senses. Leaving Hartmut alone, he bent over his friend, and, to his joy, discovered him to be whole and sound. As soon as Herwig was on his feet again, Wate asked:

"What devil possessed you to make me spare the life of that Norman robber?"

"No devil at all," replied Herwig; "the noble Gudrûn loves the Princess Ortrûn, and, for her sake, begged that Hartmut's life should be spared."

"Women, women!" cried the old warrior. "They are all alike. They have soft hearts, as easily moved as a fleecy cloud is blown by the breeze. But now let us haste, and trap the she-wolf in her lair."

At length the castle gate was burst open, and the hero of Sturmland cut his way through the small crowd of defenders to the women's apartments. There he found Gudrûn surrounded by all the frightened women in the palace, while Ortrûn and Gerlind knelt at her feet and entreated her protection.

"Where is the she-wolf?" shouted Wate. "Speak Gudrûn, and you others!"

He was awful to look upon, with his grim, stern face, his armour and sword dripping with the blood of his enemies; but Gudrûn did not quail, nor did she utter a single word to betray the cruel woman who had used her so cruelly. She sat still and quiet, full of a gentle dignity, and looked at the angry old man without blanching.

He cast a quick glance round the room in search of Gerlind, and as he did so, one of the maidens pointed to the queen. The moment he saw the glittering, snaky eyes, he caught Gerlind by the hair, and dragging her to the battlements, cut off her head, and flung both it and the body over the wall.

"Now the other!" he cried, rushing up to the terrified Ortrûn; "she belongs to the serpent's brood and must share her mother's fate."

But Gudrûn held the maiden tightly clasped in her arms, and told the grim warrior of all the love and tenderness that Ortrûn had shown her, so Wate was fain to be satisfied with the vengeance he had already wreaked.

Meanwhile the fighting outside the castle had also ceased. The Norman hero, weary to death, had surrendered with the eighty warriors that were left him.

Three days later, the victorious army went on board their ships and set sail for the land of the Hegelings, leaving Morung and his men to garrison Cassian. Hartmut, and Ortrûn with thirty of her maidens, had to accompany their conquerors. On their way they touched at Wölpensand, where Queen Hilde had had a minster built, and the bones of those who fell in the old fight buried; and there the heroes gave solemn thanks for their great victory. Ortrûn sat alone in the churchyard, looking at the graves: she thought of her slain father, and wished that she too were at rest. But Gudrûn coming up to her, took her by the hand and led her to the Moorish king Siegfried, who desired to gain her love. During the remainder of the voyage, Gudrûn managed to throw the two much together, and delighted in telling Ortrûn of Siegfried's noble and warlike deeds.

In the meantime Queen Hilde and Hergart, Herwig's sister, often sat together at a window overlooking the sea. The Hegeling army must soon return, but how would it return? and would Gudrûn have kept her troth? Hilde was not so hopeful as her young companion, for she was more used to sorrow. One day when they were at the window as usual, Hergart saw the fleet appear in the distance, and uttering a cry of joy told Queen Hilde that their friends were coming back.

Before the queen and her ladies could reach the shore, Wate had already landed, and seeing the queen, he at once told her the good news. The rest of the ships were not long in arriving, and soon Hilde had the pleasure of embracing her daughter, the long-lost Gudrûn.

Time passed and joy reigned supreme in every breast save one. Hartmut ate out his soul in sadness. Gentle Hergart pitied him, and begged Queen Hilde to use her influence to have him set at liberty, and be allowed to return to his kingdom. But Hilde explained how impossible it was to let a man go free who was sure to bear them deadly enmity, and attack them when he could. Hartmut one day by accident overheard Hergart pleading for him so tenderly and so wisely that he was deeply touched. He began to think that she was, if possible, even more beautiful than Gudrûn, and took the first opportunity he could find of speaking to her. It was not long before they learnt to love each other. Hartmut told the queen about it, and asked for her consent to his marriage with Hergart, which she at once granted, and at the same time gave him back his sword and freedom for the husband of sweet Hergart could never be aught else than the friend of the Hegelings.

A few weeks later a great marriage feast was held, in which four couples appeared before the altar to receive a priestly blessing on their vows; after which they adjourned to the banqueting-hall. Then the old minstrel, Horand, took his harp and sang his last song and told of the great deeds he had known; he sang of noble lives and noble deaths, of truth and constancy; and when he ceased, there was not a dry eye in the hall, for even the grim lord of Sturmland was seen to wipe away a tear.

The Legend of Beowulf.

The Giant and the Dragon Slayer.

Giant Grendel.

ONE EVENING while the warriors were feasting in King Hrodgar's hall, a minstrel was called upon to sing. He tuned his harp, and sang of the coming of Skiöld, the son whom Odin sent to live a human life among mortal men. He told how the babe had been seen lying on a shield floating on the waves of the sea, how he had been drawn ashore and carefully tended, and how he had become a mighty king and warrior in Jutland. He sang of Skiöld's glorious life, of the kingdom he had left to his children and grandchildren; and last of all he sang of Hrodgar, Skiöld's most famous grandson, who, like him, was the patron of all peaceful arts, the protector of all peaceful folk, and the punisher of evil-doers.

Many heroes were collected round the king that night at Hirschhalle,—so called from the gigantic antlers of a royal stag which, carved in stone, adorned the battlements. At length the time came for the warriors to separate for the night, and as there were too many of them to be accommodated elsewhere, beds were made up for them in the great hall. Two and thirty brave men lay down to sleep on the couches spread for them; but next morning, when the servants came to waken them, they were gone. The room was in confusion, here and there might be seen stains of blood, and other signs of struggle.

King Hrodgar came himself as soon as he heard what had chanced, and examined the place carefully to try and discover the cause of the disaster. He followed the bloodstains through the hall, and out of doors, and there, in the soft earth, he saw the deep footprints of a giant. The whole affair was clear to him now. He knew that the monster Grendel, who had been banished from the land by the aid of a great magician, had at length returned. When it became known that Grendel had come back, ten warriors offered to keep watch in the hall, and fight the giant if he tried to come in. Next morning they were gone. They had either been surprised in their sleep, or had not been strong enough to withstand the monster. The Skiöldungs' people were brave and fearless, so twelve other heroes immediately offered their services. Eleven of them laid themselves down to sleep in their armour, while the twelfth, a minstrel, kept watch.

At midnight the giant came, smacking his great lips, and slowly dragging his heavy body along. The minstrel saw and heard all that took place; but he could neither speak nor move; he was, as it were, paralyzed with fear, and at last sank back senseless. Next morning, when with infinite trouble they restored him to consciousness, he either could not, or would not, tell what he had seen. He picked up his arms and his harp, pointed to the stains on the floor, and strode down to the strand without a word or sign of farewell to any one. A vessel was on the point of sailing for Gothland, so he went on board, and had soon left the ill-fated shores of Jutland behind.

BEOWULF, THE BOLD DIVER.

HYGELAK, a brave and heroic man, ruled over Gothland at this time. He was surrounded by a band of famous warriors, chief among whom was his nephew Beowulf (bee-hunter, *i. e.*, woodpecker), son of Ektheov. When the harper arrived in Gothland, he found that the Swedes had invaded the country, and a great battle was about to take place. A few days later the battle was fought, and would have gone badly with the Goths had it not been for the almost superhuman prowess displayed by Beowulf, who, in spite of repeated disaster, always returned to the charge. His coolness and courage kept up the spirits of his men, and at last the Swedes had to return to their own land, mourning the loss of their king, and of many a valiant hero.

During the feast that was given in honour of this great victory, the stranger minstrel sang to the assembled warriors of the great deeds of past and present times. He sang of Siegmund (Siegfried) the brave Wölsung, and of all his adventures with giants and dragons. Then, striking yet louder chords upon his harp, he sang of Beowulf's victory, and called upon him to do yet greater things, to seek out and slay the horrible fiend of the fen, Grendel, who nightly crept into the Skiöldung's hall, and fed on the blood of heroes.

Beowulf promised to go and try to slay the monster that had done such incredible mischief. Now one of the great lords, Breka by name, was envious of Beowulf's fame, and proposed that they two should on the morrow go down to the sea, and fight the monsters of the deep. They would then see which of them was the better man; and the one that reached the shore first after the battle was over should receive the prize of victory. It was agreed that this trial of strength should take place on the morrow, and King Hygelak promised to give the gold chain he wore round his neck to whichever was the victor.

Next morning the sun rose red in the east, the stormy sea moaned, groaned, and dashed upon the shore, as though demanding a human sacrifice. The two bold swimmers stood on the strand, arrayed in their shirts of mail, their swords in their hands. When the signal was given, they flung themselves into the raging sea, and were soon lost to sight. They kept close together, that they might come to each other's help if hard pressed by the monsters of the deep, but were at length parted by waves which bore them in different directions. Breka soon found himself in calm water, where he swam about until it was time to return. Beowulf, on the contrary, was carried to a place where the waves beat fiercely against great cliffs that towered above the water, a place that swarmed with polypi, sea-dragons, and horrible nixies, all lying in wait for their prey. Gigantic arms were stretched out to grasp him, but he cut them down with his sword. Monsters of every sort tried to clutch and stifle him, but he stabbed them through their scales. A nixie clasped him in his arms, and would have dragged him down to his cave, but he stabbed the monster to the heart, and drew him to the surface of the water. After a long struggle he again reached the open sea, and then strove with all his might to reach home before the sun should quite have set. The storm was over, so that there was the less danger. Breka was the first of the bold swimmers to reach the shore. He turned with a triumphant smile to greet Beowulf, but what was is astonishment, and that of all present, when the hero dragged the monstrous form of the nixie on the sands, and stretched it out before them. The princes crowded round the hideous creature, and gazed at his enormous limbs in speechless amazement.

"Here is the gold chain," said the king to Breka. "You have won it by hard labour; but my bold nephew has done even more than you, in that he has conquered and slain one of the monsters of the deep. I shall therefore give him my good sword Nägling with the golden hilt, and the Runic letters engraved in gold, that are sure to bring good fortune to the possessor."

Beowulf was held in high honour by the Goths; but he was not satisfied with the deeds he had already done. He longed to free the royal palace of the Skiöldungs from the monster Grendel, so he presently took ship for King Hrodgar's castle, accompanied by the minstrel, and fifteen noble and courageous Goths.

On their ship touching the strand below the fortress the watchman asked them who they were, and what brought them to King Hrodgar's land. When he learnt their names and business, he was pleased, and sent them on to the king. Hrodgar also received them with joy and gratitude. The minstrel tuned his harp and sang of Beowulf's heroic deeds, and prophesied that he would conquer and slay the monster of the morass. This praise made Hunford, one of the courtiers, angry and jealous. He said it was Breka, not Beowulf, that had won the golden chain; that the Gothic hero was undertaking an enterprise that would very likely lead him to his death; and he advised him to think twice before attacking Grendel. Upon this, Beowulf exclaimed indignantly that he had won a good sword instead of the golden chain, and that it was sharp enough both to pierce the hide of the monster and to cut out a slanderous tongue. Hrodgar bade the courtier be silent, and promised the Goth that if he were victorious, he would give him rich presents, and would enter into a firm alliance with his people.

At night-fall Hrodgar and his warriors withdrew, and serving-men came into the hall to make up beds for the strangers. Beowulf felt so confident of victory that he laid aside his helmet and shirt of mail, and then gave his sword to the groom in attendance.

"I intend to master Grendel with my fists," he said; "he is unarmed, and I will meet him in like fashion."

Midnight came, and the fiend of the fen rose out of his hiding-place. He expected a feast that night, and, wrapping himself in a veil of mist, made his way to the palace. He entered the banqueting-hall, and at sight of the Goths a grin of satisfaction spread over his countenance, displaying his great teeth, which resembled boar's tusks in size and shape. At the same time he stretched out his hairy hands, which were furnished with claws like those of an eagle.

The warriors were all sunk in a sleep so profound as to seem like enchantment. Beowulf alone remained awake, and that only by a mighty effort. He watched the monster through his half-closed eyes, and saw him stand gloating over his intended victims, uncertain with whom to commence. At last he seemed to have made up his mind, for he hurled upon one of the sleepers, whom he rapidly slew, drinking his blood with evident eagerness and enjoyment. He turned next to Beowulf. But the hero seized his outstretched arm in such a firm grip that he bellowed with pain. And now began a terrible struggle between the man and the demon. The hall trembled to its foundation, and threatened every instant to fall in ruins. The sleepers awoke. They drew their swords and fell upon the monster; but their weapons glanced harmlessly off his scaly hide, and they were fain to take refuge in out-of-the-way corners, that they might not be trampled under foot by the wrestlers. At length Grendel had to acknowledge Beowulf's mastery, and now only strove to escape. With a mighty effort he succeeded in freeing himself from the hero's grasp, but at the price of one of his arms, which, torn out at the socket, remained in his antagonist's hands. Then, with a howl of rage and pain, the demon fled back to his morass, leaving a trail of blood to mark the path by which he had gone.

The Gothic hero stood in the middle of the vast hall, holding his trophy in his right hand. The rays of the rising sun streamed in at the window and lighted up his head as with a halo. His companions crowded round him and greeted him with awe and reverence. Then he fastened the trophy of his victory over the door of the hall, and, having done this, he returned thanks to All-father for having given him strength to withstand the monster. The warriors knelt round him and joined him in his praise and thanksgiving.

When the Goths rose from their knees, they saw the king and his courtiers assembled in the hall, gazing in astonishment, now at them, and now at the monster's arm over the doorway. They told Hrodgar all that had happened during the night.

The king was at first too much amazed to speak, but recovering himself he desired his nephew, Hrodulf, to bring the gifts he had prepared to reward the victor. The warrior soon returned with some servants bearing the presents, which Hrodgar gave to Beowulf with many words of gratitude for the service he had done him and the country. He then prayed the Goth to remain his friend and his son's friend as long as they all should live.

After these things the king ordered a great feast to be prepared in honour of Beowulf. While this was being done, Hunford came forward and said:

"Noble Beowulf, I wronged you yesterday evening by my scornful speech, which I never would have made had I known what you were. Will you accept my sword Hrunting? it was made by dwarfs and the blade was hardened in dragon's blood, and, in taking it, will you grant me your forgiveness and friendship?"

The two heroes shook hands in token of their reconciliation, and went together to the feast.

When the feast was over, and the warriors sat over their winecups, the minstrel sang of Beowulf's victory over Grendel, and of the alliance which had that day been concluded between the Goths and the Skiöldungs. When the song was finished, Queen Walchtheov filled the goblets of all present. To Beowulf she presented a golden cup, telling him to keep it in remembrance of her, together with a ring and a necklace that she put in his hand, saying they were the same that Hama (Heime) in the olden time stole from the Brosing (Harlung?) treasure.

"Wear them," she added, "for our sakes, but also for your own, that you may come whole and victorious out of all the battles you will have to fight during a long life."

Beowulf thanked the queen in seemly fashion, and then the Lady Walchtheov retired.

The king and his men, and Beowulf and his friends, retired to the royal apartments, and beds were spread in the hall for many warriors, who, no longer fearing a one-armed Grendel, had now flocked to the palace and filled it to overflowing.

The night, however, was not to pass as quietly as was hoped.

THE SHE-WOLF OF THE SEA.

AT MIDNIGHT a great column of water rose in the midst of the sea, and out of it came a gigantic woman, whose face was as grey as her garments. Her eyes shone like coals of fire, her bristly hair stood up on end, and her long bony arms were stretched out as though in search for prey. It was Grendel's mother, who had come to avenge her son. She came up out of the sea, crossed the morass, and entered the great hall; there she slew one warrior after another, in spite of their resistance, and slaked her thirst with their warm blood.

Deep was the sorrow of both king and people next day when they heard of the new misery that had come upon the land. Then Beowulf said that the cause of all this wretchedness was Grendel's mother, and that she would never cease to persecute the Skiöldungs as long as she lived. The only thing to be done was to seek her out in her own place, and there to slay her. This he was prepared to do. He begged Hrodgar to send the treasures that he and the queen had given him to his uncle Hygelak, king of Gothland, should he fall in his struggle with the giantess.

The whole party then went down to the shore, and Beowulf, wading into the sea, sought to find the road leading to the monster's dwelling. Finding that it was a longer way than he had imagined he came back to the shore and took leave of his friends, who one and all entreated him to give up the enterprise; but in vain.

"Wait for me two days and nights," he said, "and if I do not then return, you may know that I have been conquered by the mer-woman; but that is a matter that is in the hands of the gods alone in whom I trust."

Having thus spoken, the hero tore himself away from his weeping friends, and plunged into the raging sea with all his armour on, and with Hunford's good sword at his side.

He swam a long way. At last he saw a light deep down in the water; "Her dwelling must be here," he thought; "may the gods have me in their keeping!" He dived down, down, down to the bottom of the sea. Many a monster of hideous shape snapped at him as he shot past, but his coat of mail was proof against their teeth. Suddenly he felt himself caught as with hooks, and dragged along so swiftly that he could scarcely breathe. In another moment he found himself in the crystal hall of a submarine palace, and face to face with the antagonist he had sought.

Then began a terrible struggle. Beowulf and the giantess wrestled together for life and death. The walls of the palace shook so that they threatened to fall. The two wrestlers fell to the ground, Beowulf the undermost. The mer-woman pulled out a sharp knife to cut his throat, but Wieland's armour was too well made to give way, and Beowulf struggled to his feet again. The giantess then drew a monstrous sword, so heavy that few mortal men could have wielded it; but, before she could use it, Beowulf made an unexpected spring upon her, and wrenched the sword out of her hand. He clutched it firmly in both hands, and, swinging it with all his strength, cut off the woman's head. He felt so exhausted with his labours that he rested awhile, leaning on his sword. After a few minutes he looked about him, and saw Grendel lying dead on a couch of sea-weed. He cut off his head, meaning to take it with him as a sign of victory; but no sooner had he done so than the blood began to flow from the monster's body in a great gurgling stream, then it mixed with that of his mother's, and flowed out of the entrance door into the sea. The blade of the giantess' sword melted in it, and vanished as completely as ice in the rays of the sun. The golden hilt of the sword and Grendel's head were the only booty that Beowulf brought with him out of the depths of the sea.

His friends were collected on the shore, their hearts filled with a deadly anxiety, for they had seen the sea reddened with blood, and knew not whose it was. So when the hero appeared, they received him with acclamation.

Hrodgar and his people could find no words that would fitly express their gratitude to the hero who had saved the land from two such foes as Grendel and his mother; and when Beowulf and his warriors set out on their journey home, they were laden with blessings and gifts of all kinds.

Hygelak received his nephew with great delight, and listened to the tale of his adventures in speechless amazement and ecstasy.

BEOWULF IS MADE KING.

MANY YEARS passed away in peace and quiet. At last the Frisians made a viking raid on Gothland, burning defenseless granges and cottages. Before King Hygelak could reach the place of their depredation, and offer them battle, they had taken to their ships again and were far away. The king determined to make a descent upon Friesland and punish the marauders; he would not listen to Beowulf when he advised him to delay till better preparations could be made for the onslaught.

The Goths landed in Friesland without opposition, and, marching into the country, revenged themselves by burning many a farmstead, and taking many a castle and town. Now the Frisians were a free and warlike people, whose heroes had played an honourable part in the great Bravalla-fight; the time had come for them to preserve their homes and liberty, and they did not shun to make ready for battle. A murderous engagement took place between them and their Gothic invaders, in which the latter were defeated, and obliged to fly to their ships, terror-stricken by the loss of their king. Beowulf and the noblest of the warriors alone stood their ground, and, although severely wounded, did not join in the retreat until they had rescued and carried off Hygelak's body. Then the conquered army set sail for Gothland.

Queen Hygd was at first so overwhelmed with sorrow for the loss of her husband that she could give no thought to matters of state; but after a time she roused herself from her grief, and began to consider what was best for the nation. It was well that she did so, for while she was still wrapped up in her sorrow, the barons had been quarreling among themselves, and creating much disturbance. The royal widow therefore called a meeting of the notables, and standing up before the assembly, spoke of the anarchy into which the country was falling, and said that as her son Hardred was too young to govern the kingdom, and preserve it from civil or foreign war, she strongly advised that Beowulf should be made king. The notables all cheered, and shouted that Beowulf should be their king; but the hero came forward and said:

"And do you really think, ye men of Gothland, that I would rob the child of my uncle and friend of his rights and honours. May the gods, the avengers of all evil, preserve me from such a crime! Here," he cried, lifting young Hardred on his shield, and holding him aloft, "here is our king. I will be his faithful guardian, and will act in his name till he is old enough and wise enough to take the reins of government into his own hands."

Nobody ventured to remonstrate with Beowulf; indeed, they all knew that remonstrance would be in vain. And so the matter was settled.

Years passed on, and Beowulf kept his word. He ruled the kingdom with a strong hand, and with absolute justice; and with the help of Queen Hygd educated the young king with so much wisdom, that when the sovereign power was placed in his hands, there was every hope that he would use it for his people's good. But Hardred was not long to rule over the Goths. Like his former guardian and teacher Beowulf, the king was of a frank and honest nature, and trustful of all who had not shown themselves his enemies. So when Eanmund and Eadgils, the sons of Ohtere, king of Swithiod, came to him as fugitives, he received them with all kindness. He often tried to make them see that they had been wrong in rebelling against their father, and offered to arrange matters with him on their behalf. One day, when he was speaking to them very earnestly on this subject, Eanmund, a passionate, hot-tempered man, told him that he was too young to advise a tried warrior like him. Hardred sharply told him to remember to whom he was speaking; and Eanmund, completely losing the little self-control he ever had, drew his sword and stabbed his royal host to the heart. Young Wichstan (Weohstan) at once avenged the king's murder by slaying Eanmund; but Eadgils fled back to Swithiod, and soon after succeeded his father on the throne.

The Gothic Allthing, the assembly of all the free men of the nation, was called together as soon as Hardred's murder was made known, and by a unanimous vote Beowulf was elected king in his cousin's stead. He accepted the office, and swore to rule his people justly.

The Fight with the Dragon.

WHEN HARDRED's death was noised abroad, several of the neighbouring peoples made raids upon Gothland, but Beowulf kept so strict a watch on the borders that the enemy was beaten back at all points. Scarcely was the country freed from the attacks of these sea-wolves, when Eadgils, king of Swithiod, came at the head of a large army to avenge his brother's death. The Goths and Swedes met and fought a murderous battle, in which many men were slain, and among them King Eadgils. After the death of their king the Swedes retired to their ships, and sailed back to their own land. The consequence of this victory was a lasting peace. No vikings dared attack the well-defended shores of Gothland, and but few quarrels arose among the nobles to disturb the internal peace of the realm. Beowulf ruled the land with great justice and wisdom. No one entreating his help was ever sent empty away, and no act of tyranny remained unpunished.

Forty years or more passed after this fashion. The hero had grown an old man, and hoped that the national peace and happiness would last as long as he lived. But he was to be rudely awakened from this dream. An enemy attacked Gothland, against whom all weapons and armies were useless. This was how it happened. A dishonest slave, who feared discovery and punishment at his master's hands, fled from home, and took refuge in a wild, rocky place. When he got there, he looked about for some cave in which he might take up his abode. Coming to one, he entered, but found it already tenanted by an immense dragon, which lay stretched on the ground asleep. Behind it, at the back of the cave, were treasures of all sorts. The man looked greedily at the shining mass of jewels and gold, and thought in his heart, "If I had but a few of these treasures, I could buy my freedom, and need no longer fear my master." This idea made him bold. He slipped softly past the monster, and stole a golden pot, the knob on whose lid was formed of a shining carbuncle. He escaped safely, and going back to his master, bought his freedom. Neither of the men had the slightest notion of the harm this deed would bring down upon the land.

The dragon, which had watched over its hoard for hundreds of years, and knew each costly thing by heart, saw at once that it had been robbed. At nightfall it crept out of its hole to look for traces of the thief. Finding none, it lifted up its voice and howled so loud, that the earth shook, at the same time flames issued from its mouth and burnt up granges and homesteads far and wide. The men, who sought to put out the fire, fell victims to its fury, or else were dragged into the monster's cave, where they perished miserably. This happened night after night; the devastation had no end. Many brave warriors went out against the dragon, and tried to kill it, but none of them could withstand the fiery blasts with which the creature defended itself.

The old king heard the story of these events with infinite sorrow. He determined himself to attack the monster, and when his friends remonstrated with him on his rashness, he replied that it was his duty to defend his people from all their enemies, and that the gods would help him. He further announced that he

would have fought the dragon unarmed, as he had done the
monster Grendel, the son of the sea-witch, but that he feared he
could not make his way through the flames without such protection. He therefore had a shield made three times as thick as
usual, and so large that it covered him completely. This done, he
chose eleven of his bravest warriors to be his comrades in this
adventure, among them Wichstan, the man who avenged King
Hardred's death.

Beowulf and his companions set out on their journey, and in
due course arrived at the dragon's cave, out of which there
flowed a brook whose waters were made boiling hot by the monster's breath.

The king bade his friends wait a little way off, until they saw
whether he needed their help, and then advancing to the mouth
of the cave, he called the dragon to come forth. The great beast
came out at his call, and a terrible struggle ensued. Both combatants were hidden from view in a dense cloud of smoke and
fire. The rocks trembled and shook at the bellowing of the monster, which at the same time slashed out with its tail, whose
blows fell like a sledge-hammer both in sound and regularity.
For a moment the smoke and flames were blown aside by a puff
of wind, and Beowulf's comrades saw that the dragon had just
seized their king in its great jaws. They could not bear the sight,
and ten of them slipped aside and strove to hide behind rocks
and trees; but the eleventh brave Wichstan hastened to help his
master. His shield was burnt up in a twinkling, and he was
obliged to seek shelter behind the king. Both heroes seemed
lost. The dragon tore down Beowulf's iron shield, and caught
him a second time in its great jaws, crushing him between its
teeth with such force that the iron rings of his coat of mail
cracked like so much crockery, though they had been forged by
Wieland himself. Then Wichstan seized his opportunity, when
the beast's head was raised, the better to champ his prey, and
plunged his sword into the fleshy part of its throat under the
lower jaw. Upon this the dragon dropped the king, and encircled
both its adversaries with its tail, but Beowulf at the same

moment made a lunge at its open mouth, driving his weapon so deep that the point came out at the dragon's throat. After that they soon dispatched the monster, and then threw themselves on a ledge of rock, panting and exhausted.

When they had recovered a little, the heroes loosened their armour, and Wichstan saw that blood was oozing slowly from under the king's gorget. He wanted to bind up the slight wound; but Beowulf forbade him, saying that it would be useless, as the hurt had been given by the dragon's tooth, and the poison was already in his veins.

"I must die," he added, "but I go to my forefathers without sadness, though I am the last of my race, for my wife has given me no son and heir. I can look back on my past life with pleasure, for I have wronged no man, but have shown justice to all."

He then asked Wichstan to fetch him a drink of water, and afterwards to bring him the treasure out of the dragon's cave, that he might see, with his own eyes, the last gift he should ever make to his people.

His commands were obeyed, and a few minutes later he had passed away quietly and peacefully. Wichstan gazed at him in silent grief. Beowulf had been his dearest friend, and he felt that, with his death, his last tie to life was loosed. Meanwhile the ten warriors had come out of their hiding-places, when they found that all danger was over. On seeing what had chanced, they raised their voices in mourning; but Wichstan bade them hold their peace, or if they must weep, at least weep for their own cowardice, and not for the hero who had died at his post. He then advised them to make the best of their way to other lands, as he could not answer for their lives when the Goths became aware of the way in which they had deserted their king in his hour of need.

With bowed heads and shame-stricken faces the men turned away. They departed out of Gothland, and sought to hide their heads in countries where their names were unknown.

The body of Beowulf was borne to its funeral pile on the height called Hronesnäs, and there burnt amid the tears and sorrow of a nation. When the funeral rites had all been performed, the great treasure was taken back to the dragon's cave. For the Goths would have none of the gold their beloved king had won for them in his death. So it still lies hidden in the heart of the earth as in the olden time when the dragon guarded it from mortal ken. If it is useless to men, it is at all events not hurtful.

Legends of King Arthur and the Holy Grail

Chapter I.

Titurel.

AT THE time when the bold hero Vespasian was called away from the siege of Jerusalem, to be made emperor of Rome, there was a rich man of Cappadocia named Parille, or as the Romans called him, Berillus.

Berillus was brave in war, and wise of counsel in times of peace, so the emperor gave him large estates in Gaul. His virtues were inherited by his sons, grandsons and later descendants. One of these, Titurisone, married a noble maiden, named Elizabel, but they had no children. The knight was much distressed at the thought that a noble and chivalrous race should end with him. Once, when he was quite elderly, a soothsayer came to the castle and asked for a night's lodging which was as usual granted. That evening, when he was sitting alone with his guest, the knight began to discourse of the sorrow of his life, and the stranger told him that he ought to make a pilgrimage to the church of the Holy Sepulchre, and lay a crucifix of pure gold on the altar. Titurisone followed the wise man's advice, and he and his wife had the pleasure of having a son born to them. As the boy grew up, he showed rare gifts of mind, great piety, and unusual strength. He had received the name of Titurel at his baptism, a name that soon became known throughout the length and breadth of the land.

When the boy grew to man's estate he went with his father to fight against the heathen. He showed such marvellous prowess that his father began to praise him, and prophesy great things for his future; but the lad modestly said that he had only done his duty like others.

When the victorious army returned home, Titurel was not to be tempted to remain at court, but hastened away to his native place. Arrived there, he did not go first in search of his mother, but made his way to the chapel, dressed in the robes of a penitent. He approached the altar bare-foot, and presented the booty he had brought from the war. Having prayed for God's blessing on all his undertakings, he rose from his knees, and, going into the castle, hastened to embrace his mother.

Titurel sometimes took part in the crusade against the Saracens. His gallant deeds were so numerous that they became noised abroad, and his name was held in honour by Christians and infidels alike.

Many years passed on. Titurisone and his wife both died, leaving a large inheritance to their only son. The change in his outward fortunes made no difference in Titurel—he remained as humble in the sight of God and man as before; he had more to give away to the poor and needy, that was the only use of wealth in his eyes.

One beautiful spring morning he went out to walk in the wood. Coming to a soft mossy bank he seated himself and looked about him. Flowers filled the air with their perfume, birds were singing in the trees, and a gentle breeze whispered among the fresh green leaves. He felt full of peace and joy; it almost seemed to him as though God were speaking to him in the songs of the birds, the rustle of the foliage and the murmur of the brook. The sky was blue; one soft fleecy cloud alone was visible. He was surprised to see it coming as if towards him with extraordinary speed, and yet it was not driven by the wind. At last it sank to the earth before him, and out of it came an angel, who spoke to the hero in a deep melodious voice like the sound of the organ in church.

"Hail, chosen hero of the Most High! The Lord hath called thee to guard the holy Grail on His Mountain, Montsalvatch. Set thy house in order, and obey the voice of God."

The angel stepped back, the cloud closed round him like a silver veil, and he floated away to heaven.

Titurel went home in a state of ecstasy. He divided his wealth among his servants and those who had most need of it, after which he returned fully armed to the place where the angel had appeared to him. Once more he saw the cloud in the sky, and this time it was fringed with the gold of sunshine. It went before him, showing him the way to the goal of his pilgrimage. He went on and on through vast solitudes. At length he came to a deep dark wood, and after that to a mountain, the sides of which seemed too steep to climb. But the cloud preceded him, and he followed, dragging himself up precipitous rocks, past great abysses that made him dizzy to look into, and through thickets of thorn. Often he felt so weary he could hardly draw one foot after the other, and was brought to despair of ever reaching the top. But a voice seemed to speak to him encouragingly at such moments of weakness, and he found strength to struggle on. At length he reached the top of the mountain. He saw a bright light before him, it was the Sangreal borne in the air by invisible hands. Beneath it knelt a number of knights in shining armour. Seeing him, they rose to their feet, and cried,—

"Hail to thee, chosen hero, called to be guardian of the holy Grail!"

He did not answer, his eyes were fixed on the sacred vessel, which was like a cup of emerald-coloured jasper, encircled by a strand of chased gold. Lost in the wondrous sight, he prayed for strength to guard what was put under his charge.

And in good truth Titurel was worthy of his high calling. He, with the help of the other knights under his command, prevented any infidels from approaching the holy mountain. Many years passed away, and the vessel never came down to earth. So Titurel determined to build a castle and temple on the mountain-top worthy to hold and protect the Sangreal.

BUILDING OF THE TEMPLE.

WHEN THE grass, ferns and stones were cleared away, it was discovered that the rock, or core of the mountain, was one entire
onyx of enormous size. This was flattened into a flooring,
and polished with great care; and upon it the castle was built.
Now came the most important task of rearing the temple, but
they were in doubt as to the plan and shape that would be most
fitting.

One morning when Titurel awoke, he prayed that he might be
enlightened to know how to build the church, and when he went
out he saw the entire ground-plan clearly marked out on the
rock-foundation, and all the miraculous materials that were
wanted, ready piled up in huge stacks. So the knights worked
hard all day long, and the invisible powers worked all night. It
was wonderful how quick the walls rose, and the church was finished. It was circular in form, and had seventy-two octagon
choirs, every two of which supported a belfry. In the midst rose
a tower with many windows, and openings with pointed arches.
The topmost point of the tower was a ruby, out of which rose a
cross of clear crystal surmounted by a golden eagle with outstretched wings. Within the building, sculptured vines, roses
and lilies twined about the pillars, forming bowers, on whose
branches birds seemed to flutter as if alive. At every intersection
of the arches was a glowing carbuncle that turned night into day;
and the vaulted roof was of blue sapphire, in which a miracle of
art was to be seen. The sun, moon and stars placed there by the
builders, moved in the same order as the real luminaries in the
heavens.

In the wide inner space of the great temple a second and
smaller sanctuary was built, resembling the first, but far more
beautiful. This was the place intended for the Sangreal, should
it come down to earth.

And now the work was finished. The hour of consecration had
come. The bells rang. The priests began to chant the hymn, and
a chorus of angels joined in: "Glory to God on high, peace on
earth, good will to men." At the same moment a sweet perfume
filled the air, the sacred vessel descended and floated over the

altar in the inner sanctuary. A deep and solemn silence reigned in the mighty building. Then the invisible choir began to sing: "The glory of the Lord has arisen in Zion! Praise Him, ye faithful, and make known His holy name." The priest spoke the blessing, and the consecration was complete. Titurel did not move for some time after the others had withdrawn. He was lost in wonder and joy. He did not touch the vessel, for he had not been told to do so.

The building had taken thirty years to complete. After the consecration, a dove appeared every Good Friday carrying a wafer from the holy sacrament in its bill. It dropped the wafer into the sacred vessel, thereby keeping up the miraculous powers of the Grail, which provided food for the knights who guarded it, and healed any wounds they might sustain at the hands of the unbelievers who sometimes attacked them.

His Marriage and Descendants.

TIME PASSED on, and Titurel was four hundred years old, but no one looking at him would have thought him more than forty. One evening when he entered the sanctuary and turned his eyes upon the Grail, he saw that it had a message for him. Drawing near that he might read the letters of fire in which all such commands were issued, he read that he was to take a wife, so that the chosen race might not die out of the land. He called the knights of the Temple. They saw what was written, and said that he must obey. With one accord all fixed upon the Lady Richoude, daughter of a Spanish chief, as the most worthy maiden to be his wife. The wooing was done by solemn embassage, and neither father nor daughter was deaf to the call. The marriage took place, and on the same day Titurel received the honour of knighthood, which he had always refused before out of humility. Two children were born to Sir Titurel and his wife; a son named Frimutel, and daughter called Richoude after her mother. Twenty years later Titurel lost his wife, and was once more alone in the world, except for his children, to whom he was devoted.

Richoude, who was very lovely, married a king whose realm lay far away from her old home, and Frimutel married Clarissa, daughter of the king of Granada; by her he had five children. Two of them were sons, Amfortas and Trevrezent by name, and three daughters, Herzeleide, Joisiane, and Repanse.

Titurel was no longer able to bear the weight of his armour: he passed his time either in church or with his grandchildren. One day when he went, as he often did, to gaze at the holy Grail, he saw written in letters of fire on the rim of the vessel, "Frimutel shall be king." The old man's heart was full of joy. He called his son, his grandchildren, and all the young heroes who served the Sangreal, around him, and told them what had been ordained. He then desired his granddaughter Joisiane to place the floating Grail upon the altar; for she, as a pure virgin, could touch it. She obeyed, and then the old man put the crown on his son's head, and blessed him and the assembled brotherhood.

Titurel lived on, and saw many joyful and many sorrowful things happen. Joisiane married King Kiot of Catalonia, and died at the birth of her babe Sigune,

> Who fairer was than flowers in lusty May,
> That open their dewy cups to dawning day.

Her sister Herzeleide took the child, and brought it up with Tchionatulander, the orphan son of a friend; but after a time she lost her husband, and had to fly with her son Percival, leaving Sigune and Tchionatulander under the care of friends. But worse things than this were yet to happen. Frimutel thought his life at Montsalvatch confined and dull; he wearied of it, and went out to seek excitement in the world. He died of a lance-wound far away in the land of the unbelievers. His son Amfortas was crowned his successor, in obedience to the fiery letters that appeared on the holy vessel; but he had inherited the wild blood and roving spirit of his father; and instead of fulfilling the office to which he was appointed, he went out into the world in search of love and fame. At length he was brought back to his grandfather, sick unto death of a wound caused by a poisoned spear.

One day, while Sir Titurel knelt in the sanctuary praying for his grandson, whose life of pain was prolonged by the holy Grail appearing to him once in every seven days, he suddenly saw these words in letters of fire:—

"Murmur not, good old man; endure the load of others' sins. A chosen hero shall one day climb the holy mount. If he ask, before nightfall, of the beginning and end of this tale of woe, then shall the spell be broken, and Amfortas cured, but the new-comer shall be king in his stead."

Again and again Titurel read the mysterious words, and asked when the hero would come. He received no answer; but the words, "murmur not," shone brighter than before, and he bowed his head, leaving the future confidently to God.

CHAPTER II.

PERCIVAL (PARSIFAL).

WHEN QUEEN Herzeleide had to fly from home with her little son on the death of her husband, she retired to a small house she possessed in an out-of-the-way district, and devoted herself to the education of her boy. She never spoke to him of knightly deeds, for she feared lest when he was grown up he should leave her to seek adventures, and should die in some tournament or feud. Notwithstanding this, young Percival grew up a bold, strong youth, fearless of all danger.

One day, as he was coming home from hunting, he met some knights riding through the wood arrayed in full armour. One of them asked him a question, which Percival answered at random. Then, going up to the knight, he asked what strange garments those were that he and his companions wore, and why they had golden spurs. The knight was amused, and answered the lad's questions very kindly, adding, "If you want to know more of knights and knighthood, you must go to King Arthur's court, and there, if you are worthy, you may perchance be made a knight yourself."

Percival could not forget what he had heard and seen. He cared no more for hunting, and spent his days and nights in dreaming of swords, knighthood and battle. Herzeleide asked her son what ailed him, and when she learnt the cause of his sorrow, her heart was filled with terror lest, inheriting his father's heroic spirit, Percival might meet with his father's fate. At length she gave way to the lad's entreaties, and let him go, but with a breaking heart.

Percival felt the parting with his mother very much; but youth and hope were strong in his breast, and thoughts of the joy of meeting again soon thrust the sorrow of parting into the background.

Lost in such reflections he came to a meadow in which some tents were pitched. In one of these he saw a couch on which a beautiful woman lay asleep. She was richly dressed; her girdle blazed with precious stones, as did also the ornaments on her arms, neck and fingers. He thought, as he plucked a flower, that he might also steal a kiss from the rosy lips of the sleeping beauty; but as he did so she awoke, and was very angry.

"Don't be angry," he said, throwing himself at her feet. "I have often kissed my mother when I have caught her asleep, and you are more beautiful than my mother."

The lady gazed at him in astonishment, and listened to his boyish confidences about going to Arthur's court, being made a knight, and doing great deeds thereafter. Suddenly a horn sounded at no great distance.

"That is my husband," cried the lady; "quick, boy, get away as fast as you can, or we are both undone."

"Oh, I am not afraid," he said. "Look at my quiver; it is quite full; I could defend you as well as myself. Let me have one of your bracelets as a sign that you are not angry with me."

As he spoke he slipped the bracelet off her arm, left the tent, mounted his horse, and rode away.

Shortly after this Lord Orilus, the lady's husband, appeared, and with him many knights. When he heard from her what had happened, he fell into a passion, and swore that he would hang the "impudent varlet" if he could catch him. But though he set out at once in pursuit, he could see nothing of the youth.

Meanwhile Percival continued his journey. That night he slept in the forest, and went on his way next morning at an easy pace. As he was passing under a rock he saw a maiden sitting by a spring that gushed out of it. She wept bitterly as she bent over a dead man, whose head lay in her lap. Percival spoke to her, and tried to comfort her by saying that he could avenge the death of the murdered man, for murdered he was sure he was. He then told her his name, and she said that she was his cousin Sigune, and that the dead man was her old play-fellow Tchionatulander, who had met his end in trying to gratify a silly wish of hers—a wish she had no sooner given utterance to than she repented. She had lost a dog, and had wanted to have it again. That was the cause of all her sorrow.

"He was a real hero," she continued, "and one of the knights of King Arthur's Round Table. Your mother made him governor of her wasted lands. He conquered the robber hosts, slew their leader, wild Lahelin, and flung his ally, Orilus, Lord of Cumberland, from his horse, so that he only escaped by the help of his troopers who bore him off the field. When he promised to get me back the dog, he challenged Orilus to single combat before King Arthur and his knights, the prize of victory to be the setter that Lord Orilus had caught, and kept, when it ran away from me. The challenge was accepted, but the time of meeting was put off for a while, because Orilus was suffering from an unhealed wound. Meanwhile the Lady Jeschute, fearing for the life of her husband, sent me back the dog. Tchionatulander and I regarded the matter as settled, so we set out together to go to the sanctuary of the Holy Grail, where we were to be married. As ill luck would have it, we met Orilus and his wife, and in spite of all the entreaties of Jeschute and myself the two knights quarrelled and fought. Orilus recovered from the stunning fall; but my dear love—oh that I had died instead! It was my fault, all my fault."

"Be comforted, cousin," said Percival, "I will go to King Arthur, I will tell him your story, and ask him to make me a knight, and to take care of you. Then I will go and seek out Orilus, and avenge your wrongs."

He then took leave of Sigune, and went on his way. Coming

to a broad river he questioned the ferryman as to where he might find King Arthur's court. The man answered that he must go to Nantes, a good distance on the other side of the river; so Percival gave him the gold bracelet he had taken from the lady's arm, and asked him to set him across. This the man did, and afterwards put him in the right road.

Arrived at Nantes, the first person he met was a red-haired knight clad in red armour, and riding a sorrel steed. Percival spoke to him courteously, and asked for the loan of his horse and armour, that he might go in seemly fashion to the king and ask for knighthood at his hands. But the stranger laughed, and said, "A rustic youth in a fool's cap were the very thing to carry my message of defiance."

"Here," he continued, "take this cup to the king as a token, tell him that I challenge him and all his Round Table to deadly combat. You see that I cannot lend you my horse and armour, as I need them myself, but after the battle you will be able to pick and choose amongst the armour and horses of the slain."

Indignant at the knight's refusal, Percival rode on in silence. As he went down the principal street of the royal borough, the people all laughed at his appearance, the very boys pointed and hooted at him, and in good truth he looked ridiculous enough. The ribbons of his striped cap fluttered in the breeze, his many-coloured jacket and leather hose were very shabby, and his sorry nag limped with fatigue. At length a squire named Iwanet took his part, chased away the boys, and chid them for their discourtesy to a stranger. The young hero thanked the man, and begged him to take him to King Arthur to whom he was the bearer of a message. Iwanet at once complied with Percival's request, and conducted him to the palace. On entering the open hall where the king was seated with his knights at the celebrated Round Table, the young man turned to his companion in amazement, saying:

"Are there so many Arthurs? My mother only told me of one."

The squire smiled as he replied that there was indeed only one Arthur, and that he was the knight whose beard was beginning to turn grey, and who wore the crown on his head.

Percival now walked up the hall, and bowing to the king,

repeated the message of the red knight, adding that he wished the king would use his power and give him the red knight's horse and armour, for he liked them well.

"The boy would have the bear-skin before the hunter has slain the bear," said Arthur laughing; "but," he added, "I will give you the things you ask for, if you can get possession of them."

"Thank you, sire," answered Percival, "I shall need your gift if I am to become a knight;" so saying he bowed and took his leave.

When he returned to the red knight, he told him all that had occurred, and asked him for the horse and armour the king had given him. The knight upon this rapped him so hard on the head with the butt end of his lance that Percival fell from his nag. He soon recovered, however, and attacked the knight so viciously with his spear that he killed him on the spot. He then tried to take off the knight's armour, but in vain. Fortunately Iwanet happened to pass that way, and seeing the lad's difficulty offered to help him. Percival was soon arrayed in the full suit of armour, which he insisted on wearing above his other clothes that had been made by his mother. This done, he thanked the squire for his timely assistance, mounted the red knight's charger and rode away, he knew not whither.

After Percival had ridden a long way he came to the castle of Gurnemann, an elderly man and a brave warrior. The old chief asked the youth to come in and spend the night under his roof, and Percival accepted the invitation with pleasure. He was so taken with his host's kindly manner, that before the evening was over he felt drawn to tell him of his mother and all his adventures since he had left her. Gurnemann persuaded the lad to remain with him for some time, and began to teach him how to become a true knight and hero.

"Do not always have your mother's name upon your lips," he would say, "for it sounds childish. Preserve her teaching faithfully in your heart, and you will please her more than by talking of her continually. A knight should be modest, love one maiden only, not play at love with many women. He should help the oppressed, and show kindness to all. When he has conquered an enemy he should show mercy; and when he is conquered he should not beg for life. To face death boldly is a hero's glory, and such death is better than a dishonoured life."

With these and other words of wisdom the old man strove to fit the youth for knighthood. At the same time he gave him fitting clothes, telling him it was no disrespect to his mother to cease to wear the curious garments with which she had provided him. Time passed on, and Percival proved such an apt pupil that Gurnemann grew as proud of him as if he had been his own son.

At last he told the youth that the time had come for him to go out into the world and draw his sword in defense of innocence and right, for Queen Konduiramur was hard pressed in her capital, Belripar, by the wild chief Klamide and his seneschal Kingram. Percival was nothing loath, and at once prepared to go and help the queen.

Arrived at Belripar, which stood on the sea at the mouth of the great river, he rowed himself across the stream, his good horse swimming at his side. The castle was protected by a moat and strong walls but he gained admittance by pronouncing the password given him by Gurnemann, and was conducted into the queen's presence. She received him kindly, and he at once offered her his services. She entreated him to have nothing to do with so unlucky a cause as hers; but he was not to be persuaded to abandon her. It almost seemed as though he had brought good fortune in his train, for a few days later some ships laden with provisions managed to run the blockade, and when Percival made a sally on the enemy soon after, he unhorsed and took prisoner the seneschal Kingram, whom he set free on condition that he at once set out to tell King Arthur of his defeat at the hands of the red knight. The same fate befell Klamide himself not long afterwards.

Peace was now restored. The people were all devoted to the young hero who had freed them from Klamide, and were rejoiced to hear that he was about to marry the queen.

The wedding took place with great pomp and ceremony. In the midst of all his happiness Percival had only one sorrow, and that was that his mother was not there to share his joy. He told Konduiramur what he felt, and she agreed with him that he ought to go and bring his mother to Belripar. So Percival mounted his good horse and rode away.

QUEST OF THE GRAIL.

HE KNEW in which direction to seek is mother, but not the roads that led to her house; so it was not surprising that he lost his way several times. One day he came to a great lake which he had never seen before. He saw a man seated in a boat, fishing. The man was richly dressed, but pale and sad. Percival asked if he could get food and shelter anywhere about for himself and his tired horse, and was told that if he went straight on, and did not lose his way, he would come to a castle, where he would be kindly received. He started in the direction indicated by the fisherman, and reached the castle at nightfall, after a long and toilsome search. There he met with so much kindness and consideration, garments even being provided for him "by Queen Repanse's orders," that he was filled with amazement. When freshly attired he was taken into the hall, which was brilliantly lighted. Four hundred knights were seated on softly-cushioned seats at small tables, each of which was laid for four. They all sat grave and silent, as though in expectation. When Percival entered, they rose and bowed, and a ray of joy passed over each woeful countenance.

The master of the house, who much resembled the fisherman Percival had seen on the lake, sat in an armchair near the fire, wrapped in sables, and was apparently suffering from some wasting disease.

The deep silence that reigned in the hall was at length broken by the host, who invited Percival, in a low, weak voice, to sit down beside him, telling him that he had been long expected and, at the same time, giving him a sword of exquisite workmanship. The young knight was filled with astonishment. A servant now entered carrying the head of a lance stained with blood, with which he walked round the room in silence. Percival would have much liked to ask the meaning of this strange ceremony and also how his arrival had come to be expected, but he feared lest he should be deemed unwarrantably curious. While thus thinking, the door opened again and a number of beautiful blue-eyed maidens came in, two and two, with a velvet cushion embroidered with pearls, an ebony stand, and various other articles. Last of all came Queen Repanse bearing a costly vessel, whose radiance was more than the human eye could steadfastly gaze upon.

"The holy Grail," Percival heard whispered by one voice after another. He longed to question some one; but felt too much awed by the strangeness and solemnity of all he saw.

The maidens withdrew, and the squires and pages of the knights came forward. Then from the shining vessel streamed an endless supply of the costliest dishes and wines, which they set out before their masters. The lord of the castle, however, only ate of one dish, and but a small quantity of that. Percival glanced round the great hall. What could this strange stillness and sadness mean?

When the meal was at an end, the lord of the castle dragged himself to his feet, leaning on two servants. He looked eagerly at his guest, and then retired with a deep sigh. Servants now came to conduct Percival to his sleeping apartment. Before leaving the hall they opened the door of a room in which a venerable old man slept on a low couch. His still handsome face was framed in a coronal of white curls. His sleep was uneasy, and his lips quivered as though he were trying to speak. The servants closed the door again, and led Percival to his chamber.

When he entered the room he looked about him, and at once became aware of a picture embroidered on the silken tapestry, that arrested his attention. It was the picture of a battle, in which the most prominent figure, a knight strangely like the lord of the castle in appearance, was sinking to the ground, wounded by a spear of the same kind as the broken weapon that had been carried round the hall. Much as he desired to know the meaning of this, he determined to ask no questions till the following morning, though the servants told him that his coming had been long expected, and deliverance was looked for at his hands; and they went away, sighing deeply.

His sleep was disturbed by bad dreams, and he awoke next morning unrefreshed. He found his own clothes and armour beside his bed; but no one came to help him. He got up and dressed. All the doors in the castle were locked except those that led out to the ramparts, where his horse stood saddled and bri-

dled at the drawbridge. No sooner had he crossed the bridge
than it was drawn up behind him, and a voice called out from
the battlements:

"Accursed of God, thou that wast chosen to do a great work,
and hast not done it. Go, and return no more. Walk thy evil way
till it leads thee down to hell."

The hero turned, and looked back at the castle: a face with a
fiendish grin glared at him for a moment over the battlements,
and then disappeared. Percival put spurs to his horse, and rode
away. He journeyed all day long through bleak, inhospitable
country, and at nightfall reached a solitary cell. He dismounted,
hobbled his horse, and entered the quiet room. A woman
crouched on the floor praying. She wore a penitent's grey robe,
and her long hair lay neglected about her face and neck. Startled
by his entrance, she rose slowly to her feet and looked at him.

"What, you?" she said, "Herzeleide's wretched son! What do
you want of me? Tchionatulander's body is embalmed, and I
have laid it in this chest. Here I must kneel and pray, and do
penance till the All-Merciful sets me free."

"Good heavens!" said the hero to himself, "it is Sigune; but
how changed!"

The unhappy woman stared at him for some time in silence,
then she continued: "Wretched man, do you not know that you
are lost forever. You were permitted to look upon the holy Grail,
yet, of your own will you put aside the opportunity of freeing the
poor sufferer from his pain. Do no longer pollute this cell with
your unhallowed presence. Go, flee, till the curse overtake you."

She stood before Percival like an angry prophetess. A feeling
of dread, such as he had never known before, took possession of
him, and he staggered out of her presence and into the night.
He walked on and on, leading his horse, till at length he sank on
the ground, and found relief from his troubles in a sound and
refreshing sleep.

The sun was high in the heavens when Percival awoke. His
faithful horse was grazing near him, so he mounted and rode on
without knowing or caring whither. As evening came on, a farmer
met him, and offered him a night's lodging, which he thankfully
accepted. Next day, when he resumed his journey, he was able to

think more calmly of all that had occurred; and came to the conclusion that he ought to return to the castle, and try to expiate the
sin he had committed unconsciously. But he could not find the
way to it. He asked every one he met to show him the way to
the castle where the holy Grail was to be seen; but everyone took
him for a fool or a madman. As he rode on sadly, he met a knight
leading a woman in chains. He at once recognised the beautiful
lady from whom he had stolen the kiss when she was asleep. She
looked at him in silent entreaty, so he felt himself bound to help
her. He desired the knight to let the poor woman go, but was
answered with a scornful laugh. Upon this the fight began, and
raged hotly for some time. At last Percival was victorious. As he
was about to slay his fallen and unconscious foe, he remembered
Sir Gurnemann's teachings, and refrained. Leaving the man lying
on the ground, he turned to the lady and freed her from her
chains. By this time the fallen knight had regained his senses,
and Percival let him go after making him swear to treat the lady
for the future with all courtesy, and to go to King Arthur's court
and say that he had been defeated by the red knight. Before they
parted, Percival learned that his opponent was Sir Orilus, and
that the lady was his wife, whom, ever since that scene in the
tent, he had persecuted out of groundless jealousy. Percival
solemnly swore that the meeting had been innocent and acci-
dental, and thus he brought about a sincere reconciliation.

The hero continued his search for the holy Grail, but all in
vain. He continued the quest in summer's heat and winter's
storm, yet never seemed to get nearer the goal. One day he met
Sir Gawain, King Arthur's nephew, who asked him to come back
to court with him, and see the king, and be made a knight of the
Round Table. Percival at once consented, hoping, as he did so,
to learn something from Arthur about the holy Grail.

Sir Gawain sent a squire to announce the red knight's arrival
to his uncle, so the king came out to meet them, accompanied
by his heroes and many of the townsfolks, for all were anxious to
see the warrior of whose powers so much had been heard and of
whom so little was known. On the following day in the open
field, Percival received from Arthur's hand the sign of knighthood, and was enrolled a member of the Round Table.

Whilst the heralds were proclaiming the new knight's name and valorous deeds, a woman rode into the royal presence on a miserable nag. She threw back her veil on approaching the king, and displayed a hideous countenance, brown, yellow and grey, like a withered wolf, and her eyes glowed like burning coals out of their deep sockets.

"It is the witch Kundrie, the messenger of the Sangreal," cried many voices.

"It is even she," said the woman, "and she comes to cry woe upon King Arthur and his Round Table if they suffer the man I shall name to remain in their midst. Percival is unworthy of the honour you have shown him. He was chosen to the highest dignity, and has wickedly neglected to end the pains of the greatest sufferer upon earth. Woe unto him! Woe unto Arthur and his heroes, if the unhallowed presence of the dishonoured knight be not at once removed."

Every eye was turned upon the prophetess, and then upon Sir Percival, who, horror-stricken at what had occurred, slipped quietly out of the assemblage, and, mounting his horse, rode away. Amongst all the heroes of the Round Table there was only one who took his part, and that was Gawain. He said it was a shame to let the flower of chivalry thus depart on the word of a hawk-nosed witch.

Upon this Kundrie got into a great rage, and hurled a malediction:

"Thou wretch, the curse hath fallen upon thee too. Go, if thou dare, and find Klinschor's magic castle, where thy grandmother, thy mother, and sister, and other noble ladies lie under the spell of enchantment; free them if thou canst!"

Gawain turned, and went away without a word. He mounted his horse, and set out in pursuit of Percival.

KLINSCHOR'S ENCHANTED CASTLE.

WHEREVER THE hero went, he found people who told him they had met the red knight, and again he came up with armed men who had fought with him and whom he had conquered. So the

In the Brave Days of Old.

(After the painting by Sir John Everett Millais.)

This fascinating picture, by the master artist of his age, presents a beautiful conception of the chivalric spirit that was dominant during the Round Table period, the incident mentioned in the text affording excellent suggestion, to a creative mind, for effective portrayal. By the old tale-tellers womanhood was invested with some of the divine attributes, and the search for the Holy Grail was hardly more earnestly pursued than was the ambition of Knights to succor distressed ladies, victims of giants, dragons, enchantments, and what other powers the heroic mind could invent.

days and weeks passed on, and he still continued to follow
Percival until he lost all trace of him in the far East. At last he
heard of him again, and renewing the quest heard more of his
great deeds, but could not find the knight.

Sir Gawain thought the matter over carefully, and made up
his mind that the best way to find Percival would be to seek the
holy Grail, for which he also sought.

As he rode along, he met a knight whom Percival had
wounded. Gawain offered him help; but Kingrimursel, as the
man was called, felt too sore about his defeat to be able to
accept any kindness, and at once challenged Gawain to fight
him when his wounds were healed. Before the hero had gone
much farther he met a woman whose beauty made him forget
both the challenge and the holy Grail, and even the red knight.
And indeed she was a lady of most marvellous beauty; her dark
hair fell down her neck in curls, and her eyes gleamed like stars.
Gawain approached her and entered into conversation with her.
Finding her as wise and witty as she was fair, he told her that he
loved her; but she only laughed at him. When he persisted she
told him that if he would find favour in her sight, he must go
into the garden hard by and fetch out her white palfrey.

He went to the garden gate, and seeing an elderly man standing within, he asked him where he might find the lady's palfrey.
The man shook his head sadly as he answered:

"Ah, my friend, take care. That lady is the Duchess
Orgueilleuse, a witch who has caused the death of many a noble
knight, and for whose sake the great King Amfortas faced the
danger in which he was wounded by the poisoned spear. Throw
off her bonds while yet you can. Look, there is your horse.
Mount, and ride away."

The warning was vain: a mere waste of words. It was as
though the haughty duchess had cast a spell over Sir Gawain.
He was powerless in her hands. He brought her the palfrey, and
not noticing the supercilious way in which she refused all help
from him in mounting, followed her with passive obedience
through many lands. Many a battle had he to fight for her sweet
sake, and every now and then he could not help seeing that it
was she who brought on the fight, when otherwise there would

have been none. Yet he was always victorious, and never swerved from his fealty to the lady of his love, who was now pleased to allow him to ride beside her.

At length they reached a hill-top from which they had an extensive view over a wide valley. Opposite, there was a castle perched on the top of a high rock, and overshadowed by a gigantic pine-tree. Orgueilleuse pointed to it, and said that it belonged to Gramoflans, her mortal enemy, and the man who had slain her lover. "Now," she continued, "if you will bring me a spray of the magic tree yonder, and conquer Gramoflans, who will at once challenge you to single combat, I will be your wife."

The knight would have fought the prince of darkness himself for such a prize, so he set spurs to his horse without a moment's hesitation, and rode away in the direction of the castle. He crossed the valley, swam over a deep moat, and reached the tree. He pulled a small branch, and tried to weave it into a wreath, but as he did so, he heard a voice call in angry tones:

"What are you doing there, rash youth? How dare you touch my magic tree! I know you well, you are Sir Gawain, a knight of the Round Table. Your father slew my father long ago, and I intend to have vengeance. Meet me, therefore, in eight days time before Klinschor's magic castle. There shall twelve hundred of my warriors see me avenge my father's death. You may bring as many men, or more, if you like." So saying, the speaker turned his back upon the hero and re-entered his castle.

Gawain brought the wreath to his lady, who received it calmly. She did not waste her words in thanks, but pursued her way in silence, he accompanying her wherever she chose to go. After a time, they came in sight of two strong castles, one of which, the duchess said, was Logreis, her father's ancestral residence, and the other was Klinschor's magic castle, in which the great magician, Klinschor, kept the noble dames and damsels he had stolen, in close confinement and laden with heavy chains. She herself, she added, had only bought her freedom by giving the monster all the gold she had inherited from her father. Scarcely had she uttered these words when a grim warrior appeared, and called to Gawain to defend himself. Orgueilleuse withdrew, reminding Gawain of her promise. A few minutes later, having overthrown his adversary, the knight got into the ferry-boat, that had just returned from setting the duchess on the other side of the water, and went across. That night he lodged with the ferry-man, who told him all the gossip of the place, and particularly of the great doings of a valiant knight clad in red armour.

As darkness came on, Gawain went to the window and looked out. He saw the lighted windows of the magician's castle, at each of which a sad female face appeared. The women were a curi-ous medley. Their ages seemed to range from early childhood to grey old age. Sir Gawain turned wrathfully from the sight, say-ing that he would slay the caitiff knight, and set the wretched ladies free; but the ferryman bade him beware what he did, for Klinschor was not only very strong, but was learned in the black art. Sir Gawain, however, was not to be dissuaded from the enterprise.

He mounted his horse early next morning and set out for the magic castle, the towers of which rose dark and mysterious-look-ing before him. He was admitted into the court by a gigantic porter, who opened the door for him without making any oppo-sition. The building seemed totally deserted. Not a household utensil was to be seen anywhere, nor any woman. He wandered from room to room lost in astonishment. At last he came to a room in which a comfortable couch was spread, and as he felt tired, he thought he would lie down and rest for a little; but, to his intense surprise, the bed retreated as he advanced, and he could not get in. Rendered impatient by this he boldly leapt upon the bed, and next instant was assailed by a perfect storm of arrows, lances, javelins and heavy stones. From these he guarded himself as well as he could. Had he not been dressed in full armour, he would speedily have been slain, and even as it was he received many a wound.

The terrible hail of weapons ceased as suddenly as it had begun. A stillness as of death set in. The silence was at length broken by the heavy tramp of a peasant, who entered the room bearing a great club in his hand, and followed by a lion. The man was of enormous size, and his voice was deep and gruff.

"Quiet, Leo," he said, "I am going to break that fellow's skull before I throw you his carcase. What!" he continued in amazement, "still alive, and in full armour! Nay then, go at him your-self, good Leo." So saying, he hastened away as fast as his legs would carry him.

The lion sprang upon the hero, and tried to tear him with its claws; but almost instantly fell backwards with a howl of mingled rage and pain, for Gawain had cut off one of its fore-paws. The hero jumped out of bed, and attacked the lion with such hearty good will that he finally killed it; but the exhaustion caused by the protracted struggle was so great that he sank fainting on its carcase.

When he came to himself Gawain found a number of women bending over him, and calling him their deliverer. Among these were his grandmother, his mother, and his sister Itonie. The spell was broken, and Klinschor had fled. As soon as Gawain had a little recovered from his fatigue, he sent messengers to tell Arthur what had happened, and to ask him to come and witness the combat that was to take place between him and Gramoflans.

Arthur came, and Sir Gawain felt that his cup of happiness was full when he presented the beautiful Lady Orgueilleuse to his uncle.

At length the wished-for day of combat dawned. A knight arrived dressed in black, and riding on a coal black steed. Gawain rode forward to meet him. Their swords flashed, and they fought as beseemed noble knights in such fair company. The king and the ladies drew nearer that they might the better watch the skill of the combatants. Gradually the black knight had the better of the fight. Gawain's strength to parry the thrusts of his adversary grew less and less. Suddenly a maiden darted from amongst the spectators, and cried,—

"Noble knight, spare my brother Gawain, he is yet weak from the many wounds he received in the magic castle."

"Gawain!" echoed the stranger, raising his visor, and display-ing the well-known features of Sir Percival.

The meeting of the friends was right joyful, and while they talked, another knight came forward and asked for reconcilia-tion and friendship with the other two. This was Gramoflans, who had long been secretly betrothed to the gentle Itonie. But Gawain knew too well what depended on their combat; he knew that the lady Orgueilleuse was only to be won by defeating this man, whom she hated. He laid his hand upon his sword and would have spoken, but the great king drew near and stopped him. He promised on his word of honour to soften the heart of the proud duchess, and bring her to his nephew. Then sending for the lady, he took her apart and talked with her, and his wisdom and nobleness so wrought upon her that her anger left her, and she forgave her foe.

A few days afterwards two marriages were solemnized at the castle, and Queen Guinevere did all that she could to ensure the general happiness. Sir Percival was at the same time openly received as Knight of the Round Table; but still he was not happy. He could not forget. He heard as distinctly as of yore the curse that the witch had pronounced against him; he always saw the face of the sufferer Amfortas, the Sangreal, and further in the background his lovely wife and weeping mother. He could not endure it, so he slipped quietly away without taking leave of the king or any one. The innocent joy of his friends but increased his grief.

He rode away, a feeling of almost despair possessing him. Would he never find the holy Grail, would he never be able to right the wrong he had done so unconsciously?

PERCIVAL, TREVREZENT, AND THE GRAIL.

SUMMER AND autumn were gone, and the ground was covered with snow, when one evening Percival saw the dwelling of a recluse at a little distance. He was half frozen with cold, and so very weary that when he dismounted he could only drag himself with difficulty to the door. A tall and stately, but somewhat haggard man answered his knock, and told him to come in, while he attended to his horse.

The hermit gave him food, and spread a bed of moss for him, and while resting there, Percival began to look about him. He saw a sword with a richly carved hilt, inlaid with gold, hanging on the wall, and asked to whom it had belonged. The hermit sighed as he answered that it had belonged to him at the time when he cared for nothing but glory and love, and forgot the holy Grail, the care of which had been committed to him.

"For, stranger," he continued, "you must know that I am Trevrezent, brother of the unhappy King Amfortas, and that, like him, I devoted my life to the pursuit of fleeting pleasures. When the poisoned lance struck Amfortas, and caused him the unspeakable pain that he still endures, I laid aside my sword and armour and retired to this solitary place that I might do penance for my own sins, and perhaps even redeem my brother. Idle hope! the sufferer still endures his agony, and he that was chosen by God to save him neglected to do it, and has earned thereby the curse of perdition instead of the glorious place that was prepared for him."

"I am he who sinned so deeply, yet unconsciously," cried Percival, "but where is the justice or love of a Being that punishes the sin of ignorance with such a curse?"

"So you are Percival, the son of my sister Herzeleide," said Trevrezent. "You found the way to the Grail, but not to redemption, for you did not know the All-merciful, who only speaks in those who have received Him into their hearts. Hearken to me, and I will unfold the wondrous goodness and love He has shown to the children of men, that you may learn to endure and to trust."

Trevrezent then proceeded to tell his nephew of God's dealings with man from the beginning of time until the coming and death of Christ, and to show him what lessons might be learnt therefrom. He afterwards told him that his mother had died of sorrow not long after his departure, and that in dying she had blessed him. Continuing he told Percival that he must now seek the Sangreal with a pure heart and humble mind, trusting in God, who knew that he had repented, and whose mercy was without end.

The hero remained for some days with his uncle, who strengthened and encouraged him to perform the task that lay before him.

At last, taking leave of Trevrezent, he departed and journeyed for a great distance without seeing any trace of the holy mountain. One day he met a knight who insisted on fighting with him.

But suddenly in the middle of the fray Percival's sword broke, and he exclaimed that if he had had his father Gamuret's weapon it would not have played him such a sorry trick. The stranger then questioned him about Gamuret, and after he had heard what Percival had to say, he added:

"Then you and I are brothers, for when Gamuret was in the East, he married the Moorish queen; after her death he returned home and wedded your mother. I was brought up by my mother's relations, and am now king of the Moors. My name is Feirefiss."

So saying he opened his visor and showed Percival a dark, handsome face.

The brothers embraced with great affection, and Percival said:

"The sword that Amfortas the sufferer gave me would not drink a brother's blood; that is the first sign that God has heard my prayers. And—but was I blind?—surely I know this place! There is the lake, the rocks are here—yes, there is the road to the holy mountain. Come, brother, follow me up the steep path to the heights above, where Divine mercy awaits us."

Both heroes set out on their toilsome road with a stout heart and a willing mind; but the way was so full of difficulties that the sun was about to set before they reached the castle. On their arrival they were received like expected guests, and their horses—which they had been obliged to lead most of the way— were taken to the stable. Percival and Feirefiss were conducted straight to the hall, which was brilliantly lighted with wax candles. King Amfortas and his knights were in their usual places. The squire then came in with the bleeding lance, and was followed as before by the maidens bearing the cushion, stand, etc., and lastly, by the fair virgin, Queen Repanse carrying the holy Grail.

"Merciful Father, and our sweet Lord and Saviour," whispered Sir Percival, "teach me what I must do to bring redemption."

And it seemed to him that an angel spoke in his ear the one word, "Ask!" His understanding was now enlightened. He knew what to do. Going up to Amfortas he said:

"What ails you, great king? and why are the halls that contain the holy Grail filled with mourning and woe?"

The candles went out, but the Sangreal spread a brighter radiance than before throughout the room, and on the side of the sacred vessel appeared in letters of flame, "Amfortas is cured; Percival shall be king." At the same moment soft and heavenly music filled the air, and invisible agents sang "Glory to God on high, and on earth peace, good will to men."

The hero stood silent, his heart overflowing with joy and thankfulness. An old man now approached him with a firm step and dignified mien. He bore a crown in his hands, and this he set on the head of the chosen king, saying:

"Hail, Percival, all hail! Long have we waited for your coming. I am your great-grandfather Titurel, and have been called to make over to you the insignia of the highest honour. Now I may depart in peace. The days of my earthly pilgrimage will soon be over, and I shall rest in the Lord."

Amfortas, who was now well and free from pain, rose from his seat, and greeting Percival with solemn joy, placed the royal mantle on his shoulders, calling on him to uphold the right, and to punish all injustice and wrong.

The assembled knights joined in proclaiming the new king and in swearing to be true to him.

And the angelic choir sang in jubilant tones:

> "Hail to thee Percival, King of the Grail!
> Seemingly lost for ever,
> Now thou art blest for ever.
> Hail to thee Percival, King of the Grail!"

While Percival stood there, touched and softened by all that had happened, the door opened, and a veiled lady came in, followed by her train. As he looked at her inquiringly, she threw back her veil, and showed the face of Konduiramur, the wife he loved so well, and from whom he had so long been absent.

It was strange that the light shed by the holy Grail left one man, and one alone, in darkness. This was Feirefiss, the Moorish king, who seemed to be overshadowed by a dark cloud. he asked whence came the bright rays that lighted the hall, but did not fall upon him.

"The sacred vessel," replied old Titurel, "that received the Saviour's blood, only enlightens those who believe. You still live in the darkness of unbelief, in the bonds of the Evil One. Bow your head before Christ the crucified, the Prince of Light and Truth, and your heart also shall be enlightened."

The old man's words had a strong effect upon Feirefiss, who desired, and immediately received, baptism at the hands of Titurel; and no sooner was the rite concluded than he too could see the Sangreal, and was embraced in the radiance that emanated from it.

After that, Titurel knelt down before the sacred vessel and prayed. Having done this, he rose from his knees, and, taking solemn leave of all, told them that Sigune was now at rest. Having thus spoken, he passed out of the hall, and was no more seen by them, or by any mortal man.

Feirefiss remained for some time at the castle on the holy mount. While there, he received instruction in the Christian faith, and when he went away, he took as his wife the fair Queen Repanse, to rule with him over his own land. They had a son named John, who became a great warrior, and who formed a brotherhood, like that of the Templars, of the holy Grail; a brotherhood, strong, mighty, enduring, and of great renown.

LEGEND OF LOHENGRIN.

(LOHERANGRIN.)

THE SILVER BELL.

UNDER THE lead of Gawain and others, and lastly of Arthur himself, the knights of the Round Table sought in vain for that which lay so near, yet seemed so far, because their dim vision could not pierce the earthly mists that cloud Heaven from our view. Some said that angels had conveyed the Holy Mountain farther East, where it was guarded by Prester John; and that only when wild Saracens threatened Christendom, did the Templars appear with the silver dove on shield and helmet, and help to win the victory; then they vanished, and none knew whence they came or whither they went.

Meanwhile Percival and Konduiramur lived happily together, serving in the Temple of the Sangreal, and educating their children with the greatest care. Kardeiss, the eldest son, on reaching man's estate, was made ruler over his mother's kingdom of Belripar, and over his patrimony of Waleis and Anjou. The younger son, Lohengrin, remained at home with his parents, while the daughter, Aribadale, took the place of Queen Repanse, and bore the holy Grail from the altar to the hall and back again. It was long since any of the knights of the temple had been called by the sound of the silver bell to go out and fight against the unbelievers, for the Saracens had been completely conquered by the Christians. But one evening, when the knights were assembled round the king in the royal hall, the silver bell was heard apparently at a great distance, but coming ever nearer and nearer. It sounded like a cry for help. At the same moment the announcement appeared on the sacred vessel in letters of flame, that Lohengrin was the hero chosen by God to defend the rights of the innocent, and he should be borne whither he desired to go, in a boat drawn by a white swan with a crown upon its neck.

"Hail Lohengrin, chosen of the Lord!" cried the knights of the temple.

Percival rejoiced greatly, and embraced and blessed his son, while Konduiramur, her heart filled with joy at Lohengrin's high calling, and also with anxiety for his safety, went to fetch the armour inlaid with gold that Amfortas had once worn, and the sword that had broken during Percival's fight with his brother Feirefiss, but which had since been re-forged and tempered in the sanctuary of the Sangreal.

A squire now entered the hall, and announced that a boat lay in the lake below the mountain, which a swan with a golden crown was towing by a chain of gold. This was the sign that the hour of the young hero's departure was come. The king and queen, and all the knights accompanied him to the shore, where the boat awaited him. As he was about to embark, Percival gave him a golden horn, and said:

"Blow three times on this horn as a sign that you have arrived amongst the worldly-minded children of men, and again three times to show that you are coming home; for, if you are ever asked from whence you came, and of what family you are sprung, you must at once be up and away on your return to the holy mountain. This is the inviolable law of the brotherhood of the Sangreal."

Lohengrin sprang into the boat, and the swan swam away with it, bearing it towards the sea. The air was full of the softest strains of music; but whether it was the swan that sang or a choir of angels, Lohengrin could not tell. The music ceased when the boat reached the sea. Its place was taken by the howling of the storm, and the sound of many waters. When night came on, the young hero stretched himself in the bottom of the boat, and fell asleep, undisturbed by wind or waves.

FAIR ELSE, THE DUCHESS.

ONE DAY the youthful Duchess of Brabant had gone out to hunt. She was of such surpassing beauty that she was always called Fair Else. On this occasion she had somehow become separated from her companions, but for which accident she was not at all sorry, for she wanted to have a little quiet time for thought; so she threw herself on the grass under a great linden tree, and began to ponder over her troubles. She had many lovers, and would gladly have got rid of them all, especially of the Count of Telramund, a mighty warrior and her former guardian, who persisted in maintaining that her father had promised her to him on his death-bed. The young duchess both hated and feared the count. She had refused point-blank to marry him in spite of his threats, and he now declared that he would make war upon her, and would also bring a heavy charge against her before the newly-elected German King, Heinrich of Saxony. Else thought over all these things with a heavy heart, till she fell asleep, lulled by the humming of the bees and the soft murmur of the wind in the branches overhead. And in her sleep she dreamt. It was a strange dream. She thought that a youthful hero came to her out of the wood, and offering her a little silver bell, told her to ring it if ever she needed assistance, and he would come without delay. It seemed to her that she tried to take the bell but could not, and in the effort she awoke. While puzzling over the meaning of her dream, she became aware of a falcon hovering over her. It wheeled round her head several times, and finally perched on her shoulder. Tied round its neck was a silver bell exactly like the one she had seen in her dream. She gently detached the bell and the falcon flew away.

Soon after she returned home a messenger arrived to summon her before King Heinrich's judgment-seat at Cologne on the Rhine. She obeyed the summons with a heart at ease, for she felt herself in the keeping of a Higher Power, and trusted in the hope her dream held out to her.

King Heinrich was a man who both loved and exercised justice; but the empire sorely needed stout defenders,—hordes of

wild Hungarians ravaged the south every year,—and Count
Telramund was a mighty warrior whose assistance was of great
value to him, so he hoped that his claims would be successfully
proved.

The trial began. Three witnesses were brought to prove that
the duchess loved one of her vassals, and for a fair lady in her
position to marry a vassal was strictly forbidden by the laws of
the realm. Two of the witnesses, however, were declared false
and perjured; and the evidence of one witness was not enough.
Then the count stood up, and offered to show the truth of his
allegation against the duchess by challenging to single combat
any knight that the Lady Else might choose to defend her cause,
and appealed to God to show the right.

The challenge could not be refused, but three days' time were
allowed her to find a champion. Else looked round the hall to
see if any noble warrior would defend her, but all feared the terrible strength and skill of Count Telramund. No one moved; a
silence as of death reigned in the court. Then the maiden
remembered the silver bell. She drew it from her bosom and
rang it, and the clear sound that it gave forth pealed through the
silent hall, and passed on in louder and louder echoes till it was
lost in the distant mountains. After that she turned to the king
and said that her champion would appear at the appointed time.

The three days were over. The king was seated in his chair of
state overlooking the lists, and thoughtfully gazed over the rushing waters of the Rhine that flowed close to where the combat
was to take place. His princes and knights surrounded him, and
before him stood Count Telramund in battle array, and the fair
duchess, who looked lovelier than ever.

Three times the count called upon the champion who was to
defend the Lady Else to appear. He received no answer. All eyes
were fixed upon the king, anxious to hear whether he would now
pronounce judgment on the accused. While he yet hesitated,
distant music was heard coming over the Rhine. The sounds
were passing sweet, such as none had ever heard before. A few
moments later a boat was seen approaching the shore, drawn by
a white swan with a golden crown upon its neck, and in the boat

a knight clad in rich armour was lying asleep. As the prow
touched the land, he awoke, and sounded a golden horn three
times. The notes echoed across the river, and were lost in the
distance. This was the sign that he accepted the position of
champion of innocence. He understood what was required of
him, and disembarking, entered the lists where his adversary
was awaiting him.

Before the fight began, the herald came forward, and
demanded the stranger's name and condition.

"My name is Lohengrin," answered the knight, "and I am of
royal birth; more than that you need not know."

"It is sufficient," replied the king; "your patent of nobility is
written on your forehead."

The trumpets sounded to battle, and the combat began.
Telramund's blows fell thick and fast, and the stranger knight at
first contented himself with standing on the defensive; but suddenly changing his tactics, he attacked in turn, and with one
blow he cleft the count's helmet and head.

"God has decided," said the king, "and His judgments are
just. As for you, noble knight, will you accompany us on our
expedition against the wild invaders and command the contin-
gent that the fair duchess will send us from Brabant?"

Lohengrin joyfully accepted the proposal, and at the same
moment the Lady Else came up and thanked him for the great
service he had done her. She had recognised him from the first
moment of his appearance as the hero of her dreams, and her
heart was full of wonder and gratitude.

On the journey to Brabant, Lohengrin and Else saw a great
deal of each other, and the more they saw, the greater was their
attachment. In the castle at Antwerp they were publicly
betrothed, and a few weeks later, married.

When the bridal pair left the cathedral after the wedding,
Lohengrin told his wife that she must never question him as to
the place from whence he came, or as to his parentage, for if she
did he must leave her that very hour, and leave her forever.

They were startled out of their honeymoon by the king's call
to arms. Numerous robber hordes from Hungary had invaded

the land, so King Heinrich had determined to collect his armies at Cologne, and march against the foe. The duchess, like most of the other ladies, went with her husband to the royal city. There were many great warriors amongst the princes of the empire, and the ladies conversed of their glorious deeds and those of their ancestors; but when Else's husband was mentioned, a strange silence would fall upon the company, for rumor ran that Lohengrin was the son of a heathen magician, and that he had gained the victory over Count Telramund by his knowledge of the black art.

When Else heard the scandalous tale, she was deeply hurt, for she knew her husband's noble nature. She longed for the power of justifying him, and of making the scandal-mongers retract their words, and reverence her hero. So full did she become of these thoughts that she forgot her husband's warning, and, approaching him one day, told him of her trouble, and asked him whose son he was, and whence he came.

"Dear wife," he replied, in quiet sorrow, "I will now tell you, and the kings and all the princes, what was hidden and ought to have remained hidden forever; but remember, the hour of our parting approaches."

The hero led his trembling wife before the king and his nobles, who were assembled on the banks of the Rhine. He told them of his great father, Percival, and of his own coming to Cologne in obedience to the Divine order conveyed to him by the holy Grail.

"I would fain have fought the barbarians with you, noble king," he continued, "but destiny calls me hence. Be of good cheer—you will conquer the robbers, rule over the heathen, and win imperishable glory."

The hero spoke with the enthusiasm of an inspired seer, as he added a prophecy of the wonders time would unfold regarding the future of the empire. When he ceased, all present heard the same strange wild melody that had attended his coming, but this time sad and slow as a dirge. It came nearer, and then they spied also the white swan and the boat.

"Farewell, beloved," said Lohengrin, clasping his weeping

wife in his arms. "I had grown to love you, and life in this world of yours passing well; but now a higher will than mine tells me to go."

He tore himself away with tears in his eyes, and entering the boat, which the swan had brought close to the bank, was borne away from her sight forever.

She did not long survive the parting from her husband and when she died, she expired in the firm conviction that she was about to join her husband and see the holy Grail.

Romance of
Tristram and Isolde.

Trusty Rual and His Foster-Son.

A FURIOUS battle was raging before the gates of the castle, for
Rivalin, the lord of the place, was fighting against Morgan, his
feudal superior, whose oppression had grown too great to be
borne. Within the castle, Blancheflur, Rivalin's wife, was praying
fervently for her husband's safety, as she clasped in her weak
arms her little son that had been born while the din of battle
filled the air.

All day long it lasted. In the evening Rual, the marshal, hurried back into the castle bleeding, and called to his wife to save
what she could, and make ready for instant flight, for King
Rivalin had fallen, and the enemy threatened to blockade the
castle. Queen Blancheflur heard what he said, and with a pierc-
ing cry fell back dead. Rual, seeing that nothing could be done
for her, hurried the other women in their preparations, and,
heedless of his own unattended wounds, make ready to fly with
his master's child to a place of safety.

But though they hastened to obey the marshal, it was already
too late—the castle was surrounded, and no way of escape
remained. They carried the dead queen to another room, and
the marshal's wife took the baby for her own. The servants were
all faithful, and when Morgan took the castle soon afterwards,
he never guess that Rivalin had left a living child. The victorious
king, who honoured Rual for his fidelity to his late master, made

him governor of the kingdom he had just subdued, and then went back to his own place.

Time passed on, and the foster-parents were delighted with the good qualities their pupil developed. They had had him christened Tristram, or Trista (Sorrowful), because of the sad circumstances that had attended his birth. Rual himself taught him all knightly exercises, and engaged tutors to instruct him in music, languages, and many other accomplishments.

One day some foreign merchants landed on the coast, and offered their wares for sale. Young Tristram often went down to see them, and questioned them about their country, and about the many strange lands they visited. The boy's unusual beauty and the great knowledge he possessed aroused their cupidity. They determined to steal him, and sell him in some foreign country where he would bring a good price. So once, when he was on board their ship, they quietly raised the anchor, and set sail. Rual pursued them, but they escaped, owing to the greater swiftness of their vessel. Another danger, however, threatened to overwhelm them. A terrific storm came on, worse than any they had ever encountered before. They thought it a sign of God's wrath, and were filled with fear and awe. In the perturbation of their souls they swore to set the boy free, and they kept their word. They put him ashore on an unknown coast, feeling assured that with his uncommon gifts he would soon make a livelihood. They were not mistaken. A troup of pilgrims happening to pass that way, Tristram joined them, and accompanied them to the court of King Mark of Cornwall. The king took the boy into his service as page, and grew very fond of him.

Meantime Rual had sought his foster-son everywhere, and was broken-hearted at not being able to find him, or hear any news of him. He wandered from one country to another, begging his way. At last, footsore and weary, he arrived at King Mark's court. Tristram greeted him with joy and took him to the king.

When Mark heard who the supposed beggar was, he exclaimed angrily:

"What! Are you the former marshal of the traitor Rivalin, who stole away my sister Blancheflur?"

"Sire," replied Rual, "love made him do so. The Lady Blancheflur had been secretly married to my master before she went away from here. She and her husband are both dead, and this youth," laying his hand on Tristram's shoulder, "whom I have brought up from his infancy, and whom I have sought for years, is their only child."

The king was astonished to hear this tale, and was pleased to find that his favourite page was in reality his nephew. Rual remained in Cornwall with his foster-son, for, his wife being dead, he did not care to return home, and again endure Morgan's despotic sway.

Tristram grew up to be a tall and handsome man, a brave warrior, and a noble knight, as much beloved in peace as in war. But although he lived a full and joyous life, he could not forget his native land, and often mourned over the thought that his fellow-countrymen and rightful subjects groaned under the tyranny of a foreign oppressor. He at last explained his feelings on the subject to his uncle, who gave him men and ships, telling him to go and set his people free, but making him promise to return to Cornwall afterwards, as he had appointed him to succeed him on the throne.

The expedition was successful. Morgan was defeated and slain, and Tristram was crowned King of Parmenia. He remained for a year longer in his native land, settling all differences, and arranging matters for the good of his subjects. Having done this, he made Rual governor of the realm and returned to Cornwall as he had promised.

ISOLDE (YSEULT, ISOUD.)

ON HIS arrival there, he found every one in great distress. King Gurmun of Ireland had, during his absence, invaded Cornwall, and, with the help of his brother-in-law Morolt, a powerful chief and great warrior, had subdued the country, and forced King Mark to pay him tribute; and a shameful tribute it was. By the treaty with Gurmun, the Cornish king was bound to send thirty handsome boys of noble birth to Ireland every year, to be sold

as slaves for the benefit of the Irish king. On the very day of
Tristram's return, Mark was about to deliver the thirty boys into
the hands of grim Morolt, Gurmun's messenger, who had come
to receive them.

Tristram was very angry when he heard the news, and told the
knights they were cowards ever to have consented to such an
arrangement. Then going straight to Morolt, he tore up the
treaty, saying it was too inhuman to be kept. Morolt's only
answer was to draw his sword and challenge him to single combat. He accepted, and the fight began. After some time, Morolt,
having severely wounded Tristram, cried:

"Yield, Sir Tristram; I feel pity for your youth. Yield, and my
sister, Queen Isolde, shall cure your wound, for she alone can
heal a wound made by my poisoned blade."

"Death rather," exclaimed the young knight, and making a
mighty effort, he split his adversary's head open from crown to
jaw.

This settled the matter. The Irish returned home sadly, bearing with them the corpse of their hero, while the victor went
back to his uncle's palace. His wound was washed and bound,
but it would not heal. It continued to fester, in spite of the use
of balm, and other herbs of well-known excellence. An experi-
enced doctor who was called in to see the patient, said that only
the Irish queen Isolde, and her daughter of the same name, possessed the art of drawing such poison out of a wound. So
Tristram determined to go to Ireland in the guise of a minstrel,
and seek healing at the hands of the queen, although he knew
that Gurmun had sworn to kill him and every Cornishman who
had the misfortune to fall into his hands.

At length he reached the Irish court, and there he played and
sang so beautifully that the queen sent for him, and begged him
to teach his art to her young daughter Isolde. The minstrel
found the princess an attentive pupil; and while teaching her,
and listening to her sweet voice as she sang some plaintive ditty,
he would even forget for a time the pain of his wound. And she,
in learning from him, learnt to love him with all the strength of
her innocent young heart.

The days went on, and the pain of his wound grew worse and

worse. Then he told the queen of his suffering, and asked her to heal him. This she at once consented to do, and a few weeks later he was cured. He now sang with greater power than before, and the king was so charmed with his music that he would have liked to keep him forever at his court. But, fearful of discovery, Tristram determined to be gone while yet there was time.

On his return to Cornwall, Tristram was joyfully received by all save the great lords, who knew that King Mark would make him his heir, and they did not wish to have a foreigner rule over them. They desired the king to marry, and Tristram, finding what was in their minds, himself advised his uncle to choose a wife, saying that the Princess Isolde of Ireland would be the most suitable person for him to wed. After some deliberation, it was agreed that Tristram should go to King Gurmun as his uncle's ambassador, to ask for the hand of the princess.

Arrived in Ireland, he set out for the royal residence. On the way he heard heralds proclaiming that the king would give his daughter in marriage to whoever slew a dragon that was devastating the land, provided he who rescued the country were of noble birth.

Tristram sought out the dragon, and, after a long struggle, killed it; then cutting out the tongue of the creature, as a proof that he had really slain it, he turned to go; but the pestiferous breath of the monster so overpowered him that he sank backward into the morass out of which the dragon had come.

Struggle as he might he could not free himself, for he had sunk up to his shoulders. While in this miserable plight, he saw a horseman approach, cut off the head of the dead monster, and then ride away.

The horseman was sewer (head waiter) at the palace. He showed the king the dragon's head, and boldly demanded the meed of victory. The queen, who knew the man well, and held him to be a coward, did not believe his tale; so she went with her train to the dragon's hole, and discovered the real hero in the morass. His bloody sword, and the dragon's tongue showed that it was he who had done the deed. He was quite insensible when he was taken out of the morass and carried to the palace. The princess at once recognised him to be the minstrel who had before visited Ireland, and hoped that his birth was sufficiently good to enable him to win the prize. The queen gave him a sleeping potion, and told him to keep quiet. Then taking her daughter into the next room, she showed her the horrible tongue of the lind-worm, and the sword with which the creature was slain.

"Look," she said, "the minstrel is the real hero of this adventure, and not that cowardly sewer."

She left the room, adding that the truth would soon be known. Isolde took up the sword and examined it. She saw that a bit of the blade was broken off.

"Merciful heaven," she cried, "surely he cannot be the—" She ceased, and took from a drawer the splinter of steel she had drawn out of the wound on her uncle's head. She fitted the splinter to the blade, and saw that it was as she had feared.

"Ha," she went on, trembling with anger, "he is the murderer of my uncle Morolt. He must die, die by my hand, and be slain with his own weapon."

Seizing the sword in a firmer grip, she went into the room where Tristram was sleeping, and swung the sword over her head; but as she did so, he smiled as in a happy dream, and she could not do the deed. Then it seemed to her that she saw her uncle looking at her reproachfully, and she nerved her heart to strike, but at that moment her hand was seized by her mother, who had entered unnoticed.

"Wretched child," she cried, "what are you doing? Are you mad?"

Isolde told the queen that this was Tristram, her uncle's murderer; and the mother answered:

"I loved my brother dearly, but I cannot revenge him, for this man has saved our people from the dragon, and a nation is worth more than a single man, however dear to our hearts."

Isolde confessed that her mother was right, and let her resentment die.

When Tristram had recovered, he did not show the dragon's tongue in proof of what he had done, but challenged the sewer to trial by combat. Now the man had often fought before, but when he saw Tristram come forth to meet him in the lists, his heart died within him, and he confessed his guilt. King Gurmun thereupon ordered the recreant knight's shield to be broken, and sent him forth a banished man.

Tristram then fetched the dragon's tongue, and was at once proclaimed victor amid the acclamation of the people.

Great was the astonishment of all, when Tristram, instead of claiming the princess' hand, proceeded to woo her for his uncle King Mark, of Cornwall. Gurmun had such a dislike to King Mark that he would have refused him as a son-in-law point-blank, if Queen Isolde had not taken part in the debate, and shown the wisdom of giving way. So Tristram received a gracious answer from the king, and was content. No one thought of asking the maiden if she were willing to marry the old King of Cornwall. She was a princess, and princesses were never allowed a choice, when reasons of state demanded that they should marry some particular person.

THE LOVE-POTION.

THE PRINCESS went on board Tristram's vessel, which was about to sail for Cornwall. Her dresses and jewels were there also, and as soon as her old nurse and faithful companion came down to the ship, they were to set sail. Brangäne was closeted with the queen, who wished to say a few last words in private.

"Look, Brangäne," said the mother, "take this goblet, and keep it carefully. It contains a drink made of the expressed juices of certain plants, and is a love-potion. See that my daughter and her husband both drink it on their marriage day, and all will yet be well."

The nurse promised to be careful, and took leave of the queen.

Wind and weather were favourable to the voyagers. One day when Tristram had been singing and playing to the princess for a long time, and trying his best to distract her thoughts from dwelling on her dead uncle, her old home, and the unknown future, he became so thirsty that before beginning another song he was fain to ask for something to drink. One of the attendants opened a cupboard, and finding there a goblet with a drink all ready prepared, supposed that the nurse had made it in case it were wanted, and took it to Tristram, who handed the cup first to Isolde that she might pledge him, as was the custom. The princess raised the cup to her lips and drank a little; but finding it very good, she put it to her lips again, and drank half the contents. Then she returned it to Tristram, who finished it at a draught.

Their eyes met, and they knew that they loved each other.

When Brangäne came in a few minutes later, and saw the empty goblet upon the table, she burst into tears, and bemoaned what had occurred, saying that the queen had given her the love-potion to administer to Isolde and King Mark upon their wedding-day. But the princess comforted her by asserting that no harm was done, for human beings had free will, and could struggle against enchantment. And struggle they did; but their love was strong.

The ship reached the harbour, and King Mark came down to meet his nephew and his bride. He was much pleased with the appearance of the princess, whom he welcomed with all ceremony. The marriage took place, and King Mark thought himself a happy man.

All went quietly for some time, so carefully did the nurse conceal her lady's love for Sir Tristram; but after a time people began to whisper, and at length the whisper reached the ears of the king. At first he would not believe the truth of what he heard, but afterwards the thing was proved to him so clearly that he could no longer doubt. He determined to bring the lovers to trial. Meanwhile Brangäne had discovered that the king knew all; she therefore warned Tristram, and fled into the forest with him and Isolde. There they hid themselves in a cave for a long time. But winter was coming on, and the nurse feared for her darling's life if she remained in such a place during the frost and snow.

One day as they were talking over what were best to be done, King Mark suddenly appeared amongst them. Brangäne stepped forward, and assured him that the stories that he had been told were all gossip; and the king, who loved both Tristram and Isolde, willingly believed her, and took them home with him.

But the effect of the philter had not yet passed off, nor had the young people conquered their love. Whispers again arose about the court, and Tristram could not call any of the whisperers to account, for he knew that he had dishonoured the name of knight, and had ill repaid his uncle's kindness. Isolde, too, was miserable. They both made up their minds that they must part, and as they said farewell, it was with the fervent hope that the magic potion would have lost its power by the time they met again.

Tristram went away. He wandered through Normandy and Alemannia; he fought many battles, and led a bold, adventurous life, but he could not forget Isolde. At last he came to the kingdom of Arundel, and there he found King Jovelin and his son Kaedin hiding, in a thatched cottage in a great forest, from the bands of robbers who had overrun the land. It was late in the evening when he arrived at the solitary house, where he met with a kind reception. The lovely daughter of his host, curiously enough, was also named Isolde, to which was added the appellation of "la blanche mains." It did him good to be with the maiden and her father. He promised them his aid, and for this purpose went to visit his own kingdom. There he found his presence much wanted, for old Rual was dead, and all was confusion in the land. His first action was to re-establish order and good government, after which he called out his troops, and marched to Arundel to help King Jovelin. He fought the robbers there, chased them out of the land, replaced the king on his throne, and made friends with Kaedin. Weeks passed, and he became engaged to Isolde of the white hand. He vainly hoped that being married to another woman would cure him of his love for the Queen of Cornwall, and he knew that the princess loved him.

His betrothal did not bring him peace. His affection for the Lady Isolde grew no stronger, so in despair he put off his marriage, and, unable to feign a love he did not feel, went out to seek death at the hands of the robber hordes that had again invaded the country. He conquered them, and forced them to fly. On his return from this expedition, his marriage day was fixed; but one evening he was induced to accompany his friend Kaedin on a dangerous adventure, and during the combat to which this led, he received a spear thrust in the breast. He fell senseless to the ground. Kaedin carried him out of the fight, and took him home to the palace, where Isolde succeeded in bringing him to himself again.

Everyone hoped that he would soon recover from his wound; but instead of that he grew worse. One day he said that the Queen of Cornwall had a remedy that would cure him, if she could only be induced to bring it. Kaedin at once set off for Cornwall to appeal to her compassion. No sooner had the queen heard his tale than she persuaded King Mark to let her go to Arundel, and cure his nephew. Armed with his permission, she started on her long journey by sea and land, and never rested till she arrived at King Jovelin's palace. There she was greeted with the sad words, "You have come too late—he is dying." They led her to his couch, and she knelt down and took his hand. A slight pressure showed that he knew who she was; next morning he opened his eyes, gazed at her with a sad and loving look, and then died. She bent over him and kissed him, and in that kiss her spirit passed away. They were buried three days later under the same grave-mound in the distant land of Arundel.

A CATALOG OF SELECTED DOVER
BOOKS IN ALL FIELDS OF INTEREST

CONCERNING THE SPIRITUAL IN ART, Wassily Kandinsky. Pioneering work by father of abstract art. Thoughts on color theory, nature of art. Analysis of earlier masters. 12 illustrations. 80pp. of text. 5⅜ x 8½.   23411-8

ANIMALS: 1,419 Copyright-Free Illustrations of Mammals, Birds, Fish, Insects, etc., Jim Harter (ed.). Clear wood engravings present, in extremely lifelike poses, over 1,000 species of animals. One of the most extensive pictorial sourcebooks of its kind. Captions. Index. 284pp. 9 x 12.   23766-4

CELTIC ART: The Methods of Construction, George Bain. Simple geometric techniques for making Celtic interlacements, spirals, Kells-type initials, animals, humans, etc. Over 500 illustrations. 160pp. 9 x 12. (Available in U.S. only.)   22923-8

AN ATLAS OF ANATOMY FOR ARTISTS, Fritz Schider. Most thorough reference work on art anatomy in the world. Hundreds of illustrations, including selections from works by Vesalius, Leonardo, Goya, Ingres, Michelangelo, others. 593 illustrations. 192pp. 7⅛ x 10¼.   20241-0

CELTIC HAND STROKE-BY-STROKE (Irish Half-Uncial from "The Book of Kells"): An Arthur Baker Calligraphy Manual, Arthur Baker. Complete guide to creating each letter of the alphabet in distinctive Celtic manner. Covers hand position, strokes, pens, inks, paper, more. Illustrated. 48pp. 8¼ x 11.   24336-2

EASY ORIGAMI, John Montroll. Charming collection of 32 projects (hat, cup, pelican, piano, swan, many more) specially designed for the novice origami hobbyist. Clearly illustrated easy-to-follow instructions insure that even beginning papercrafters will achieve successful results. 48pp. 8¼ x 11.   27298-2

THE COMPLETE BOOK OF BIRDHOUSE CONSTRUCTION FOR WOODWORKERS, Scott D. Campbell. Detailed instructions, illustrations, tables. Also data on bird habitat and instinct patterns. Bibliography. 3 tables. 63 illustrations in 15 figures. 48pp. 5¼ x 8½.   24407-5

BLOOMINGDALE'S ILLUSTRATED 1886 CATALOG: Fashions, Dry Goods and Housewares, Bloomingdale Brothers. Famed merchants' extremely rare catalog depicting about 1,700 products: clothing, housewares, firearms, dry goods, jewelry, more. Invaluable for dating, identifying vintage items. Also, copyright-free graphics for artists, designers. Co-published with Henry Ford Museum & Greenfield Village. 160pp. 8¼ x 11.   25780-0

HISTORIC COSTUME IN PICTURES, Braun & Schneider. Over 1,450 costumed figures in clearly detailed engravings–from dawn of civilization to end of 19th century. Captions. Many folk costumes. 256pp. 8⅜ x 11¾.   23150-X